Olivier Mentz, Tracey McKay (Eds.)

Unity in Diversity

EUROPA LERNEN

Perspektiven für eine Didaktik europäischer Kulturstudien

Die wissenschaftliche Schriftenreihe „Europa lernen – Perspektiven für eine Didaktik europäischer Kulturstudien“ besitzt ein Double blind Peer-Review-Verfahren durch die Mitglieder des wissenschaftlichen und redaktionellen Beirats.
The scientific series "Learning Europe – Perspectives for a didactics of European Cultural Studies" undergoes a double blind peer review process through the members of the scientific and editorial board.

Band / Volume 7

LIT

Unity in Diversity

European Perspectives on Borders and Memories

edited by

Olivier Mentz and Tracey McKay

LIT

Cover image: *United Diversity Wordwide*

Co-funded by the
Erasmus+ Programme
of the European Union

This publication has been co-funded with support from the European Commission within the Erasmus+ KA2 project "Border Education – Space, Memory and Reflection on Transculturality" (BE-SMaRT; project number VG-SPS-BW-14-001602-3). It reflects the views only of the authors, and the Commission cannot be held responsible for any use which may be made of the information contained therein.

This book is printed on acid-free paper.

Bibliographic information published by the Deutsche Nationalbibliothek
The Deutsche Nationalbibliothek lists this publication in the Deutsche Nationalbibliografie; detailed bibliographic data are available on the Internet at http://dnb.d-nb.de.

ISBN 978-3-643-90962-6 (pb.)
ISBN 978-3-643-95962-1 (PDF)

A catalogue record for this book is available from the British Library

Klosbachstr. 107
CH-8032 Zürich
Tel. +41 (0) 44-251 75 05
E-Mail: zuerich@lit-verlag.ch   http://www.lit-verlag.ch
Distribution:
In the UK: Global Book Marketing, e-mail: mo@centralbooks.com
In North America: International Specialized Book Services, e-mail: orders@isbs.com
In Germany: LIT Verlag Fresnostr. 2, D-48159 Münster
Tel. +49 (0) 2 51-620 32 22, Fax +49 (0) 2 51-922 60 99, e-mail: vertrieb@lit-verlag.de
In Austria: Medienlogistik Pichler-ÖBZ, e-mail: mlo@medien-logistik.at
e-books are available at www.litwebshop.de

Inhalt

Tracey McKay

A Short Introduction to the BE-SMaRT Project and Case Studies

Borders? I have never seen one.
But I have heard they exist in the minds of some people.
Thor Heyerdahl

The idea for this book was born out of the Erasmus+ BE-SMaRT Project (Border Education – Space, Memory and Reflection on Transculturality) which was itself inspired by a paper that appeared in the academic journal, Progress in Human Geography, 2006, 'The lines that continue to separate us: borders in our 'borderless' world', by David Newman. In this paper Newman pointed out how

> we live in a world of lines and compartments. We may not necessarily see the lines, but they order our daily life practices and strengthen our belonging to, and identity with places and groups, while ... perpetuating and re-perpetuating notions of difference and 'othering'. (Newman 2006, 1)

While many people will be familiar with the concept of a 'border' as a line on a map, whose primary function is to delineate and demarcate territory, Newman's paper called for a much broader appreciation of 'borders' as dynamic human phenomenon, socially constructed, and strongly influenced by perceptions.

The BE-SMaRT Project through the intellectual outputs of the individual case studies, some of which are presented in this volume, seeks to move discussion beyond the physical and highly visible lines of 'border' separation towards a much richer inter-disciplinary appreciation of the bottom-up 'bordering processes' affecting the lives of people on an everyday basis in different parts of Europe. While the BE-SMaRT Project recognises the continued relevance and importance of geo-political and territorial borders in Europe, it calls for traditional border concepts, largely but not exclusively associated with geography and the demarcation of space, to be seen as one aspect of a more fluid, inter-disciplinary and multi-faceted discourse. This thinking is reflected in the different individual case studies chapters presented here. Drawn from a range of different contexts the individual contributors explore the different ways that borders help create (or indeed reflect) difference and constitute the separation lines not only between states and geographical spaces, but also social and cultural distinctions; that is to say the distinctions between, 'us' and 'them', the 'here' and 'there', and the 'insiders' and 'outsiders'. The authors recognise the importance of border demarcation as the process through which the criteria of belonging (or indeed non-belonging) is defined; be that citizenship of a country, membership of a specific social or economic group, or religious and cultural affiliation. The theme of 'crossing borders' be they – economic, political, territorial, social, cultural, linguistic, gender – has been to the fore in both academic and popular discourse. While it is true that some 'borders' are extremely difficult to cross, a range of other 'borders' types can and are regularly 'crossed'. The metaphor of 'bridges', as points of contact for border crossing, whether those borders are geo-political, territorial economic, social, cultural, linguistic or gender is significant, and by addressing these in this volume we seek to encourage critical reflection encountering difference across different borders in Europe.

As Newman's paper suggests

> discussion concerning the nature of borders as bridges and points of interaction is of relevance in the sense that borders can become transformed into the frontiers (in the most positive sense of the term) where people or groups who have traditionally kept themselves distant from each other, make the first attempts at contact and interaction (Newman 2006, 8).

In a similar vein, and until relatively recently, the concepts of 'borderland', 'frontier' and 'transition zones' were largely restricted to discussions of real tangible spaces where lives were 'divided' or 'marked out' by territorial borders. More recently these spatially grounded concepts have been applied to a wide range of border crossings by people whose lives have hitherto been divided. Of course, none of this should be taken to imply that the act of border crossing is necessarily easy or straightforward, or that it will necessarily lead to positive and life affirming outcomes. Indeed, as Newman's (cf. ibid., 9) work cautions, the experience of meeting the 'Other' for the first time, especially after a long period of fear, suspicion and distrust can heightened mutual feelings of animosity. What is significant about the diverse case studies examined through the BE-SMaRT Project, and presented here in this book, is that they examine border crossings by, and across, different social, ethnic, religious, cultural, gender, linguistic groups.

In so doing the case studies employ a range of methodologies intended to uncover the meaning and significance of 'borders' and 'memories' in a range of European contexts. They are attentive to the life-stories, memories, as well as the lived experiences arising from the unique situations within the BE-SMaRT Project partner countries. They seek to uncover the real-life and diverse experiences of different people in different parts of Europe that will have resonance for students and teachers within Initial Teacher Education settings. They incorporate a range of 'borders narratives' and 'border' representation in cultural media, film, museum spaces, textbooks, the lecture theatre and the classroom. Significantly these individual case studies have formed the basis of the 'dilemmas' approach utilised within the BE-SMaRT Study Module. However, it is also the case that each individual case study stands in its own right as a contribution to learning and teaching in higher education, and for that reason they have been included in this publication.

In the chapters that follow the contributors (most of whom are BE-SMaRT consortium partner members) seek to examine the much broader process of 'bordering' and the ways in which different types of 'borders' are demarcated, constructed (often in peoples' minds) and managed, as well as the categories of difference or separation they create and maintain. In this respect the link with memory studies has proven critical. The case studies seek to provide a broad inter-disciplinary understanding of 'borders', incorporating the critical intersection with memory studies, in an effort to better understand how individuals and groups perceive and experience the borders in their everyday lives.

Border Concepts: Alexander Drost's chapter "Borders: a narrative turn" (pp. 14-33) provides comprehensive reflection on border concepts, practices and how these have been communicated over time and through space. As he explains, since the 19th century a complex academic discourse has developed around what appears on the surface to be a very simple question, what is a border? Whereas in the past discussions about 'borders' tended to take place within discrete disciplinary contexts more recently the debate itself has been enriched by crossing disciplinary borders.

> Churchyard walls, the border of the nation state, ethnic, or religious boundaries – are all borders and order life. [...] In this way, borders form spaces, in which people can identify themselves in accordance to a common culture, language, and tradition, distinguishing and separating one social group from another. (p. 14)

Drost's chapter provides a strong theoretical and contextual framework for the chapters that follow. After a short discussion on border concepts his chapter provides critical reflection and insights on 'bordering processes', he addresses the formation of borders over the centuries, paying particular attention to the national or state border. He reviews the 'spatial turn' taken by the humanities and social sciences at the close of the 20th century and the impact which cross-disciplinary thinking and sensitivity to 'border narratives' has had for our understanding and appreciation of the subject. Towards the end of his paper he offers readers "a little detour" (p. 27), as he puts it from, European integrated borderlands to a contemporary borderland situation on the Thailand/Myanmar border. Using this example he illustrates how two border narratives, one of a national border of European descent and the other of a historical/cultural borderland co-exist today side-by-side.

Sweden: As an immigrant society, Sweden has experienced both internal migration and migration to and from the country. To that end members of the society have generated memories from different geographical and social settings. In her chapter "Social Memories and Identities: how staff in museums and Initial Teacher Education can create critical learning experiences" (pp. 150-168), Laila Niklasson, examines 'bordering', social memories and identities in the case of Finnish immigrants to Sweden, exploring how social memory can be used facilitate dialogue between museums and initial teacher education thus creating 'critical learning experiences'. Contextually her chapter opens with an account of how a border was created between Sweden and Finland, presenting an overview of migration trends between the two countries. Her case study focuses on 'The Legacy' (Arvet) – a travelling exhibition that was displayed in Västmanland´s Museum, a regional museum in Sweden – which sought to represent how second and third generation immigrants from Finland perceive their Finnish legacy and how they maintain it in Sweden. Informatively this case study traces the changes that have taken place in Swedish museums, from 19th century concerns with the 'nation' and nationalism, to multiculturalism of the 20th century, as well as the evolving role of museums in education, outreach and constructivist learning. 'The Legacy' (Arvet) exhibition with its emphasis on immigrant life stories provides rich opportunities for exploring a range of pertinent themes linked to European 'border' 'identity' and 'belonging'. As Niklasson points out museums and initial teacher education both aim to create critical learning experiences; her case study reflects on the ways in which 'The Legacy' (Arvet) exhibition created several interesting points of intersection for student-teacher discussion and reflection.

Slovenia: In their chapter, "Yugonostalgia among young Slovenes" (pp. 133-149), Bostjan Rogelj, Katja Vintar Mally and Tatjana Resnik Planinc point out how the Socialist Federal Republic of Yugoslavia was born in the maelstrom of war at the end of 1943; its existence and development closely tied to the Yugoslav Communist Party, which was led for many years by Josip Broz Tito. Under Tito's leadership Yugoslavia changed from an agrarian to an industrialized country whose citizens enjoyed a relatively high standard of social rights. However, during its latter years the communist party was unable to respond to new economic challenges and in the face of economic and social problems Yugoslavia officially disintegrated in 1992. As the authors suggest over its fifty-year history Yugoslavia faced a series of highs and lows, successes and failures, lighter as well as darker moments. While some inhabitants experienced a 'good life' relatively free from cares and worries, others endured economic hardships and political repression. So, it is the case today that varied, indeed even diametrically opposed, memories of life in the former Yugoslavia are found to co-exist. In this case study Rogelj, Vintar Mally and Resnik Planinc take these 'varying memories' as the central subject of their research. They focus in particular on young people that grew up after the collapse of Yugoslavia and examine the memories they hold. Through their research the authors sought to ascertain if indeed any memories of the former Yugoslavia were actually evident amongst this younger generation. Having identified that this was the case, they explored: the extent to which memories of Yugoslavia were evident in their daily lives; which memories were most often preserved, how and by whom these memories were transferred to the younger generation. This chapter is helpfully structured in three parts; the first sets the theoretical frameworks for the research, exploring the concept of nostalgia before moving on to present the results of a survey and interviews conducted with young people in Slovenia. The chapter concludes with a presentation and summary of the research.

The theme of 'borders' and 'border crossing' – be they economic, political, territorial, social, cultural, linguistic, or gender – has been to the fore in both academic and popular discourse. With respect to the latter much of the discussion had been couched in quite negative vocabulary, as if 'border crossing' was something to be deeply suspicious about. This has been most evident in mass media representations of recent 'border crossings' by refugees fleeing into Europe. The themes of border, memory and migration have been fundamental to the work of the BE-SMaRT Project. In her chapter on "Thinking, teaching and learning about migration processes – the case of Slovenia" (pp. 118-132), Mojca Ilc Klun connects borders, memory and education, documenting how migration is a truly global phenomenon that is an important part of our lives. Therefore, it is vital that the topic of migration is appropriately incorporated into the educational experiences of young people. Drawing on extensive material from three different studies she undertook between 2014-16, Ilc Klun provides a fascinating insight into what young people in Slovenia think about migration, and how this research can be used to generate interest and engagement in the classroom. Her first study focuses on a survey of over 1,000 Slovenian students from primary and post-primary schools exploring their knowledge about migration processes, their perceptions and personal opinions about migration processes. The second explores the knowledge and perceptions of 75 undergraduate students from the Geography Department, at the University of Ljubljana, regarding migration experiences in Slovenia in 2015/16. As Ilc Klun explains the use of unstructured written essays provided the opportunity to collect the students' thoughts and feelings about migration. In the last study she presents draws on 'life story' research carried out with over fifty people of Slovenian descent now living in the USA, Canada, Australia and New Zealand. As Ilc Klun's paper demonstrates an urgent need exists in Europe to educate young people about migration processes, the causes and consequences of these processes and the acceptance of cultural, religious, linguistic and other diversities in order to develop intercultural dialogue. As her paper also points out, to do so effectively will require teachers to engage with concepts of 'borders' and 'memory' in ways that speak directly to learners' experiences.

Northern Ireland: Traditionally borders have constituted barriers, their function being to prevent 'us' from crossing to 'there'; as such, what lies on the other side of the border remains only partially visible and mostly unknown. In this context ignorance or at best partial knowledge, often inaccurate and biased, is left unchallenged to fuel perceptions and contribute to mindsets (cf. Newman 2006). However, when borders are opened or efforts are made to cross them, the 'Other' – that which hitherto had been mysterious and unknown – can be encountered for the first time (cf. ibid., 9) The BE-SMaRT case studies presented here suggest that 'border crossing' experiences are worthy of closer scrutiny because they help to throw light on what happens when the 'Other' is brought into a more normalised reality. This is particularly important where the 'Other' has been perceived in negative, threatening or violent terms, where conflict and war has been a feature of lived experience, or where the transition to a post-conflict society is underway. In this volume Tracey McKay's paper "Crossing Borders in Initial Teacher Education: a case study on students' perceptions of the Orange Order and education in a conflicted society" (pp. 169-192) explores students' perceptions of cultural otherness in a divided society. The north of Ireland exemplifies a range of border issues including a sovereign and territorial dispute over the 'contested' border which separates the northern six counties (of Northern Ireland) from the 26 counties of the Republic of Ireland. At the same time the deeply divided nature of society in Northern Ireland means that ethnic and cultural 'borders', to one extent or another, impact on most aspects of daily life, including education. While peace lines and indeed other 'territorial' markers on the cultural landscape speak of inclusion, exclusion and belonging, they are also symbolic indicators of the 'borders' that exists in the minds of citizens separating the 'us' from the 'them', the 'insiders' from the outsiders'. In the context of Northern Ireland physical, tangible 'geographical borders' really matter but so too do the perceptions that shape the 'borders of belonging' that exist inside people's heads. This case study examines the perceptions of and attitudes towards the Orange Order (a Protestant fraternal organisation) held by students from a mainly Catholic/Nationalist background, currently enrolled in a four year initial teacher education programme at St Mary's University College, a mainly 'Catholic' teacher training college located on the Falls Road in west Belfast. It examines the students' reflections on crossing what is largely perceived as a hard-edged cultural border to participate in a workshop to raise awareness about the 'Other', reflecting the extent to which memories, both individual and collective, influence and shape perceptions and attitudes. McKay's chapter closes with a short reflection on the need for continued, courageous and imaginative 'border crossing' within initial teacher education to help achieve the peaceful, equitable and shared society set out in the Good Friday Agreement.

Given recent media discourse one could be forgiven for thinking that the only borders that matter in Europe today are political or territorial. However, for many people in Europe the borders that are most apparent in their everyday lives are often invisible. All borders, both tangible and intangible, start with an idea that they are needed; thus all borders are social constructs, intended to meet a perceived 'need'. For many people it is the intangible or invisible borders, deeply etched in their thinking that inform perceptions, which in turn, temper feelings and attitudes and drives behaviour. As the BE-SMaRT case studies included in this volume illustrate just because a border cannot always be seen (or pointed out in tangible space) does not mean that it does not exist or have very real impacts; "if we really want to know what borders mean to people, then we need to listen to their personal and group narratives" (Newman 2006, 12). Angela Vaupel's chapter, "Borderlines" (pp. 60-96), offers a critical comparison of the representation and displayed experience of borders in contemporary youth films from both Germany and Ireland. As Vaupel explains, films are cultural expressions and, in many ways, mirrors of society. They communicate social values, experienced realities and interests, and consider how societies construct both historical and contemporary meaning. In the context of Border and Memory Studies, cinematic narratives provide insightful seismographic exploration into the depiction, imagination and commemoration of European borders after WWII. While these narratives explore national and political borders, they often also attempt to identify, challenge, and imagine frontiers of another kind: social, ethnic, religious, and gendered. These boundaries occur on international, national, communal, and individual scales, providing the opportunity for reflection on what it means to think, live, and – especially regarding the experience of young people – to grow-up between boundaries. By adopting a comparative approach in the analysis of four selected contemporary films from Ireland and Germany, Vaupel's chapter discusses these representations, relating her findings to key values of film education. The case study focuses in particular on the border-experiences and memories of young people as displayed in the two German films *Westwind* (2011) and *Am Ende kommen Touristen* (2007), both directed by Robert Thalheim, and in the two

Irish films *'71* (2014) and *Mickybo and Me* (2004) directed by Yann Demange and Terry Loane, respectively.

The rationale of the BE-SMaRT Project has been to understand Europe from the lived experiences and practices of students (the future citizenship educators of tomorrow's Europe) and their families. By adopting a bottom-up approach, with a focus on individual border narratives and experiences, reflecting the ways in which borders impact on daily life practices, the aim has been to show that 'Europe' is not some abstract subject to be learnt about in school or university. Rather, as the contributors to this volume suggest, it is a work in progress that encompasses past and present heritages, where all types of borders and the memories that inform and sustain our thinking are important and thus worthy of sustained critical reflection.

Germany: As Chloé Faucompré's paper "Cross-border cooperation between a researcher and teachers to optimise the teaching of the neighbours language" (pp. 97-117) explains there is a tendency in France to associate 'border regions' with bilingualism, primarily due to the country's proximity with other countries. In the Upper-Rhine region, where her research is focused, joint bilingual courses are in place on both sides of the French-German border, with the neighbour's language being systematically taught as the first foreign language. However, a recent and worrying trend related to mutual declining interest in learning the 'neighbouring' language provided the inspiration for her timely research. In this paper Faucompré reflects on her work to reassess educational practice in this particular border region in an attempt to remedy waning interest in 'neighbouring' language learning. Her work focuses on the cities of Strasbourg (Alsace) and Freiburg (Baden-Wurtemberg), where daily life is characterised by the daily cross-border flow of inhabitants. This cross-border interaction, as her chapter explains, has an important impact on representations of the neighbouring language and culture; these representations are not always positive owing to a continuous cohabitation with the 'Other', but they are critically important and need to be taken into account in the teaching and learning of German and French in this particular context. Faucompré's contribution to this volume is significant on at least two fronts; firstly her concretisation of a theoretical model seeks to make otherwise abstract ideas and concepts accessible for language teachers in a 'border region' context. While her critical reflection on the actual process of setting up a co-operative partnership between teachers and herself as the 'researcher' in this cross-border, regional context is informative of the opportunities and challenges facing those involved in modern European language education today.

In his paper "Old Dreams creating New Borders: the problems of EU Regional Policy and the future development of European Teacher Education" (pp. 34-59) Hans-Peter Burth reflects on the potential of the BE-SMaRT Project to serve as an interface between European Teacher Education, European Citizenship and Border Studies. Taking as his starting point the BE-SMaRT Project aim to develop a bottom-up reflective approach to memory and traditional concepts of Europe's borders in the professional development of teachers, he documents the important links between BE-SMaRT, European Teacher Education, European Civic Education and Border Studies. He demonstrates the various ways that the BE-SMaRT Project can meaningfully contribute to European identity, European knowledge, European multiculturalism, and European citizenship. His chapter moves to present an insightful review of European Cohesion policy (its origins, its impacts on processes of convergence and divergence in the EU and its challenges) before drawing the reader's attention to the opportunities and challenges which this presents for educators, including the BE-SMaRT Project. He issues a timely reminder

> that a critical analysis and reflection of the political aim of Europeanisation is necessary. Especially if you want to create and promote an affirmative and supportive attitude towards the EU by teacher education you will have to check carefully the assumptions and empirical facts that underlie your notions of Europeanisation as a central premise for European education. (p. 55)

His chapter concludes that the constructivist approach of the BE-SMaRT with its bottom-up cognitive approach to understanding borders and bordering processes represents real progress. Yet, he wisely cautions, that

> [q]ualitative cultural studies exploring individual border experiences and correlating collective memories and history (as used e.g. in BE-SMaRT) must not be separated from such a comprehensive picture of the process of Europeanisation that functions as a reference point (pp. 55f.).

To that end he urges educators not to lose sight of the fact that 'borders' can and do create their own reality that are experienced as objective social, political and economic facts. This he suggests becomes obvious when we look at the different lifestyles, the types of infrastructure, access to resources that enable or constrain wealth and development within the EU member states and its regions. As he reminds readers, "the chances, options and problems created by borders are not 'all inside our head'" (p. 56). Therefore, with one eye on the future and the other on the regional inequalities, setbacks and delays now shaping the European project, Burth acknowledges the contribution of education (including the BE-SMaRT Project) to achieving the old dream of a unified, peaceful, cooperative and cohesive Europe. As he says "it is the task of programs of European teacher education such as BE-SMaRT to impart such a utopian perspective into the heart and mind of teacher students" (p. 57).

Thus, by drawing together a range of different experiences and perspectives in this book, we hope to engage students' curiosity about borders, memory and identity issues across Europe. We hope that the case studies presented here will promote critical thinking and encourage student-teachers to become active citizens empowered by knowledge, enlivened by critical debate and inspired by the interdisciplinary thinking evidenced in the case studies themselves. Furthermore, it is hoped that the inclusion of the individual case studies within the BE-SMaRT Study Module will lead to new ways of thinking about, reflecting on and ultimately learning about borders. The BE-SMaRT Project consortium is committed to the ongoing development of 'border education'; to that end Olivier Mentz has directed the writing of a Memorandum on Border Education which is included in this publication (pp. 193-212).

We hope that by bringing together the case studies from the various partner countries in this focused volume we will make an active contribution to border education. Through them we seek to encourage student-teachers and teacher-educators to reflect on 'borders' and the intersections with 'memories'; to inspire them to move away from thinking about 'borders' only as a line on a territorial map and to begin to appreciate them as fluid, constantly changing entities, being (re)produced through everyday life experiences of people in a wide range of places that have been and continue to be informed by equally diverse types of memories and experiences. Finally, we hope that by sharing our case studies here that we might inspire ongoing research on 'borders', 'memories' and 'identities', in Europe and beyond, amongst student teachers and teacher-educators within initial teacher education.

Alexander Drost

BORDERS: A NARRATIVE TURN – Reflections on Concepts, Practices and their Communication

Introduction

What is a border? A complex academic discourse has developed since the 19th century that aims to answer what on the surface appears to be a simple question. Although initially conducted within discrete disciplinary contexts, the debate has recently crossed disciplinary borders and now links different aspects, meanings, influences and characteristics of various kinds of limits and their impact on social, economic and cultural life. Churchyard walls, the border of the nation state, ethnic, or religious boundaries – are all borders and order life. They include or exclude people, concede or restrict privileges, or regulate flows of commodities and people. In this way, borders form spaces, in which people can identify themselves in accordance to a common culture, language, and tradition, distinguishing and separating one social group from another. This was and is also the basis for the organization and identity of states, although the academic debate gradually drifted away from compartmentalization through lines, walls and fences, to emphasize instead the permeability of borders in the context of integration and globalization. Cultural exchange has moved into the centre of the debate. Even the notion that borders and boundaries are vanishing has found adherents across disciplines, particularly in the fields of economics and politics. The inter-/ trans-disciplinary debate has expanded the concept of the border by introducing the concept of the borderland **as** another important border concept for explaining historical and current developments of cultural diversity and exchange. However, more recent counter-narratives have challenged the perspective of expanding borders. Narratives of orders created by traditional, more restrictive bordering convince in the light of crisis, terror and growing uncertainty. Nevertheless, the ambivalence of order and freedom withstands simplistic concepts of restriction. As a result, the narratives about borders and their functions in political, cultural and social debate have become as important as the borders themselves.

The present synopsis adds to the ongoing discourses about borders and how they have evolved over time. After a short introduction concerning the scope of concepts mentioned in this chapter as well as some preliminary reflections about bordering processes, this chapter continues by addressing the formation of borders over centuries. In earlier times borders had not yet been represented by fixed lines. This is the age of the flexible frontier that lasted from the Middle Ages up until around 1800. The chapter then takes a first turn towards the most significant border concept for our spatial thinking, the national or state border. The next turn then refers to the more recent 'spatial turn' in the humanities and social sciences at the close of the 20th century. A variety of border concepts emerged that questioned whether the idea of the nation state border can remain relevant in the post-modern period. The final part of this chapter draws attention to the power of narrative at and across the border with two narratives about the Thai-Myanmar (Burmese) border, a border region which provides a good working example of borders in otherwise historical borderlands.

Border Concepts

The development of historical and current concepts of borders shows a fundamental change in how and why people and societies order their spaces through borders and boundaries. Since antiquity, meanings of exclusion and security have been expressed tangibly through walls and ramparts, to the extent that these are also manifested as metaphors in language. However, we will concentrate here on the development of borders and borderlands since the middle ages, particularly focusing on the role of statehood. In contrast to universal concepts in predominantly religious thinking of the Middle Ages, the concept of bordered space emerges as an antithesis. This bordered space formed initially a religious and later also a socio-cultural entity. The further development of the concept leads to the congruence of territory, stately sovereignty and society. This concept dominates our spatial thinking, which is strongly bound to the border of the nation state. Topographic-territorial border concepts manifest a so-called "territorial trap" (Agnew 1994). Symbolic and metaphorical understandings of border have been trying to extricate border concepts from the "trap" since the 1990s (cf. Paasi 2005, 118). Besides frontier (cf. Turner 1921, 27-37; Anderson 1996), 21-43) and national borders (cf. Demandt 1991; François, Seifarth & Struck 2007; Duhamelle, Kossert & Struck 2007; Kaplan, Carlson & Cruz 2009, Tagliacozzo 2016), concepts like the contact zone (cf. Krieger & North 2004a; Burke 2000; White 1991), the border as a product of social interaction (cf. Paasi 2005; Houtum, Kramsch & Zierhofer 2005, 1-13), or the borderland (cf. Anzaldúa 1987; Martinez 1994; Hämäläinen & Truett 2011; Lee & North 2016), and most recently the borderscape (cf. Mezzadra & Neilson 2013; Brambilla 2015) have provided new impulses for the debate on border concepts and their either diminished or increased importance in the order of today's societies.

Order and Space

Borders are constructions and depend on the interpretation of people who use them as a tool to order their world. In this way, people create a certain order in an otherwise indefinite or borderless world. Henk van Houtum emphasizes the ordering function of borders, which should be comprehended as dividing lines detached from space and time (cf. Houtum & Naerssen 2002, 126). Bordering supports spatial ordering on different levels. Hereby, the focus lies on the accentuation of difference between things, for instance, differences between states and their territories, but also differences between cultural societies within one territory. By emphasizing 'difference' between 'self' and 'other' (othering) we also become aware of the borders of our own identity. At the same time, we mark spaces of action and influence (cf. Houtum & Naerssen 2002, 126; Houtum, Kramsch & Zierhofer 2005, 1-13; Migdal 2004, 5f.).

Differentiation on various levels clearly demonstrates the multidimensional character of borders (cf. Balibar 2002, 81-84). Besides geographical and political space, borders also structure social, cultural or economic spaces and thus help people and societies to locate themselves. Furthermore, the ordering function of borders, in the sense of van Houtum, points to the mental dimension in the process of bordering. It is daily practice to interpret existing borders and adjust them in a de- and rebordering process, particularly when someone ascertains his or her identity (cf. Houtum, Kramsch & Zierhofer 2005, 1-3; also Paasi 2002, 139-141; Yuval-Davis, Wemyss & Cassidy 2016).

For a long time, topographic models offered the most comprehensible explanations for understanding borders and the social world they created. Border stones, city walls, fortresses, custom stations, battle lines, or lines on a map are real products of the mind, offering protection, demarcating property, creating an exclusive space. The same pattern of interpretation can be applied for example to coast lines, deserts or forests, which should not be understood as so called 'natural boundaries'. These borders emerge also from an interpretation and communication process in which certain characteristics can be ascribed to water, mountain or deserts but those characteristics can be either dividing or connecting (cf. Berg & Houtum 2003, 2).

Since antiquity, manifestations like the Limes or the Great Wall of China have also influenced imaginings of protection and exclusion. Whilst during the Middle Ages strict social boundaries in universally organized societies dominate spatial concepts, it is particularly the conflict driven emergence of the early modern states which bound the ends of empires and transformed the concept of border significantly.

From frontiers to state borders: In the borderland

The European frontier of the Middle Ages can mainly be understood as a line of battle. However, the term frontier can also be applied to fringes of power in empires and monarchies. These spaces did not necessarily form clearly delimitated sovereignties, ethnicities or cultures. The medieval frontier is a rather ambiguous concept – my understanding here draws on the studies of Daniel Power (1999), Naomi Standen (Power & Standen 1999) and David Abulafia (2002). The frontier is a space of mostly violent interaction, in which religious, power-political or sovereignty conflicts are fought. In connection with these conflicts, the territories of defeated powers were occupied and social and cultural patterns were transferred in order to promote allegiance to the new rulers (cf. Abulafia 2011, 5-20; Power 1999, 106ff.). These battles often initiated considerable spatial shifts in the boundaries of fealty, at that time particularly in relation to conflicts with other religions at the fringes of Christian Europe in the Mediterranean, in Spain or in the Baltic Sea Region (cf. Moreno 1999, 34ff.; Mažeika 2002, 153ff.; for background information on the Baltic Sea see North 2007, 196-249; on the Mediterranean Sea see Abulafia 2011, 318-333). These spatial shifts caused also diverse overlaps of cultural and political spaces. Against this background, the frontier of the Middle Ages could never simply be drawn as a line. Its manifestations stretched from open spaces between two powers to single markers in the form of fortresses at the periphery of empires. Besides its political function to order space, the frontier also functioned as a marker of religious limits. These frontiers were not bound to a particular territory and the presence of the frontier often only became really apparent during periods of conflict. Therefore, the medieval frontier had a rather mobile character as a zone between rivals. The frontier could not be fixed in space and if so, then only for a short period of time. The frontier often disappeared with the disappearance of the conflict.

The ambiguity of the frontier also characterizes the violent negotiation of Europe's borders during the Early Modern Period. Administrative, cultural and religious loyalties and spaces overlapped and formed different complex spatial units like dominions (earldoms, dukedoms, kingdoms), national-cultural spaces (French speaking cultural space, etc.), maritime networks (Baltic Sea Region), religious spaces (Catholic south, Protestant north, multi-confessional Poland-Lithuania). The political spaces and enclaves which appeared due to the double loyalties of rulers are a case in point (cf. Duchhardt 1997): consider the fact that between 1648 and 1815 the King of Sweden was also a duke of the Holy Roman Empire due to his rule over Pomerania (cf. Kent 2014, 74).

The reign of Phillip II of Spain in the Low Countries constitutes a fine example for the development of the early modern concept of borders. In the course of the Dutch Revolt from 1568 onwards the shifting line of battle between the northern and southern provinces of the Low Countries became more and more fixed and was finally confirmed as a state border in the Peace of Westphalia in 1648. Furthermore, the spatial overlaps of administrative, political and monarchical loyalties ceased to exist between Spanish-Habsburg, Austrian-Habsburg and the Holy Roman Empire and a clearly demarcated state, a republic of 17 provinces was established. The frontier developed into a territorial border, which besides symbolically representing a border between a protestant north and a catholic south also marked a border between a prosperous north and in economic terms a declining south (cf. Deursen 1993, 205; Israel 1995; North 1997, 22-36).

However, even though territorial border formation was a characteristic process in early modern Europe, the mobile frontier did not disappear. Especially during the European expansion into Asia and the Americas, the frontier as cultural or civilizational border became a characteristic element of European global migration processes. Frederick Jackson Turner developed his idea of the American frontier against the background of European settler colonisation and expansion into the western territories in North America. He was convinced of a special position of the United States in the world due to the continuous interaction between civilization and wilderness at the North American frontier (cf. Turner 1921, 2f.). James C. Scott and Willem van Schendel observed comparable interaction patterns between civilised valley and unruled hill areas in South and Southeast Asia (cf. Scott 2009, 54; Schendel 2005, 282-285). Furthermore, the European frontier was transferred into Asia through several conflicts between European rivals in the spice trade. In this way, European border concepts were transferred into non-European areas where indigenous societies seem to have problems to translate the meaning of these concepts into their own systems of meaning (cf. Drost 2013).

Another important concept that characterises spatial delimitation and fragmentation is the borderland. Overlaps of political, cultural and religious identities created borderlands in which concrete borders were less manifest. At the fringes of empires for instance, the distance to the imperial power, e.g. the King of Sweden, let evolve local or regional orders, which were obviously loyal to the king but also took the advantage of distance to pursue their own goals. Local estates, for example in the multicultural Swedish-Russian borderland of Livonia successfully retained their privileges in the Early Modern Period and thus maintained the historical space of Livonia, which disappeared in the period of nation state building in the 19th century. The southern Baltic Sea Region represented an overlap of different local spatialities which experienced different cultural transfer processes, starting with Christian crusaders and the Hanseatic network followed by the Swedish expansion and the growing importance of the Polish-Lithuanian Empire (cf. North 2007, 157, 196-199, 203ff.; North 2011, 66-77 and 136-143). Recent research on a post-national Europe let us re-encounter some of these historical spaces as sub-national or transnational regions (cf. Thormählen 2004, 76; Stokłosa 2006, 117ff.). Furthermore, these encounters point to the dominance of the model of the 'nation state' and its borders in our spatial imagination, which conceals the multi-dimensional character of religious, political, economic, social and cultural borders in the Early Modern Period. A different approach towards spaces and borders might offer better explanations for historical and current bordering processes in Europe. One such concept has been proposed by Gloria Anzaldúa who describes the borderland as cultural spaces of interaction and exchange, in which specific social structures are engendered (cf. Anzaldúa 1987, Preface).

Demarcation and Frame of Reference: The Border of the Nation State

The post-national and post-colonial border concepts can be understood as a reaction to the concept of the border of the nation state, which emerged in a period of crises.

The crisis of the Ancien Régime in the end of the 18th century contributed to a climate of greater ideological freedom in which enlightened ideas and emerging patriotism were seeking new stable orders. Rational thinking may have initiated the development of new socio-political orders as alternatives to monarchic models but liberty also fostered a feeling of uncertainty and insecurity (cf. Schmidt 2009, 11-14). This transitional phase of indefinite political structures (revolutions) ended up in a spatial reorganisation of Europe and the emergence of the nation state as a new spatial unit with clear national borders. This process can be roughly located in the 19th and 20th century. It is not very easy to define the nation state due to many different historical discourses. However, there are some important characteristics which also determine our ideas about national borders.

Jürgen Osterhammel, for example, thinks of a political community which has a common identity that is ideally built on common language and common destiny. This is the basis of a world order in which the 'nation state' forms the basic unit. In this basic unit, the community aspires to autonomy within a clearly defined and demarcated territory and needs state structures to secure this autonomy (cf. Osterhammel 2009, 582). The achievement of such an order of the world in nation states is a self-sufficient economic space and a homogeneous culture with common values and symbols. Furthermore, the nation state survives only with an internationally successful diplomacy, resp. to other nation states (cf. Reinhard 2000, 447f.). The ideal of common values, symbols, ethnic and law continues to dominate our spatial imagination and the construction of borders even today (cf. Schulze 2004, 189-208; Dann 1996, 149-158), although, as Wolfgang Reinhard states, most nation states are multi-national if we consider, for instance, minority policy (cf. Reinhard

2000, 447f.). However, the nation state has a great impact in imagining societies whose members have formed strong territorially fixed borderlines at the peripheries of their state structures and are considered equal citizens of that state. More or less strict border regimes control the permeability of these borders. Visa and custom checks regulate flows of commodities and people in accordance with socio-political principles which follow strict definitions of 'internal and external' or 'self and other'.

The process of forming the fixed borderline of the nation state contributed to the disappearance of the frontier character of borders, real and imagined. Borderlands remain only as no man's land or defence zones, whereby these peripheries developed into economically weak areas because of the disruptive effect of demarcation on economic activity.

From the 'Iron Curtain' to the Re-ordering of Space: In the Borderland

The next demarcation level in bordering was achieved by Cold War and for example the construction of the Berlin Wall. This border was an impenetrable material manifestation of the ideological divide between East and West in the 20th century. The term border could not encompass the dimensions of this form of bordering. If we call on the dividing and connecting function of borders, the 'Iron Curtain' was a border to represent a non-relationship. With the disappearance of the 'Iron Curtain' in Europe, a new and more intense discourse on borders and their construction started. The political and cultural developments nurturing this discourse, however, started earlier.

Since the middle of the 20th century, new transnational structures have emerged in following the founding of the European Union. Firstly, these developments contributed to the re-bordering of a common European economic market which opened up the formerly nationally controlled economies of the member states. As transnational economic interaction of the Western European states was intensified, economic borders became more permeable and the national economic space ended up in a European single market, leaving or overcoming the imagined unity of political, cultural and economic spaces in the nation state.

With the fall of the 'Iron Curtain' and in connection with intensifying globalization and accompanying American cultural expansion, the unity of social, political and cultural spaces in the nation state was called into question, especially in Europe. Intensified migration and transfer processes too had and have a strong impact on exchange and regional as well as trans-regional integration processes in Europe since 1989/90/91.

Nevertheless, it would be wrong to see national borders as unimportant and to paint a picture of a borderless world as some observers had (cf. O'Dowd 2003, 13). Rather, the permeability of state borders and intensified economic and administrative European integration have changed perspectives on borders and border concepts and thus contributed to a re-interpretation of the role and impact of borders. Commodity flows, migration and transnational institutions as well as the emphasis on common values have contributed to the imagination of an apparently borderless space in 21st century EU Europe. In this context, the demarcatory character of borders was replaced by an understanding of borders as bridges due to the opening of the nation state model. This interpretation of the border has facilitated a redefinition of the periphery, from an economically weak area to one that could profit from intensified flows of commodities and migration (cf. Schack 2007, 9-17). Borderlands could be cast as innovative centres because of the first hand experiences with the neighbour and new ideas. Furthermore, by stressing the conjunctive elements of the relationship between neighbours rather than the dividing ones, the perspective highlights the emergence of hybrid cultures through cultural interaction (cf. Morehouse 2004, 26-32; Clement 2004, 41f.).

Richard White (1991) and Homi Bhabha (1994) have both described hybridisation processes at the borders of colonial empires and helped to develop early interpretation patterns for the change in the nature of European and global borders with their concepts of the 'middle ground' or 'third space'. These concepts supported also a wide range of research on cultural transfer and the description of integration patterns on several levels of the European integration process at the end of the 20th century. In these descriptions, historical regions – like the Mediterranean, or the Baltic Sea Region – re-emerged in the regional development literature and practice, as actors saw regional coherence due to traditional connections via trade, art, education or religion as a socio-economic resource (cf. Krieger & North 2004b; North 2011; Abulafia 2011). In analysing these historical structures, concepts like 'Cross-border-Cooperation' or 'Global Governance' were used to describe current cross-border phenomena (cf. Anderson, O'Dowd & Wilson 2003).

However, the open, unbounded space is not an option. Borders still have their importance in life. With Paasi (2005) we understand borders as 'social practice' and observe that people may cross any national border freely but also that these people have regularly to negotiate their own identity and thus live in a continuous bordering process. In this context, ethnic, religious, local or regional localization and bordering processes take place all the time and it seems that the newly emerging cultural-symbolic borders have a stronger impact and demarcating character than the border of the nation state ever had (cf. Migdal 2004, 5f.). Examples like the urban enclaves of ethnic minorities in Berlin, Paris, or London confirm this development as much as the right wing polemics about religious minorities and their conflicts with a Christian Europe. Cultures of dialogue and negotiation form the new border regime, regulating the penetration and permeability of cultural boundaries.

In this sense, the Anzaldúan 'borderland' (1987), in which identity and its borders are negotiated in a daily practice, becomes an important concept to describe current interpretations of borders.

Furthermore, the spatial units changed considerably in EU Europe. The protective and barrier function of the border of the nation state has moved to the external borders of the integrated Europe. To the inside, new models like "global governance" or new spatial orders can be tested and borderlands emerged as contact zones, development or innovation spaces. In this way, the model of the nation state was transformed from its ends, the borders. But, the nation state has not (yet) become obsolete. Between integration and identity preservation, the nation state has rather an ambivalent position. Whilst a transformed border concept sharpened our awareness for (re-)emerging symbolic, social and cultural borders as utility for identity formation in a continuous European integration process, the narrow concept of state and territorial borders celebrate a revival in multi-layered deterrence strategies (cf. Godenau & López-Sala 2016, 151), for instance at EU borders. This also affects the perception of borderlands as peripheries of the state again and thus borderland categories, which – at least in Western Europe – we almost forgot. Oscar J. Martinez (1994, 5-10) developed four of these borderland categories: (1) The *Alienated Borderlands*: a closed border area with little or no interaction in a rather unstable border situation. (2) The *Co-Existent Borderlands* with contacts across a border between two more or less socially and economically complementary but still cautious partners. (3) The *Interdependent Borderlands,* in which these partners show a higher degree of integrated and friendlier interrelations. (4) The *Integrated Borderlands* as the highest degree of interrelations between states and the free movement of goods, people and ideas. Raimondo Strassoldo (2000) related these four types of borderlands to the different stages of state formation from the initial phase of state building to a consolidation phase of co-existence and finally a phase of integration as we experienced in Europe. However, the ambivalent perception of different phases of integration and disintegration of social, cultural and political spaces shed light on the temporal character and historicality of border concepts. The interpretation of borders is strongly connected to the problems and perspectives of people and societies in a certain period of time. This points on the one hand to the volatility of borders, and on the other to certain border narratives. They are a key element in mediating and communicating certain concepts of and perspectives on borders.

Border Narrative Turn

Considering occurrences like the refugee crises, global and regional ecological problems, or national extreme movements we are probably experiencing a turning point in political and cultural terms right now. As the last examples of increased border control and different stages of integration suggest, we may want to evaluate our current narratives of open societies, integration and cross-border mobility. Furthermore, we want to know how these narratives were put in place, for what reason and how this influences our understanding of events.

European states have been engaged in a fundamental political and cultural transformation process since the fall of the iron curtain, the expansion of the EU and globalization. Economic globalization and their local entanglement as "glocalization" (Bauman 1998, 43; Ritzer 2003, 194) stimulated as many opposing stories as narratives of advocacy. For about two decades, we perceived these processes as chance and positive turn in the course of history. Political, social and cultural actors and decision makers took the opportunity to praise the advances of borderless societies in the terrestrial and digital world, announcing economic strength and stimulating cross-cultural, cross-border activities. The emerging border studies are a result of this process. As we have seen, academic discourse supported narratives of the devaluation of state borders and the re-emergences of cultural ones. Research hereby tried to overcome the spatial atrophy in the humanities and implemented the ideas of the spatial turn. This approach offered possibilities to perceive for instance (historical) regions again as cultural, political and economic entities beyond national and territorial frames (cf. Belokurova & Nozhenko 2013, 34f.)

However, the power political, social and cultural preconditions seem to have changed in the most recent course of history. The narratives in favour of transnational developments seem to have lost their explanatory power. Global and European crises (banking crises, Russian annexation of Crimea, refugee crisis, Brexit, election of Trump) somehow relinquished beliefs of interconnected, transnational and transcultural spaces and borderlands. These phenomena encouraged the return of nationalism and scepticism against cross-border cultural contacts. Their narratives seem to convince growing numbers of people around the world and hereby implicitly supported the shift of former liberal governments towards more conservative perceptions of and narratives about border regimes and the control of borderlands. Furthermore, these 'new' narratives predict a different future.

In this this context, the questions are: Which story are we about to tell about a border? What kind of future we are predicting with this story? And also, who is telling the story to whom?

A little detour from our European integrated borderlands takes us to a modern borderland situation at the border of Thailand and Myanmar. Two narratives of the 21st century exist side by side, one of a national border of European descent and the other of a historical cultural borderland.

The border situation between both countries is characterized by a long history of political and military conflicts, comparable to the history of many borders in Europe. It is a historical borderland of imperial military campaigns. These are now embedded in national stories about the military strength of Thailand. The most obvious material representation for this is the shrine of King Naresuan at each border post. He became the guard of the Thai army and is vividly remembered for his campaigns against the Taungoo Empire and King of Ava in 16th and 17th century Burma to overcome Ayutthaya's subjugation and to strengthen its power in the region. Most importantly, he reasserted Siam's independence from the Burmese. When the King of Ava invaded the Shan region in today's Northern Myanmar and Thailand, Naresuan raised an army to counter this attack. However, he fell ill in Chiang Mai province and died in 1605 in what is now the Shan state (cf. Wyatt 2000, Baker 2005). His military strength is resembled in the shrines along the border, hereby also empowering the Thai soldiers guarding a national border, which conceptually is a rather new idea in this region. The shrines of Naresuan are always facing Myanmar, against the 'enemy'. The enemy can hereby be defined as 'Burmese' but not necessarily as Shan or Wa, the actual inhabitants on both sides of this border.

While the (military) frontier history is still present in monuments and shrines the official narrative of this border is deeply rooted in the European ideas of bordering states. The unofficial narrative gives an account of a cultural borderland situation.

The first narrative, vividly presented at the border post of Doi Ang Khang, tells the story of a national border as national defence line. Trenches, tunnels, sand bags and shelter in camouflage colour offer the ultimate border experience for Thai and foreign tourists. It represents military strength and power before a canvas of Burmese dreariness on the other side. Maps show the exact borderline to the visitor. The border at this border post is a reflection of an image of a nation state border imagined in Bangkok or Naypyidaw. It is an alienated borderland, closed for interaction. At the same time, this border scene is educating the visitor about a border, which otherwise cannot be recognized outside this border post in the jungle of Chiang Mai region. The barbwire fence is less a necessity at this point than a demonstration.

Beyond the architecture of this border post, the second narrative derives from the historical borderland of hill tribes and their cultures. This borderland situation comes closest to the conceptual ideas of Gloria Anzaldúa and Anssi Paasi. It is a borderland of Shan and Wa people, living on both sides of the border. It is also a narrative of Chinese and Vietnamese refugees from the 1950s and 1970s, and, of course, of Thai people. They engage in traffic across this actually closed border, anticipating the ideas of an integrated and multicultural border region beyond any national divide. They participate, often illegally, in the social and cultural negotiation of this border. Shan, Wa, refugees and Thai do not only experience the national border differently, but also interpret its existence from a much longer, pre-national narrative of openness and their own bordering practice, which includes particularly cultural markers when acting across the border. Language and appearance mark the belonging to a particular social ad ethnic group. Furthermore, Buddhism unites many ethnic groups across the national border.

However, both narratives about the national border and the cultural borderland exist. The situation and the person, who tells the story, determine which one is told.

It is a tentative establishment, distribution and updating of narratives. They are characterized by a certain elasticity and fuzziness due to the relation between narrative and users of this narrative. Narratives require interpretation and hereby offer to narrators as well as to the audience a certain liberty in applying semantics to the facts and the arrangement, which were presented in the story (cf. Schmied 2014, 21). Furthermore, the underlying uncertainty principle asks for a permanent re-contextualization of the given facts and happenings in the development of the plot. Temporality produces coherence. However, temporality demands also continuously semantic shifts.

While Bangkok is in favour of a story about a strong national border represented in a few closed and barb wire fenced border posts, the numerous local tribes and refugee communities engage locally and under the eyes of military and police in trade and traffic across this border. They do so away from the border posts, usually on traditional paths and trails through the uncontrollable jungle. Their narratives include a borderland situation of openness and contact. Therefore, the semantics applied to this border shift between closed and open, depending on whom you ask for his/her story.

References

Abulafia, D. (2002). Introduction. Seven Types of Ambiguity. In D. Abulafia & N. Berend (eds.). *Medieval Frontiers. Concepts and Practices*. Aldershot, 1-34.

Abulafia, D. (2011). *The Great Sea. A Human History of the Mediterranean*. Oxford.

Agnew, J. (1994). The Territorial Trap. The Geographical Assumptions of International Relations Theory. *Review of International Political Economy*, 1/1, 53-80.

Anderson, J.; O'Dowd, L. & Wilson, T. M. (eds.; 2003). *New Borders for a Changing Europe. Cross-border Cooperation and Governance*. London.

Anderson, M. (1996). *Frontiers. Territory and State Formation in the Modern World.* Cambridge.

Anzaldúa, G. E. (1987). *Borderlands. The New Mestiza*. San Francisco.

Bhabha, H. K. (1994). *The Location of Culture*. New York.

Baker, Ch. (ed.; 2005). *Van Vliet's Siam*. Chiang Mai.

Balibar, E. (2002). *Politics and the Other Scene*. London, New York.

Bauman, Z. (1998). On Glocalization: or Globalization for some, Localization for some Others. *Thesis Eleven*, 54/37, 37-49.

Belokurova, E. & Nozhenko, M. (2013). Regional community-building and cross-border interaction. In H. Eskelinen, I. Liikanen & J. W. Scott (eds.). *The EU-Russia Borderland. New contexts for a regional co-operation*. Abingdon, New York, 31-43.

Berg, E. & Houtum, H. van (2003). Prologue: A Border is not a Border. Writing and Reading Borders in Space. In E. Berg & H. van Houtum (eds.). *Routing Borders Between Territories. Discourses and Practices*. Aldershot, 1-12.

Brambilla, C. (2015). Exploring the Critical Potential of the Borderscapes Concept. *Geopolitics*, 20/1, 14-34.

Burke, P. (2000). *Kultureller Austausch*. Frankfurt.

Clement, N. C. (2004). Economic Forces Shaping the Borderlands. In V. Pavlakovich-Kochi, B. J. Morehouse & D. Wastl-Walter (eds.). *Challenged Borderlands. Transcending Political and cultural Boundaries*. Aldershot, 41-62.

Dann, O. (1996). *Nation und Nationalismus in Deutschland 1770-1990*. München.

Demandt, A. (ed.; 1991). *Deutschlands Grenzen in der Geschichte*. München.

Deursen, A. Th. van (1993). De Republiek der Zeven Verenigde Nederlanden (1588-1780). In J. C. H. Blom & E. Lamberts (eds.). *Geschiedenis van de Nederlanden*. Amsterdam, 117-177.

Drost, A. (2013). Grenzenlos eingrenzen. Koloniale Raumstrukturen der Frühen Neuzeit in den Konfliktfeldern zwischen Asien und Europa. *Themenportal Europäische Geschichte*. Online: http://www.europa.clio-online.de/essay/id/artikel-3735 [last accessed 20 July 2017].

Duchhardt, H. (ed.; 1997). *Der Herrscher in der Doppelpflicht. Europäische Fürsten und ihre beiden Throne*. Mainz.

Duhamelle, Ch.; Kossert, A. & Struck, B. (eds.; 2007). *Grenzregionen. Ein europäischer Vergleich vom 18. bis zum 20. Jahrhundert*. Frankfurt.

François, E.; Seifarth, J. & Struck, B. (eds.; 2007). *Die Grenze als Raum, Erfahrung und Konstruktion. Deutschland, Frankreich und Polen vom 17. bis 20. Jahrhundert*. Frankfurt.

Godenau, D. & López-Sala, A. (2016). Multi-layered Migration Deterrence and Technology in Spanish Maritime Border Management. *Journal of Borderlands Studies 31/2,* 151-169.

Hämäläinen, P. & Truett, S. (2011). On Borderlands. *Journal of American History*, 338-361.

Houtum, H. van & Naerssen, T. van (2002). Bordering, Ordering and Othering. *Tijdschrift voor Economische en Sociale Geografie 93/2,* 125-36.

Houtum, H. van; Kramsch, O. & Zierhofer, W. (2005). Prologue. B/ordering Space. In H. van Houtum, O. Kramsch & W. Zierhofer (eds.). *B/ordering Space*. Aldershot, 1-13.

Israel, J. (1995). *The Dutch Republic. Ist Rise, Greatness, and Fall, 1477-1806*. Oxford.

Kaplan, B.; Carlson, M. B. & Cruz, L. (eds.; 2009). *Boundaries and Their Meanings in the History of the Netherlands*. Leiden, Boston.

Kent, N. (2014). *A Concise History of Sweden*. Cambridge.

Krieger, M. & North, M. (2004a). Kultureller Austausch zwischen Westeuropa und dem Ostseeraum. Eine Einleitung. In M. Krieger & M. North (eds.). *Land und Meer. Kultureller Austausch zwischen Westeuropa und dem Ostseeraum in der Frühen Neuzeit*. Wien, 1-8.

Krieger, M. & North, M. (eds.; 2004b). *Land und Meer. Kultureller Austausch zwischen Westeuropa und dem Ostseeraum in der Frühen Neuzeit*. Wien.

Lee, J. W. I. & North, M. (eds.; 2016). *Globalizing Borderlands Studies in Europe and North America*. Lincoln.

Martinez, O. J. (1994). *Border People. Life and Society in the U.S.-Mexico Borderlands.* Tucson.

Mažeika, R. (2002). Granting Power to Enemy Gods in the Chronicles of the Baltic Crusades. In D. Abulafia & N. Berend (eds.). *Medieval Frontiers. Concepts and Practices*. Aldershot, 153-71.

Mezzadra, S. & Neilson, B. (2013). *Border as Method, or, the Multiplication of Labor*. Durham.

Migdal, J. S. (2004). Mental Maps and Virtual Checkpoints. Struggles to Construct and Maintain State and Social Boundaries. In J. S. Migdal (ed.). *Boundaries and Belonging. States and Societies in the Struggle to Shape Identities and Local Practices*. Cambridge, 3-20.

Morehouse, B. J. (2004). Theoretical Approaches to Border Spaces and Identities. In V. Pavlakovich-Kochi, B. J. Morehouse & D. Wastl-Walter (eds.). *Challenged Borderlands. Transcending Political and Cultural Boundaries*. Aldershot, 16-39.

Moreno, E. M. (1999). The Creation of a Medieval Frontiers. Islam and Christianity in the Iberian Peninsula. Eighth to Eleventh Centuries. In D. Power & N. Standen (eds.). *Frontiers in Question. Eurasian Borderlands, 700-1700*. London and New York, 32-54.

North, M. (1997). *Geschichte der Niederlande*. München.

North, M. (2007). *Europa expandiert 1250-1500*. Stuttgart.

North, M. (2011). *Geschichte der Ostsee. Handel und Kulturen*. München.

O'Dowd, L. (2003). The Changing Significance of European Borders. In J. Anderson, L. O'Dowd & T. M. Wilson (eds.). *New Borders for a Changing Europe. Cross-border Cooperation and Governance*. London, Portland/Oregon, 13-36.

Osterhammel, J. (2009). *Die Verwandlung der Welt. Eine Geschichte des 19. Jahrhunderts*. München.

Paasi, A. (2002). Bounded Spaces in the Mobile World. Deconstructing „Regional Identity". *Tijdschrift voor Economische an Sociale Geografie 93/2,* 137-48.

Paasi, A. (2005). Boundaries as Social Practice and Discourse. The Finnish Russian Border. In P. Ganster & D. E. Lorey (eds.). *Borders and Border Politics in a Globalizing World*. Lanham, 117-36.

Power, D. (1999). French and Norman Frontiers in the Central Middle Ages. In D. Power & N. Standen (eds.). *Frontiers in Question. Eurasian Borderlands, 700-1700*. London and New York, 105-127.

Power, D. & Standen, N. (eds.; 1999). *Frontiers in Question. Eurasian Borderlands, 700-1700*. London and New York.

Reinhard, W. (^{2}2000). *Geschichte der Staatsgewalt. Eine vergleichende Verfassungsgeschichte Europas von den Anfängen bis zur Gegenwart*. München.

Ritzer, G. (2003). Rethinking Globalization: Glocalization/Grobalization and Something/Nothing. *Sociological Theory 21/3,* 193-209.

Schack, M. (2007). *Grenzen und Grenzregionen. Soziale Differenzierungen im Raum*. Aachen.

Schendel, W. van (2005). Geographies of Knowing, Geographies of Ignorance. Jumping Scale in Southeast Asia. In P. H. Kratoska, R. Raven & H. Schulte-Nordholt (eds.). *Locating Southeast Asia. Geographies of Knowledge and Politics in Space*. Singapur, 275-307.

Schmidt, G. (2009). *Wandel durch Vernunft. Deutsche Geschichte im 18. Jahrhundert*. München.

Schmied, W. (2014). *Elemente der Narratologie*. Berlin.

Schulze, H. (^{2}2004). *Staat und Nation in der europäischen Geschichte*. München.

Scott, J. C. (2009). *The Art of Not Being Governed. An Anarchist History of Upland Southeast Asia*. New Haven, London.

Stokłosa, K. (2006). Two sides of the border and one regional identity: the identity problem in the German-Polish and the Ukrainian-Slovak border regions. In T. Lundén (ed.). *Crossing the border. Boundary relations in a changing Europe.* Eslöv, 117-133.

Strassoldo, R. (^{2}2000). National Border Relations. In E. F. Borgatta & R. J. V. Montgomery (eds.). *Encyclopedia of Sociology*. New York et al., 1931-1639.

Tagliacozzo, E. (2016). Jagged Landscapes: Conceptualizing Borders and Boundaries in the History of Human Societies. *Journal of Borderlands Studies 31/1,* 1-21.

Thormählen, L. (ed.; 2004). *Entwicklung europäischer Grenzräume bei abnehmender Bedeutung nationaler Grenzen*. Hannover.

Turner, F. J. (1921). The Significance of the Frontier in American History. In F. J. Turner (ed.). *The Frontier in American History*. New York, 1-38.

White, R. (1991). *The Middle Ground. Indians, Empires, and Republics in the Great Lakes Region, 1650-1815*. Cambridge.

Wyatt, D. K. (ed., 2000). *The royal chronicles of Ayutthaya*. Bangkok.

Yuval-Davis, N.; Wemyss, G. & Cassidy, K. (2016). *Bordering Polity*. Cambridge.

Hans-Peter Burth

Old Dreams creating New Borders: The problems of EU Regional Policy and the future development of European Teacher Education

Introduction: BE-SMaRT as an interface between European Teacher Education, European Citizenship Education and Border Studies

Regarding European societies with a focus on social cohesion, the Erasmus+ project BE-SMaRT aims to develop bottom-up reflective educational approaches to challenge memories and "traditional" concepts of Europe's borders in the professional development of teachers. Thus BE-SMaRT aims to explore and discuss borders in an inclusive manner by examining the interdisciplinary aspects of borders and their impact on (young) peoples' life-experiences and constructions of identities within more and more globalized societies: "BE-SMaRT stimulates teacher students and teachers in service to critically think about the role of mental borders in everyday life actions and practices of European citizens." (BE-SMaRT Application 2014, 32)

By doing so BE-SMaRT can be regarded as an interface between European Teacher Education, European Citizenship Education and Border Studies (cf. Mentz 2017, 199f.). In this introductory chapter I want to illustrate the versatile links between BE-SMaRT and these different disciplines.

Being a concept of European Teacher Education BE-SMaRT can be regarded simultaneously as tool within the wider field of *European Citizenship Education* (cf. Eis 2007; Lösch 2009, 855f.). In its strong normative version (cf. Dürr 2005, Mickel 1999, Kelbling 2002), European Citizenship Education aims at creating an emotional identification with the European Union (EU) and the imparting of a European competence to European citizens including a cognitive, sensuous and conative dimension (cf. Dürr 2005, 20f). Quite similarly

> teachers in the European Union not only educate future citizens of their particular member state, but also support them in becoming future generations

> of European citizens. They work within a national framework, which emphasizes the need for a national identity as a basis for transnational awareness within European society. (Schratz 2014, 18)

Correspondingly BE-SMaRT aims at "opening teacher education from its traditionally national orientation to a European dimension" (BE-SMaRT Application 2014, 36), and encourages teacher students to become active European citizens that assume responsibility in creating "a more socially just, inclusive and successfully functioning European society" (ibid., 92).

Trying to answer the question "What is a European teacher?" Austrian educationist Michael Schratz makes some suggestions how the attribute of "Europeanness" inside European Teacher Education can be specified.[1] By this means BE-SMaRT's implicit targets concerning the imparting of European identity and European Citizenship to teacher students can be made more explicit. Especially the following aspects of Europeanness that are also mirrored in the BE-SMaRT contributions are suited to illustrate the program's character as an interface between European Citizenship and European Teacher Education. These dimensions are:

- European identity:
  The European Teacher
  > would see himself/herself as someone with roots in one particular country, but simultaneously belonging to a greater European whole [...] This co-existence of national identity and transnational awareness provides a valuable perspective on questions of heterogeneity. Diversity within unity is, therefore, a key aspect of a developed European identity with an open mind toward the world at large. (Schratz 2014, 18)
- European knowledge:
  > On the governance level, there is knowledge about Europe that is expected from an educated European citizen and is already taught at primary level [...] On the higher education level, there is debate regarding 'a Europe of knowledge', which has reflected the synergies and tensions between European research and higher education policies [...] In the realm of teaching, the

[1] For similar reflections refer to Mentz 2010 and 2011.

question arises of whether a European Teacher has to have some knowledge of other European education systems and, possibly, of educational policy matters on the EU level [...] Does s/he have a knowledge of European and world affairs and is s/he aware of European history (histories) and its (their) influence on contemporary European society? (ibid., 18)

- European multiculturalism:
  A European Teacher engages with the multicultural nature of European society. He/she has an active relationship with his/her own culture and is open towards other cultures. He/she knows how to behave in other cultures in a confident and non-dominant way. He/she works with heterogeneous groups, sees heterogeneity as valuable and respects any differences. He/she copes with the challenges of the multicultural aspects of the knowledge society and works to promote equal opportunities. (ibid., 19)
- European citizenship:
  A European Teacher should act as a 'European citizen'. He/she should show solidarity with citizens in other European countries and shares values such as respect for human rights, democracy and freedom. His/her critical teaching should foster autonomous, responsible, and active citizens of a Europe of tomorrow. (ibid., 20)

These dimensions are suited to lay the foundations for a European Teacher Education that overcomes the shortcomings and restrictions of the national orientation that dominates teacher Education in Europe so far (cf. Mentz 2017, 198f.). It is obvious that these competences of a European Teacher comprise empirical and theoretical knowledge concerning Europe as well as practical attributes, such as a certain lifestyle formed by a personal European identity and appropriate pro-European attitudes and beliefs. In this connection, the theoretical and normative reference point of such dimensions as European identity, European multiculturalism and European citizenship is the process political science refers to as 'European Integration'. The sociological concepts within European Studies (cf. Rumford 2009) however use the more general term 'Europeanisation' to characterize the political and socio-economic development from the European Economic Community to EU. Thus 'Europeanisation' can be interpreted as the creation of supranational spaces that are steadily turning external national borders into internal ones through processes of inclusion and homogenisation of living conditions (cf. Hettlage & Deger 2007, 18). In contrast to national concepts of Teacher Education, the central premise of European Teacher Educations is an affirmative and supportive position towards the process of Europeanisation.

Europeanisation is not only a central premise of European Teacher Education. From the comprehensive perspective of Border Studies, Europeanisation appears as supranational feature of the EU and is characterized by "making the premise of territorial sovereignty increasingly irrelevant [...] suggesting bordered nation-states will disappear or increasingly function as substate units with a larger federal structure" (Diener & Hagen 2012, 109). By reflecting the individual mental representations of borders during this process of Europeanisation in the mind of European teacher students and discussing its relevance for their professional profile BE-SMaRT creates also a linkage between European Teacher Education and the general discipline of Border and Memory Studies.

In historical perspectives, the initial point of Europeanisation is the Preamble of the Treaty of Rome (1957) where „the member states stated their determination to lay the foundations for 'an ever-closer union among the peoples of Europe'" (Cini & Borragan 2016, 7). During the process of Europeanisation since the last 60 years this goal has led to the emergence of the EU as a unique supranational political unit. Though often ignored by political science as well as by the media coverage on the EU, Regional Policy has become since the mid-seventies a central instrument to promote a harmonious economic and social development throughout the EU. Besides the institutional arrangements of the Common Market (1993) and the Schengen Treaty (1995) and the creation of the European Economic and Monetary Union (2002) European Cohesion Policy can be regarded nowadays as a core policy of the EU and one of the most significant manifestations of the multifaceted phenomenon Europeanisation.

From the perspective of European Teacher Education concepts such as BE-SMaRT, the scientific occupation with the European Regional Policy makes it possible to broaden the notion of Europeanisation and its implicit understanding of borders. Thus, the concept of borders not only comprehends physical phenomena such as national, ethnic, linguistic and gender borders and the correlating experience of border crossing but also refers to immaterial ones such as socio-economic borders and the consequences of political attempts to eliminate them. Furthermore, it becomes obvious in a methodological perspective that there is a close and necessary connection between such disciplines as European Teacher Education and European Citizenship Education and the results of empirical research on the EU they are referring to. In doing so, the traditional geographical and historical knowledge about Europe, which is regarded as essential for concepts of European Teacher Education (cf. Mentz 2017, 208), is completed by socio-political and economic knowledge of the EU. Therefore, it is worthwhile to have a closer look on European Regional Policy understood as a central manifestation of Europeanisation.

In the following second chapter I will present the central political and economic features of European Cohesion Policy – describing its origins, its impact on processes of convergence and divergence in the EU and its problems. Chapter 3 will then show the specific implications of European Cohesion Policy as manifestation of Europeanisation for the design of concepts of European Teacher Education such as BE-SMaRT.

Creating an "ever closer union": EU Cohesion Policy as a manifestation of Europeanisation

The guarantee of peace and the promotion of wealth are the overarching normative goals of the European integration process (cf. Brasche 2013, 330f.). The EU is assuring all of its current and future member States the compliance with these goals. The endeavour to foster a harmonious development of the EU without disparities can be traced back as early as the Roman Treaties of 1957. Article 2 of the Roman Treaty states:

> It shall be the aim of the Community, by establishing a Common Market and progressively approximating the economic policies of Member States, to promote throughout the Community a harmonious development of economic activities, a continuous and balanced expansion, an increased stability, an accelerated raising of the standard of living and closer relations between its Member States. (Treaty Establishing The European Economic Community 1957, Art.2)

Since the last forty years, European Regional Policy has become a central instrument to promote a harmonious economic and social development throughout the EU and by this can be regarded as a central manifestation of Europeanisation.

The establishment of European Cohesion Policy

The European Economic Community (EEC) of the late 1950's was aiming at the promotion of market integration by eradicating all trade barriers. According to the prognosis of the Neoclassical Growth Theory that was popular at the time, the free market would ultimately lead to the convergence of income levels. The European Social Fund was established to meet the needs of those groups of workers that would be excluded from the integration and convergence process. At the time, the relevant analytical entities were the Member States of the EEC. However, it was soon discovered that the free market was not able to portray a complete picture of the common European market. During the 1970s, the market remained very fragmented because of the persisting non-tariff trade barriers (i.e. technical standards, exchange rates, consumer preferences) (cf. Marzinotto 2012, 4). The Neoclassical Growth Theory stipulated that poor regions would grow faster than wealthy regions because of their higher equity return. However, given the remaining fragmentation of the market it became clear that some regions were suffering from more disadvantages than others due to the economic integration. Thus, the establishment of the European Social Fund in 1975 can be interpreted as the beginning of a 'proper' European cohesion policy. It was aiming to compensate the potential losers of the integration process (cf. Hagen & Mohl 2009, 2).

Current cohesion policy was not established until 1988 right after the accession of Spain, Portugal and Greece to the EU (cf. Marzinotto 2012, 4). It was thought of as a sort of compensation for the establishment of a common European market (1987-92). At the time, people believed that the integration of the market would strengthen regional disparities because mobile production factors would migrate to the core regions that had the highest rate of return on investments. In light of these circumstances, the establishment of the Cohesion Fund in 1994 can be interpreted as a compensation payment that was asserted by the veto power of the 'poor' EU states (cf. Hagen & Mohl 2009, 5).

With the enforcement of the first cycle of cohesion policy from 1989-2003, the underlying purpose of the Social Fund was changing: The regional promotion was no longer limited to compensation payments for the losers of the integration process. It was rather exceeded to provide public goods (i.e. infrastructure, research and development) in peripheral regions in order to advance the conditions that determined the rate of return on investments (cf. Marzinotto 2012, 4). Therefore, this policy change was supposed to strengthen the cohesion between states and to reduce disparities in wealth between EU member states (cf. Knodt & Corcaci 2012, 108f.).

Article 174 of the Treaty on the Functioning of the EU is defining the goal of the structural policy as an instrument for regional balance:

> In order to promote its own harmonious development, the Union shall develop and pursue its actions leading to the strengthening of its economic, social and territorial cohesion. In particular, the Union shall aim at reducing disparities between the level of development of the various regions and the backwardness of the least favoured regions. (Treaty on the Functioning of the European Union, Art. 174)

Thus, EU Cohesion Policy can also be characterized as a regional policy.

Since 2010 the government debt crisis of the Euro-Zone has been dictating most of the discussions in the public sphere over the last couple of years, overshadowing the development of the EU Regional Policy. However, in the face of the eastward enlargement of the EU, the relevance of the Regional Policy for the success and acceptance of the European economic integration cannot be underestimated (cf. Knodt & Corcaci 2012, 108). The share of the overall EU budget that is being spend in the name of EU Regional Policy has grown from 1.4% in 1965 to 46% today (cf. Brasche 2013, 363; Axt 2016, 16): There has been no comparable growth in financial capital in any other policy field in the EU.

The structure of the EU's Regional Policy in the current funding period of 2014-2020[2]

Between 2014 and 2020, a total of over € 351.8 billion is and will be invested in EU regions. The level of support and the national contribution are adapted to each region's level of economic development (cf. European Commission 2014, 3). The current funding period of EU Regional Policy differentiates between 3 types of regions:[3]

- Less Developed Regions (GDP < 75% of the EU-27 average)
- Transition Regions (GDP 75-90 % of the EU-27 average)
- More Developed Regions (GDP > 90% of the EU-27 average)

The basis for the allocation of funds within the scope of EU Regional Policy was carried out by a classification of the EU member states into regional entities on different levels that were determined by Eurostat, which is called NUTS (*nomenclature des unités territoriales statistique*) (cf. Knodt & Corcaci 2012, 140f.; Brasche 2013, 334). EU Regional Policy constitutes the largest part of the EU budget for 2014-20 (€ 351.8 billion out of a total € 1082 billion):

> These resources are used to finance strategic transport and communication infrastructures, to favour a transition to a more environmentally friendly

---

[2] The following section is based on information given by the European Commission (2014). As the document illustrates the aims of the several funds of EU Regional Policy (and not its impact) it can be regarded as a neutral and appropriate source.

[3] Gross domestic product (GDP) is a monetary measure of the market value of all final goods and services produced in a period (quaterly or yearly). GDP per capita means GDP divided by the average population for the same year.

> economy, to support small and medium-sized enterprises (SMEs) in becoming more innovative and more competitive, to create new and lasting job opportunities, to reinforce and modernise education systems and to build a more inclusive society. (European Commission 2014, 3)

Serving as a promoter for further public and private funding, the overall impact of regional EU investment for 2014-20 is likely to be more than € 500 billion. Regarding the regional disparities both across the EU and within member countries „[r]egional policy is also an expression of solidarity between EU countries as it dedicates the bulk of its funding to the EU's less developed regions" (ibid., 3).

- The diverse funds that constitute the financial fundament of European Regional Policy are called *European structural and investment funds (ESIFs).* Primarily essence these are *the Regional Development Fund (ERDF), the European Social Fund (ESF) and the Cohesion Fund* (CF). Being called the Structural Funds the ERDF and the ESF are

  > designed to invest in economic and social restructuring across the EU and thereby reduce gaps in development between European regions, for example in terms of infrastructure and employment (ibid., 6).

  On the other hand, the CF aims at investing in transport networks and environmental projects.
- Regarded in detail, the ERDF

  > invests in growth-enhancing sectors to foster competitiveness and create jobs in all EU regions and cities. ERDF actions are designed to address economic, environmental and social challenges, with a special focus on sustainable urban development [...] The ERDF pays particular attention to [...] areas naturally disadvantaged from a geographical perspective (ibid., 7).

  Being also part of the European territorial cooperation, the ERDF

  > promotes and finances cross-border, transnational and interregional cooperation [...] covering a wide range of issues including joint transport infrastructure, innovation and communication networks, cross-border trade, joint management of natural resources and the linking of urban and rural areas (ibid., 7).
- The ESF however

  > aims to assist jobseekers by ensuring they have access to appropriate training to enhance their employability [...] The ESF also invests in projects which

aim to combat discrimination [...] and to help marginalised communities integrate into society. It also invests in the efficiency of public administrations and public services to ensure that relevant institutions deliver on education, employment, social and other policies (ibid., 7).

- In addition, the CF

  invests in transport networks and the environment in EU countries with a GDP lower than 90 % of the EU-28 average [...] The fund actively promotes green economic growth while reducing economic and social disparities by improving regional connectivity and accessibility. In particular, the fund supports the trans-European transport network (TEN-T), which is essential for the proper functioning of the internal market and for facilitating the circulation of people and goods within and beyond the EU by land, sea and air. The Cohesion Fund invests in climate change adaptation and risk prevention, the water and waste sectors and the urban environment. It can also support projects related to energy efficiency and the use of renewable energy in companies and public infrastructures (ibid., 7).

Figure 1 (p. 44) recaps the most relevant details of European Cohesion Policy in the current 2014-2020 period.

Disparities in the EU

The starting point of any discussion about the necessity of a European Regional Policy is the question, whether there are any significant disparities concerning wealth and development throughout the states and regions of the EU.

Now, empirical data confirms that there are poor and rich regions within the EU. Taking the year 2009 as an example for the analysis, it can be observed that there are distinct disparities regarding wealth and development between EU member states and EU regions (for the following cf. Brasche 2013, 354ff.).

The term 'wealthy country' in this context refers to those countries whose majority of population lives in regions that obtain more than 125 % of the average gross domestic product per capita (Luxembourg, Ireland, Netherlands, Finland, Austria, Belgium, Denmark, Germany, Sweden, Spain, France).

Figure 1: European Cohesion Policy 2014-2020 (source: EU Commission 2013)

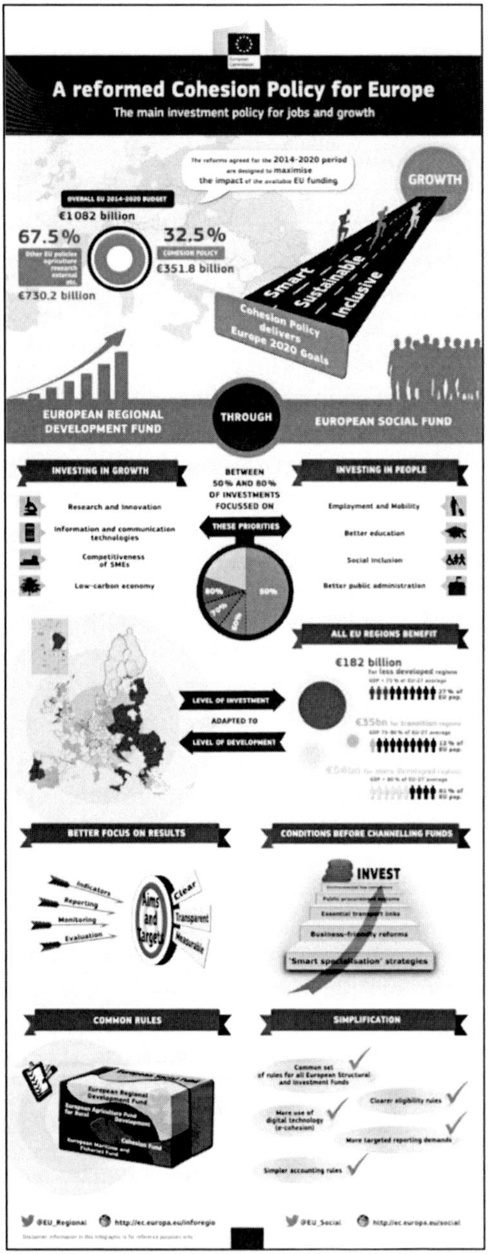

The term 'wealthy country' in this context refers to those countries whose majority of population lives in regions that obtain more than 125% of the average gross domestic product per capita (Luxembourg, Ireland, Netherlands, Finland, Austria, Belgium, Denmark, Germany, Sweden, Spain, France).

A 'strong centre' regarding the gross domestic product per capita can be observed in those countries in which only a small percentage of the population lives in either 'poor or wealthy regions' (Great Britain, Cyprus, Malta). 'Polarized countries' refers to those countries in which a significant percentage of the population lives in either poor or 'wealthy regions' (Italy, Czech Republic, Slovakia). Countries are being characterized as 'poor' when most of the population lives in regions that obtain less than 75% of the average gross domestic product per capita in the EU (Greece, Slovenia, Portugal, Hungary, Bulgaria, Poland, Romania, Estonia, Latvia, Lithuania).[4] The most developed regions of the EU can be found in the South of Germany and Great Britain, Northern Italy and Belgium, Luxembourg, the Netherlands and Austria. The same is transferable for big cities such as Madrid, Paris, Prague and Bratislava. The least developed regions can be found in the south of Europe, the new Eastern states of Germany and the transformation countries. In the light of the described disparities it can be argued that from an empirical perspective there is a necessity for a Regional Policy that addresses the wealth gap through transfer payments.

Macro economical reasoning for and political legitimation of EU Regional Policy

It is not only of academic interest whether the necessity of a Regional Policy of the EU can be argued from a macro economical perspective. If anything, there is a political dimension to this question since it implies the need for political legitimation:

---

[4] See for a similar result for the year 1999 (cf. Dauderstädt 2016, 12).

> If it can be proven by reference to the theory of regional development, that disparities will decrease on its own – meaning they will be regulated through the market – there is no [political, HPB] legitimation for compensation payments or regional funds to harmonize regional disparities. However, if it can be proven that the market integration is increasing regional disparities, this would imply that there is a political legitimation for regional compensation payments and the promotion of underdeveloped regions. (Brasche 2013, 341)

Applying the External Trade theory to the economic relations between regions it could be argued from a macro economical perspective that an unregulated market is decreasing disparities between regions. According to David Ricardo, countries will benefit from trade if each country is exporting goods where one party has a price advantage compared to the other party. Referring to the modern external trade theory there will be no persisting distinct disparities between the income and capital between countries (regions) since the integrated market will harmonize these disparities with time (cf. ibid., 341).

However, the premises of this model are idealized since they cannot be corroborated empirically. A reality check that is considering returns to scale, external effects and varying costs of transportation shows that a polarized and disparate development of regions is possible (cf. ibid., 344ff.). Thus, according to so-called New Economic Geography (Krugman) and related economic approaches "an ongoing market integration might increase regional disparities under certain circumstances" (Brasche 2013, 345). Hence, from the perspective of a more realistic macro economical model it could be argued that there is a legitimation for the justification of EU Cohesion and Regional Policy. Looked at that way it would make sense to accompany the EU's market integration by a Cohesion Policy that is promoting development processes through transfer payments from rich to poor countries (cf. Dauderstädt & Keltek 2016, 4).

Convergence and divergence in the EU

While disparities (as shown previous) depict a certain distribution of wealth at a specific moment in time, the concepts of convergence (or divergence) allow for a dynamic perspective on the development of the distribution of wealth of EU member states and regions during a specific time frame (cf. Brasche 2013, 336). In the context of the EU, convergence refers to the alignment of the per capita income, which is also described as 'cohesion' (cf. Dauderstädt 2016, 12). In macro-economics there is a distinction between two different kinds of convergence (cf. Brasche 2013, 337; Dauderstädt 2016, 12):

- Beta-convergence occurs when poor countries grow faster than rich ones which is also described as 'a pursuit race'.
- Sigma-convergence refers to the downward trend in the relative differences in incomes towards the alignment of incomes.

Thus beta-convergence is a necessary but not sufficient condition for sigma-convergence.[5]

Looking at the development of income in EU countries, it is evident that after 1999 there was a clear tendency towards convergence (except for the development before 1985 and after 2010). Especially the poor countries in the South as well as the newly acceded countries in Middle- and Eastern Europe showed a higher growth rate between 1999 and 2012 than the rich Northern EU countries. Thus, this development can be interpreted as beta-convergence (cf. Dauderstädt 2016, 13; correspondingly Adam & Mayer 2016, 194).

However, the focal perspective for the EU is not the development of income between EU member states but the development of income between *regions* of the EU. The convergence of the development of incomes between regions (so-called 'cohesion') has been the core normative goal of EU politics since the 1970s. Nevertheless, the income differentials between regions are still a lot more profound than between EU member states. The high-income disparities result from the concentration of development in big cities and growth zones (i.e. capitals) (cf. Dau-

[5] Ibid.

derstädt 2016, 14).[6] In terms of the average of the EU, regional disparities increased (cf. Adam & Mayer 2016, 192). Between 2000 and 2014, there was even a bigger increase of regional disparities within the respective member states. Therefore, standard deviation[7] of the 22 countries of the EU-28 which are divided into NUTS2-regions was averagely 106% whereas the regional disparities in the member states in Middle and Eastern Europe were leaping (in Romania over 300%).

To arrive at significant statements about the development of convergence in the EU as a whole, the trend towards increasing disparities within countries and the trend of partial convergence between countries must be combined. Dauderstädt takes the ratio between the income of the richest and the poorest fifth as an indicator: The calculation shows that disparities were decreasing until 2009 and shortly increasing in 2010 before they started to stagnate: "While in the past the interstate income convergence was able to compensate for the interstate divergence, this has stopped in 2010." (Dauderstädt 2016, 15; see also Dauderstädt & Keltek 2016, 1f.) It becomes evident that since 2010, convergence as an overarching income development within the EU as intended by the EU Commission cannot be achieved since the level of income in the poorest fifth of the EU has not increased faster than the income level of the richest fifth of the EU (cf. Dauderstädt & Keltek 2016, 3). At the same time the situation of the distribution of income, which is re-

[6] "Figures from 2011 [...] show that the gross domestic product (GDP) of EU regions ranged from 29% of the then EU-27 average in Severozapaden (Bulgaria) and Nord-Est (Romania) to 321% of the average in Inner London (United Kingdom). This highlights the need for a strategic and targeted investment policy which tailors EU investment to individual regions" (European Commission 2014, 3).

[7] "Standard deviation is a measure of the dispersion of a set of data from its mean. It is calculated as the square root of variance by determining the variation between each data point relative to the mean. If the data points are further from the mean, there is higher deviation within the data set" (Investopedia 2017).

garded as a core consideration by the EU Commission, has been marked by divergence.

Furthermore, it is problematic that even the existing convergence between EU countries cannot be ascribed clearly to their EU membership in a causal way (cf. Dauderstädt 2016, 14). And also, a deepening of integration won't give reason to expect more convergence: Even in the Euro-Zone which is high-integrated by a common currency divergence has been dominating since 1999. Empirically it is obvious that Europeanisation is shaped by simultaneous processes of convergence and divergence.

Evaluating EU Regional Policy: contradictory analyses and inconsistent results

Given these still existing disparities between the EU member states and the regions within each country there is, of course, the question of the effectiveness of EU Regional Policy:

> European Cohesion Policy is [only, HPB] successful if disparities between regions decrease. Therefore, the convergence process of EU regions is a question of high political importance and it has attracted the interest of several researchers. (Mohl 2016, 2)

Looking at economic research on the effectiveness of EU regional funding, however, one will notice that there is no consistent picture. This has both substantive and methodological reasons:

> There are many studies on the expected and actual effects of EU regional aid [...] which refer to individual points, programs, funds, regions or countries [...] The results can be obtained but not to a clear result plus they also come to different and partly contradictory results. In view of the complexity of the subject matter, the heterogeneity of the subject matter and the multitude of methodological approaches, this can not be expected otherwise. (Brasche 2013, 375)

Having a closer look at the newest findings, Philipp Mohl came to the same assessment:

> However, whether the potential success regarding economic growth and convergence results from EU Cohesion Policy is an open question in applied

> econometric research. While some authors do find evidence of a positive impact of structural funds on economic growth (for example, Beugelsdijk and Eijffinger, 2005; Dall'erba, 2005; Ramajo, Marquez, Hewings and Salinas, 2008), others only find weakly-positive (for example, Esposti and Bussoletti, 2008), no statistically significant (for example, Dallerba and Le Gallo, 2008) or even a negative impact (for example, Eggert, von Ehrlich, Fenge and Konig, 2007). (Mohl 2016, 2)

The lack of consensus regarding the impact of EU Regional Policy is also described by Bachtler *et al.* (2016, 2) and Crescenzii & Giua (2017, 21).

In his own econometric study of the funding period 1999-2006, Mohl as well was only able to show limited positive effects of the EU Regional Policy:

> - EU Cohesion Policy seems to be only conditionally effective, since only Objective 1[8] payments do, in fact, promote economic growth [...]
> - EU aid only has a positive and statistically significant employment effect for the high-skilled, but not for the low-skilled part of the population [...]
> - And despite the principle of additionality EU Cohesion Policy payments seem to crowd out national public investment [...] (Mohl 2016, 158)

Also, other current researches regarding the effectiveness of the EU Regional Policy come to nonuniform result: Analysing the long-term effectiveness of EU Regional Policy from 1989 to 2012, Bachtler *et al.* could show positive policy results concerning infrastructure, entrepreneurship and tourisms but only mixed effects on environmental measures and social, community and territorial development (cf. Bachtler et al. 2017, 17). According to Crescenzi and Giua, some studies focused on the contextual aspects of EU Regional Policy show a condi-

[8] During the 2000-2006 programming period of European Regional Policy "Objective 1 regions" were called those areas and regions of the EU "lagging behind in their development [...] where the gross domestic product (GDP) is below 75% of the Community average" (European Commission 2015). In this programming period more than 2/3 of the appropriations of the Structural Funds (more than EUR 135 billion) were allocated to help these areas (ibid.).

tioned, limited or non-significant policy impact (cf. Crescenzi & Guia 2017, 24f.). Further studies however identify a stronger performance for objective-1 funds (less-developed countries) while „Beugelsdijk and Eijffinger (2005) concluded that Cohesion Policy has a positive impact on European regional growth" (ibid., 24). Other studies presented by the authors pursue a counterfactual analysis strategy and illustrate a positive impact of Cohesion Policy on the employment growth of 'Objective 1' regions (cf. ibid., 28).

In their research overview of econometric studies analysing the effects of Cohesion Policy, Pienkowski and Berkowitz document heterogeneous results as well:

> The majority of the reviewed econometric studies found a positive, although usually small impact of structural funds on regional growth, especially in less developed regions [...] A small number of studies found no significant impact on regional growth, or even a negative impact. (Pienkowski & Berkowitz 2017, 62)

On the other hand, several studies conclude that Cohesion Policy is effective or modestly effective. Additional studies argue that the effectiveness of Cohesion Policy has improved and could be even more improved (cf. ibid., 62 and 64). Overall the results of Pienkowski and Berkowitz concerning the effectiveness of Cohesion Policy as well remain inconsistent and contradictory – in spite of the broad scope of documented studies.

The central problem of EU Regional Policy can thus be summed up with a statement by Brasche: "Both can be observed: prosperity without regional funding and regional funding without prosperity" (Brasche 2013, 379). Coming to this résumé, it leaves a disillusioning conclusion about the effectiveness of the EU-Policy:

> Given the long-term stability of the disparities, the current regional support could be considered a failure because it could not achieve its main objective. At best, the evidence that the disparities would have developed even more unfavorably without the EU funding – an evidence which is hardly verifiable – could lead to a positive assessment of the funding. (ibid., 377)

What do these unexpected and unwanted research results concerning European Cohesion Policy imply for the process of Europeanisation as a whole? And how can concepts of European Teacher Education like BE-SMaRT can handle these empirical findings on their reference point Europeanisation? These questions will be answered in the last chapter of this article.

Old Dreams creating New Borders: the implications of EU Regional Policy for BE-SMART and future European Teacher Education

What do we learn from this analysis of EU Cohesion Policy for the design of concepts of future European teacher education such as BE-SMaRT? Which premises have to be checked, which methodological principles have to be readjusted?

As we have seen, concepts of European teacher education rest on a notion of Europeanisation (as implicit or explicit assumption) that in a normative perspective aims at promoting the process of European Integration and overcoming borders and its implications in the mind of European teachers. An essential condition and premise for achieving this normative aim is an adequate empirical picture of the process of Europeanisation in its different shapes and forms of appearance.

Against the background of European knowledge as one of the four dimensions that constitute European teacher education, the previous chapter has made clear that it is necessary to regard the more complex aspects of European institutionalism and EU policies such as regional or economic policy as well. After all, European teacher education takes place at universities and not on primary or secondary schools. It must convey to teachers and teacher students a realistic picture of Europeanisation and teach them the essential competences and values to deal with their own future in the European society of the 21st century. Furthermore, the imparting of European knowledge to teacher students can't refer only to European education policy (as Schratz 2014 writes) but has to cover as well other European policy fields that are in the centre of Europeanisation.

Hence it becomes obvious that Europeanisation (and European Regional Policy as one of its manifestations) is not only the subject of the cognitive dimension of European teacher education (so called "European Knowledge"). On a meta-level, Europeanisation functions as well as a methodological, theoretical and normative premise that has significant implications for the design of concepts of European teacher education such as BE-SMaRT.

In the following, four of these implications that can be derived from our analysis of European Regional Policy will be presented:

1. The central assumption of European teacher education says: The creation of a European union that is shaped by the promotion of cross-border processes and the teardown of physical and mental borders is predominantly threatened by the appearance of new forms of anti-European, neo-nationalistic and populist politics as we have witnessed during the last years. This is true (cf. Mentz 2017, 195ff.). However, our analysis of European Cohesion Policy has shown moreover that the process of Europeanisation meanwhile has reached a new level of complexity characterized by a high degree of inconsistency and asynchronicity. Thus, the process of Europeanisation *itself* creates new and immanent socio-economic borders in Europe in an unexpected way.[9]

   In other words: Nowadays we can watch how the old dreams of an "ever closer" European union (manifesting themselves in policies that aim at inclusion such as the EU Cohesion Policy) create new borders within Europe. And these borders are not only external frontiers (as

[9] And these new borders are not only the result of a failed management of divergence. Thus far as European Cohesion Policy is not only restrained to the funding of weakly developed regions but also covers more wealthy EU regions it creates new divergences due to the regions' different options to absorb subsidies.

they are produced e.g. by the EU Migration Policy that nowadays is making the headlines)[10] but internal ones like the borders created by the process of socio-economic divergence that shapes the interior of the EU. Summing up we can say that after sixty years of European integration these new features of Europeanisation let appear this process no more as self-fulfilling prophecy but as a non-linear process being characterized by delays, setbacks and paradoxes which are partly self-created. The shortcomings of European Regional Policy show the obvious problems of the EU to deal with these phenomena. And the latter casts a shadow over the process of Europeanisation as the central normative ideal of European Integration.

2. In view of the contradictions and the lack of efficacy that characterize the EU Cohesion Policy it becomes clear that programs of European teacher and European citizenship education cannot afford to draw an entirely positive and uncritical picture of European integration and Europeanisation as desirable political aims. Numerous publications of the EU commission dealing with the impact of European Cohesion Policy are full of self-praise while ignoring the problems and failures of this policy. Thus, it becomes obvious that a critical analysis and reflection of the political aim of Europeanisation is necessary. Especially if you want to create and promote an affirmative and supportive attitude towards the EU by teacher education you will have to check

[10] „Yet paradoxically, we seem to find ourselves in a situation where previous efforts to reduce the political importance of borders by removing border controls may now actually be serving to increase the political importance of borders within the EU and beyond. A number of emergency and temporary border control measures were implemented in recent years. It now appears that many of those temporary measures will continue for the foreseeable future. Migration to and within Europe has, of course, been a matter of some controversy for some time, but now migration has come to dominate political discourse. And for much of the public and some politicians, borders appear to offer a quick fix." (Hagen 2017, 21)

carefully the assumptions and empirical facts that underlie your notion of Europeanisation as central premise for European education.

3. From this follows that European teacher education and European citizenship education have to be orientated to a broad technical and interdisciplinary knowledge concerning the institutions and policies of the EU and its society. Otherwise the didactical reflections of European teacher education would be incomplete. Qualitative cultural studies exploring individual border experiences and correlating collective memories and history (as used e.g in BE-SMaRT) must not be separated from such a comprehensive picture of the process of Europeanisation that functions as a reference point. Nevertheless, it becomes clear that empirical research concerning the EU itself sometimes is ambiguous as well as the research on European Cohesion Policy has shown.
4. It is incontestable that the constructivist approach of BE-SMaRT (and recent border studies as a whole) understanding borders primarily as mental concepts of people gathering border experiences is a real progress compared to the traditional notion of borders as physical entities. On the other hand, one cannot ignore that borders nonetheless create their own reality that can be experienced as objective social, political and economics facts and interactions (cf. Mentz 2017, 205f.). This becomes obvious when we look at the different lifestyles, the varieties of infrastructure and the different resources enabling various ways of living and career which are determined by the divergent structure of wealth and development that characterizes the internal socio-economic structure of the EU member states and its regions. Thus, the chances, options and problems created by borders are not only „all inside our head" but real external structures as well.

Conclusion

Nonetheless the analysis of European Regional Policy makes clear that the socio-economic and political borders created by the processes of divergence in Europe – as any borders – only can be overcome by individual learning, the rearrangement of mental border images and the surmounting of othering stimulated by the readiness of ordinary citizens to be open for new experiences within border areas. This bottom up perspective on borders chosen by programs of teacher education such as BE-SMaRT requires – as any innovative politics – a utopian element. Especially in the face of the setbacks and delays that nowadays shape the process of Europeanisation. Characteristic for such a utopian perspective is a point of view that won't stop at the surface of socio-political processes but searches for the deep structure consisting of hidden potentials and implicit options. And it is the task of programs of European teacher education such as BE-SMaRT to impart such a utopian perspective to the heart and mind of teacher students.

Viewed in this utopian light, Europe sometimes appears like the apparently inaccessible mistress the bucolic Shepherd is dreaming of in the poem by German rococo poet Johann Peter Uz (dating from 1755). The poem ends with a deep sigh and simultaneously with the firm promise never to give up: "Welch süßem Traume geb ich Raum, Der mich zum Schäfer machet! Die traurige Vernunft erwachet: Das Herz träumt fort und liebet seinen Traum." (Uz 1980, 130)[11] The same goes as well for the old dream of a united Europe and for future European teacher education promoting it.

References

Adam, H. & Mayer, P. ([2]2016). *Europäische Integration*. Konstanz, München.

Axt, H.-J. (2016). EU-Struktur und Kohäsionspolitik: Hilfreich oder nutzlos? *ifo Schnelldienst, 17/2016, 69. Jg, 15.09.2016,* 16-18.

Bachtler, J. & Begg, I. & Charles, D. & Polverari, L. (2016). *EU Cohesion Policy in Practice: What Does It Achieve?* London.

[11] "Sad sanity is awaking. The heart is dreaming on and loves its dream."

Bachtler, J. & Berkowitz, P. & Hardy, S. & Muravska, T. (eds.; 2017). *EU Cohesion Policy. Reassessing performance and direction.* Milton Park, New York.

Bachtler, J. & Berkowitz, P. & Hardy, S. & Muravska, T. (2017). *Introduction: reassessing the performance and direction of EU Cohesion Policy in 2014–20.* In J. Bachtler et al. (eds.). *EU Cohesion Policy. Reassessing performance and direction.* Milton Park, New York, 1-9.

Bachtler, J. & Begg, I. & Charles, D. & Polverari, L. (2017). *The long-term effectiveness of EU Cohesion Policy: assessing the achievements of the ERDF, 1989-2012.* In J. Bachtler et al. (eds.). *EU Cohesion Policy. Reassessing performance and direction.* Milton Park, New York, 11-21.

BE-SMaRT Application (2014). *ERASMUS+ KA2-Application "Border Education – Space, Memory and Reflections on Transculturality".*

Brasche, U. (^{3}2013). *Europäische Integration. Wirtschaft, Erweiterung und regionale Effekte.* München.

Cini, M. & Borragàn, P.-S. (2016). *European Union Politics.* Oxford.

Crescenzi, R. & Giua, M. (2017). *Different approaches to the analysis of EU Cohesion Policy: leveraging complementarities for evidence-based policy learning.* In J. Bachtler et al. (eds.). *EU Cohesion Policy. Reassessing performance and direction.* Milton Park, New York, 21-33.

Dauderstädt, M. (2016). Konvergenz und Divergenz in der Europäischen Union. *ifo Schnelldienst, 17/2016, 69. Jg, 15.09.2016,* 12-15.

Dauderstädt, M. & Keltek, C. (2016). Kein Fortschritt beim sozialen Zusammenhalt in Europa. *WISO DIREKT, 11/2016, Friedrich-Ebert-Stiftung,* 1-4.

Deger, P. & Hettlage, R. (eds.; 2007). *Der Europäische Raum: Die Konstruktion europäischer Grenzen.* Wiesbaden.

Diener, A. C. & Hagen, J. (2012). *Borders. A very short introduction.* Oxford.

Dürr, K. (2005). Die Europäisierung der europäischen Zivilgesellschaft. *Aus Politik und Zeitgeschichte 36/2005, 5. September 2005,* 16-21.

Eis, A. (2007). Education for European Democratic Citizenship. In D. Lange & V. Reinhardt (eds.). *Basiswissen Politische Bildung.* Baltmannsweiler, Bd. 2, 154-164.

European Commission (2013). *A reformed Cohesion Policy for Europe.* Online: http://ec.europa.eu/regional_policy/en/information/publications/posters/2013/a-reformed-cohesion-policy-for-europe [last accessed 11 July 2017].

European Commission (2014). *The European Union Explained: Regional Policy.* Online: http://europa.eu/pol/index_en.htm [last accessed 19 June 2017].

European Commission (2015). *Regional Policy – Inforegio – The European Commission.* Online: http://ec.europa.eu/regional_policy/archive/objective1/index_en.htm [last accessed 20 June 2017].

Hagen, J. (2017). The Meaning of National History and Borderlands for Identity and Border Education. In A. Vaupel (ed.). *Borders, Memory and Transculturality. An Annotated Bibliography on the European Discourse*. Münster, 12-24.

Hagen, T. & Mohl, Ph. (2009). *Econometric Evaluation of EU Cohesion Policy – A Survey.* Discussion Paper No. 09-052. Zentrum für Europäische Wirtschaftsforschung. Online: http://ftp.zew.de/pub/zew-docs/dp/dp09052.pdf [last accessed 18 June 2017].

Hettlage, R. & Deger, P. (2007). Europäischer Raum und Grenzen – Eine Einleitung. In P. Deger & R. Hettlage (eds.). *Der Europäische Raum: Die Konstruktion europäischer Grenzen.* Wiesbaden, 7-24.

Investopedia (2017). *Standard Deviation.* Online: http://www.investopedia.com/terms/s/standarddeviation.asp [last accessed 17 June 2017].

Kelbling, M. (2002). Grenzgänge im neuen Europa: Internationale Jugendbildung zwischen Rückzug und Aufbruch. *kursiv, Heft 2,* 18-21.

Knodt, M. & Corcaci, A. (2012). *Europäische Integration. Anleitung zur theoriegeleiteten Analyse.* Konstanz und München.

Lösch, B. (2009). Internationale und europäische Bedingungen politischer Bildung – Zur Kritik der European Citizenship Education. *Zeitschrift für Pädagogik, 55/6, 849-859.*

Marzinotto, B. (2012). *The growth effects of EU Cohesion Policy: A meta-analysis.* Bruegel Working Paper, No. 2012/14.

Mentz, O. (2010). The European Challenge – How to integrate European competences in Geography in Higher Education. *European Journal of Geography 1 (2010)*, 61-69.

Mentz, O. (2011). Ohne geht es nicht! Argumente für eine europäische Dimension in der Lehrerbildung. In O. Mentz & A. Surdeko (eds.). *Europa – Einsichten und Ausblicke.* Münster, 54-88.

Mentz, O. (dir; 2017). Memorandum of the BE-SMaRT project on Border and Memory Education in Teacher Education Curricula. In T. McKay & O. Mentz (eds.). *Unity in Diversity. European Perspectives on Borders and Memories.* Münster, 193-212.

Mickel, W. W. (1999). Die internationale Dimension in der politischen Bildung. In W. W. Mickel (ed.). *Handbuch zur politischen Bildung*. Bonn, 639-642.

Mohl, Ph. (2016). *Empirical Evidence on the macroeconomic effects on EU Cohesion Policy.* Wiesbaden.

Pienkowksi, J. & Berkowitz, P. (2017). Econometric assessments of Cohesion Policy growth effects: how to make them more relevant for policymakers? In J. Bachtler et al. (eds.). *EU Cohesion Policy. Reassessing performance and direction.* Milton Park, New York, 55-69.

Rumford, Ch. (2009). *The Sage Handbook of European Studies.* London.

Schratz, M. (2014). The European Teacher: Transnational Perspectives in Teacher Education Policy and Practice. *Center for Educational Policy Studies Journal, Vol. 4, No. 4,* 11-27.

Treaty establishing the European Community Rome 25 March 1957 (1957). Online: https://www.cvce.eu/content/publication/1999/1/1/cca6ba28-0bf3-4ce6-8a76-6b0b3252696e/publishable_en.pdf [last accessed 16 August 2017].

Treaty on the Functioning of the European Union (2007). Online: http://eur-lex.europa.eu/legal-content/EN/TXT/?uri=celex%3A12012E%2FTXT [last accessed 18 June 2017].

Uz, J. P. (1890). Der Schäfer. In *Sämtliche poetische Werke.* Stuttgart, 130. Online: http://www.zeno.org/nid/20005827396 [last accessed 20 June 2017].

Angela Vaupel

Borderlines: A critical comparison of the representation and displayed experience of borders in contemporary youth films from Germany and Ireland

Introduction

This study seeks to be attentive to cinematic representations of geopolitical and social types of borders, and the correlation of space with memories affecting peoples' lives. For the films discussed, it specifically means a focus on the representation of space and collective memory connected to a divided Germany in *Westwind* (dir. Thalheim 2011), and the memory and legacy of the Holocaust extending to the complicated relationship between Germans and Poles as a result of WW II presented from a largely West-German perspective in *Am Ende kommen Touristen* (dir. Thalheim 2007). A similar emphasis is employed for the two Irish-themed films, both to do with the Northern Ireland conflict commonly known as 'the Troubles' and the memories thereof. In *Mickybo and Me* (dir. Loane 2004), the focus is on children's perspectives and experiences of crossing ethnic-cultural borders between the two main cultural communities in a segregated Belfast which are deemed to belong to different 'political faiths', i.e. the Unionist/British and Nationalist/Irish communities who, by and large, still live in geographically defined territories of the city. The film *'71* (dir. Demange 2014) thematises the issues of borders, otherness, and the life-threatening dangers that are often connected to the crossing of borders.

The crossing of borders is intrinsically linked to intercultural exchange in the broadest sense, as well as to collective memory connected to space. Borders represent not only the marking of territorial boundaries but also ideologies and differing personal experiences, e.g. life stories. In each of the film narratives, the main characters are severely affected by the act of crossing borders, literally and metaphorically, and by the drawing of such boundaries in the first place: the illegal crossing of the border between East and West prior to German reunification in *Westwind* aids individual romance and freedom but also tears a family (twin sisters) apart. The legal crossing of the border between Germany and Poland as part of a borderless European Union in *Am Ende kommen Touristen* results in a blossoming love story between a young German male and Polish female but also symbolises a 'return' of a new generation of Germans to the infamous place of German genocide in Auschwitz[1], which complicates the young couple's relationship. *'71* presents an accidental crossing of largely invisible borders by a young British soldier dropped into a violent and seemingly murky conflict in Belfast, who literally has no sense of the right way out and survives only by navigating his way intuitively through enemy lines and betrayal with the help of the exact people he has been trained to consider as 'the other'. In reality, of course, it is the soldier himself who is 'the other' in an ethnic sense as he is English and not a native of Northern Ireland, and who is perceived as alien by both tribal communities in Northern Ireland. He is equally foreign in a 'place sense' as he has no mental map of the (ideologically) different territories unlike the indigenous population of a segregated Belfast. The innocent and naïve crossing of borders, physically by crossing a bridge leading from Republican into Loyalist territory as well as socio-culturally by forming a childhood friendship across the sectarian and social class divide, is the centre of the narrative in *Mickybo and Me* within Belfast as the epicentre of sectarian violence.

The films' narratives are anchored in specific historical events and, despite their fictional plots, they refer to real-life experiences that many of the audiences will be able to relate to. In fact, many of today's viewers are likely to have some personal experience linked to the history of a divided Germany, of coming to terms with the Nazi past, of having un-

---

[1] In the film aptly referred to as the grandson's return to his grandfather's crime scene by Polish Holocaust survivor Stanisłav Krzemiński.

dertaken *Zivildienst*[2], or of having been affected by the Troubles. If not personally then indirectly by means of these events marking extended family histories, the legacy of these histories on contemporary lives, or as reflected in mass media and education. In addition to individual memories, there is the collective memory each community (East or West German, Polish, Jewish, Nationalist or Unionist, British or Irish) holds and promotes, and which become disseminated by education, cultural expressions of identity, political representation and the media.

Borders, Boundaries, Third Space and Film

Research on (the visual) representations of migrants has identified how dominant discourse has historically excluded migrants by locating them in a condition between two places. Their 'inbetweenness' keeps these individuals in a status as foreign, outsider, between two cultures (at least) and, therefore, belonging to none (cf. Adelson 2002). Inner-European migration is included in this observation despite the core principle of the EU's free movement of people and attempts at cultural union also: it is argued that "transnationalism in Europe is not leading to a cultural space unified along the same model of the nation-state" (Halle 2014, 5), although the boundaries of the EU are considered an 'interzone' that offers possibilities. Taking these findings into consideration, it becomes obvious that it is not just the immigrant from foreign destinations who is seen as in a state of 'inbetweenness' but rather any outsider to the dominant group, be it European or non-European, national or non-national. This differentiation does not even end at local level as can be seen in the Irish-themed films where the 'local' itself is divided by

[2] The *Zivildienst*, or alternative civilian service, was compulsory for 18-20 years old German males in West Germany until suspension of conscription in 2011. It was a means for conscientious objectors to fulfil their national service typically in the fields of health and social work or environmental protection.

territorial, cultural and social segregation. Precisely, one could include additional aspects of otherness that may put individuals in an outsider position such as disability, gender, sexual orientation, age, etc. Thus, in addition to the physical presence of borders and boundaries (e.g. the Iron Curtain, peace walls between Protestant and Catholic neighbourhoods in Belfast, the Auschwitz memorial site as a place distinct from Auschwitz town), it is this multi-faceted notion of social-cultural boundaries that inform otherness and which need to be challenged in order to find an "interzonal space" (ibid.) or, indeed, a shared identity.

Film has historically been the privileged medium for the imagining of such shared communities, perhaps today more so than ever, as our world is cinematic and our collective (post-) memories are largely informed by moving images. European cinema, which developed from the need of national cinemas to reach out beyond national boundaries due to shared technological, artistic and cultural developments as well as because of a shared continental social history, narrates directly international experiences of contact and transformation. Unlike print culture which is bound immediately to linguistic and ethnic-national communities, film proved capable of crossing borders and appealing to divergent communities from its beginnings – not only in the literal sense of bi-/multinational film collaborations and distribution, but also socially as the dim environment of the movie house and the affordability of consuming films in public places enabled the togetherness of the sexes and social classes, of immigrant and indigenous populations, and of old and young. The four films discussed in this study share and challenge the theme of otherness by establishing 'shared' or 'third' spaces, i.e. physical and/or ideational interzones "of transit, interaction, transformation, and contentious and contested diversity" (ibid., 23).

By utilizing spatial awareness we try to understand why things exist in specific locations. Geographical space is often considered as land in relation to ownership-usage in which space is seen as property or territory. While most cultures in Western civilizations usually assert the rights of the individual in terms of ownership, other (tribal) cultures may identify with a communal approach to land-ownership, while still other cultures, such as Australian Aboriginals, rather than asserting ownership rights to land invert the relationship and consider that they are in fact owned by the land. However, analyses of conflicted spaces often privilege one group, identity or place over the other instead of focusing and examining potential connections. Thus, the concept of space is closely connected to notions of otherness and often closed to alternatives or more positive imaginings of how space can connect by creating shared identities and conflict resolutions (cf. Mavroudi 2013). Space, if imagined as dynamic, in-between and potentially connecting, can be transformative and can have a positive role to play in interrogating us/them relationships, power inequalities and othering in (conflicted) regions.

This view of space closely connected to othering is central to the 'third space' theoretical framework, which emerged from the sociocultural tradition in psychology and which Homi K. Bhabha applied directly to the postcolonial condition with its "unequal and uneven forces of cultural representation" (Bhabha 2004, 245). Relating Bhabha's expanded concept of 'third space' to the representation of space, place, borders and boundaries in film signify how film can display third, 'shared' in-between and open-ended spaces beyond the us/them divide by challenging notions of space, place and time in the narrative. It also demonstrates how film as a cultural medium may function as a 'third space' in itself by allowing spectators from all social strata emotional and cognitive responses, and to move towards a "spatial politics of affects" (Thrift 2004) where boundaries are transgressed and 'inbetweenness' becomes empowering (cf. Mavroudi 2013).

From Divided Memory to Common Memory in German Films

The restoration of the German nation after more than 40 years of division placed the history and memory of Nazism and the Holocaust at the centre of a quest for a new and 'shared' German identity. Prior to German reunification in 1990, the Nazi past had been mainly interpreted in two different ways in East and West Germany: "one was a straightforward narrative of victory over fascism, the other a complex narrative of guilt and collective shame" (Berghahn 2006, 294). A further aspect adding to the complexity of an all-German *Vergangenheitsbewältigung*[3] is the third and following generations' historical distance and access to the memory of the Third Reich, which became mediated and led to memory being replaced by 'postmemory' (ibid., 296). The term 'postmemory' describes the passing-on of memories to those born after the (traumatic) events to be remembered by means of stories, images, and behaviours (cf. Hirsch 2012). Typical of postmemory films is their contribution to the discourse of normalisation and ideological hegemony by narrating the past in a way that converts 'bad history into a good story' (cf. Berghahn 2006) as demonstrated in commercially successful films such as *The Harmonists* (Levy 1998) or *The Pianist* (Polanski 2002). This can also be argued to be the case for both of the examined German films, albeit perhaps in an expanded manner: the discourse of *Vergangenheitsbewältigung* becomes replaced with an alternative *Gedächtniskultur* ('memorial culture') suggesting a broadening of historical perspectives to include the views and experiences of post-war generations; specifically German memory debates on the Stasi and the legacy of Socialism or the issue of West German cultural hegemony since unification. This is evident in the specific West-German (post-) memory perspective of *Am Ende kommen Touristen* and the memories attached to the experience of Germany's division into two opposing states in *Westwind*. Both films, therefore, approach memory from a perspective that is less geared towards the past whilst still honouring it.

The local setting of the film narratives is not Germany but Poland and Hungary respectively. Both countries are strongly connected to German memory: Poland because of its 'shared' ethno-cultural history with Ger-

[3] Translated as 'coming to terms with the past'. The term refers to the negatives of German history and public debates of traumatic events, in particular related to the Nazi era, that raise sensitive questions of collective culpability.

many since the Middle Ages (especially with regard to the regions of Silesia and Pomerania) but more so because of the German WW II occupation of Poland, which is forever linked with Auschwitz as the place and symbol of German mass murder and ethnic megalomania. Similarly, Hungary also shares parts of its history and population with Germany, e.g. the ethnic minority of the Danube Swabians as a result of the Habsburg Empire's resettlement politics after the Ottoman wars. More importantly, the country is remembered as the Eastern bloc state that allowed thousands of East German citizens to flee the GDR in 1989 by crossing Hungary's border with Austria, before the fall of the Berlin Wall. Therefore, borders, boundaries and perceptions of otherness are already closely associated with the very name of the countries featuring as the films' locations, whether these borders are actually visibly displayed or not.

Westwind

Westwind is a German fiction film directed by Robert Thalheim in 2011 and inspired by true events happening one year before the fall of the Berlin Wall. In summer 1988, the young non-identical twin sisters and East German athletes Doreen (Frederike Becht) and Isabel (Luise Heyer) participate in a training camp for competitive GDR rowers at Lake Balaton in Hungary where they make the acquaintance of two young West German males on holiday, Nico (Volker Bruch) and Arne (Franz Dinda). While Nico and Isabel merely flirt, Doreen and Arne quickly fall in love. In order for Doreen and Arne to stay together, the young people develop a plan to smuggle the twins into the West by crossing the Hungarian-Austrian border in the boys' car.

The film opens with a train journey showing a seascape slowly emerging into the camera frame and two young women practicing Hungarian. Later, while browsing a well-stocked record store (a hint towards Hungary's process of democratic reformation), the twin sisters miss their bus connection and accept a lift offered to them by two young men in their

Volkswagen Beetle. On sighting the Beetle, the girls whisper "Westdeutsche" ("West Germans") and the camera zooms in on the car's Hamburg number plate[4]. This serves as a setting of the scene, furthered by their conversation during the journey which contains references to 1980s UK pop music (e.g. Depeche Mode, The Cure) instantly creating a common link between the young people. The use of British 1980s music throughout the film not only demonstrates internationality, i.e. that music is borderless and connects people worldwide as a lingua franca, but also illustrates the universality of youth and the importance of music in youth culture as well as the mnemonic aspect of memories connected to sounds, tastes or smells. Thus, in *Westwind* the music provides the soundtrack of a generation, irrespective of national, gender or ideological borders. Indeed, presenting the four protagonists' similarity as youth instead of pointing towards dissimilarities due to their life-experiences shaped by opposing political systems is the strength of this film: the East German women look as 'fashionable' as Westerners in terms of their outfits or their '80s style make-up, and they behave in no way different to their West German counterparts other than that they have to meet with them in secret as contact with Westerners (*Westkontakt* in GDR-terminology) is considered as damaging to the sisters' sports careers.

It is certain vocabulary, used mockingly at times, that reminds us of the ideological context of expressions rather than that of mere regional linguistic variation. For example, on delivering the sisters to their training camp, one of the boys mocks it as a "sozialistische Kaderschmiede"[5]; or when using the East German word "Trinkröhrchen" instead of West German "Strohhalm" for a straw, the girls become 'outed' as East German ("Zonis"). These linguistic nuances climax in Niko's toast to Isabel: "Ist doch erstaunlich, wir kommen aus zwei verschiedenen Welten und

[4] Until 2015 all West German vehicle licence plates used to indicate the place where the vehicle was registered.

[5] „socialist cadre unit"

können uns ganz normal unterhalten. Nie wieder Faschismus!"[6] Evidently, there are several layers to Niko's toast as he refers to the existence of two Germanys and the reason for its division (namely fascism) into two states of contrasting ideological views. On a meta-level, he mocks the socialist state's habit of using pretentious political slogans even in commonplace situations and the GDR's founding myth as an anti-fascist state (and, therefore, its absolution from any culpability for Nazism). Niko's good-humoured mockery is accentuated by the scenes' location of an almost empty restaurant including a bored waiter not keen to serve them: a typical situation in many restaurants in socialist countries that has become the subject of many West German anecdotes about visits to the GDR.

Doreen's feelings for Arne interfere with the sisters' close relationship. From the very start of the film the twins' closeness is very apparent; at times they even speak synchronously and when asked whether it is not unnerving for them to be often perceived as one person, Isabel responds with "ist total schön"[7]. Whereas initially it seems the sisters do everything in unison, e.g. their coxed pair rowing and weight training in perfect rhythm, sleeping in beds rearranged side by side, jointly spent evenings at the camp fire or secret escapes over the camp's fence together, this starts to change in correspondence with Doreen and Niko's developing romance: their rowing rhythm suffers to the point where Isabel exercises in a single scull boat; she now sits alone at the camp fire listening to East German 'Liedermacher'[8] songs in comparison to Doreen spending her nights with Arne listening to The Cure. Furthermore, Isabel who originally covered for Doreen's unauthorized absences eventually tells on her sister. "Kannst du bitte mal wieder normal werden?"[9], is her

[6] "It's remarkable, we're coming from two different worlds but converse quite normally. Never again Fascism!"
[7] "it's absolutely beautiful"
[8] singer-song writers
[9] "Will you please behave normally again?"

desperate plea once she realizes that Doreen is seriously thinking of eloping with Arne to the West. Isabel's angry reaction to her sister's love affair is more to do with the strong bond between twins and the recognition of the importance of their unique attachment and possible interdependency than with jealousy. In addition to mourning the pending loss of her twin, Isabel anticipates the disruption of their sheltered, mapped-out future because it will be impossible for her to remain a cadre athlete after her sister's escape. In other words, it is not only Doreen whose life will change dramatically and who faces an uncertain future in the West but also Isabel, whose life in the GDR will become severely affected by the authorities' punishment of those considered as guilty by association.

The Hungarian-Austrian state border is shown only once in the film's final sequence when the Volkswagen with the hidden Doreen on board waits its turn in the long queue at the checkpoint. Niko tries his best to ease the tension of this situation by telling a joke, yet his joke acquires a metaphorical meaning much owed to the border locality: a rabbit wants to cross the street and asks for help to get to the other side, "but you're already on the other side" is the reply it gets from the other animals across the street. While the audience hears Niko telling the joke, the camera view is on a parallel queue where border guards search a car by almost taking it apart. In the following scene then, it is Doreen who phones her sister from 'the other side'. Apart from the film's final sequence, references to borders are presented more subtly: a camp fence, which the young people secretly climb in both directions; a volleyball net separating West German from East German team players; visual comparisons of the basic functionality of the girls' training camp versus the relative luxury of the boys' hotel. Other boundaries are plentifully on show, for instance, the girls' only means of transport by foot or public transport versus the group of West Germans' traveling by car (West German car makes); the independent boys and their spontaneous actions versus the girls' restrictive training timetable and conformity. Hungary literally signifies as the 'third space' for the young people as it was, at the time, only countries not aligned to the Cold-War military blocs (*blockfreie Staaten*) like Yugoslavia, or moderately reformed socialist countries like Bulgaria and Hungary that were open to tourists from both East and West Germany. In addition to granting the opportunity of East-West encounters in the first place, this 'third space' quality of Hungary becomes obvious in a dialogue between the sisters early in the film when Isabel worries about the negative effects their acquaintance with West Germans might have, to which Doreen stubbornly retorts: "Wir sind aber in Ungarn und nicht in der DDR"[10]. Recurring views of the seemingly limitless seascape of Lake Balaton contribute to a sense of liberty.

Although the narrative is presented from a predominantly West German perspective, it largely avoids political doctrine as its representation of the East German characters is unbiased. For instance, the coach and the camp's staff are not ideological hardliners but regular people: the coach is lecturing the sisters out of honest concern for their well-being and it is he who aids Doreen in her flight by reporting the wrong type of getaway car to the authorities. In comparison, the West German characters (especially Arne) remain somewhat underexposed and one-dimensional throughout the film. Although the narrative suggests a collective German memory with regards to Hungary's role in bridging (and eventually in overcoming) German national division, it is the love-across-the-divide story of the plot that adds a deeply personal memory which is unrepresentative for the unified nation. *Westwind* was nominated for the German Film Awards in 2012. Reviewers of the film particularly praised the director for his successful avoidance of cultural stereotyping (i.e. *Ossi/Wessi* clichés) and political dogmas, as well as for the film's "intense emotionality" (Gansera 2011).

[10] "But we are in Hungary and not in the GDR"

Am Ende kommen Touristen

Thalheim's 2007 second feature film works through the filmmaker's own experience as a *Zivildienstleistender* (a conscientious objector; in German abbreviated as *Zivi*) in the 1990s when serving at the International Youth Meeting Centre in Oświęcim/Auschwitz. The film narrative focuses on *Zivi* Sven's (Alexander Fehling) daily observations and experiences at the Auschwitz concentration camp's museum, in particular on his cautious relationship with Holocaust survivor and former camp inmate Stanisłav Krzemiński (Ryszard Ronczewski) who lives and works on the memorial site restoring authentic suitcases left behind by the Jewish victims of German genocide in the Auschwitz/Birkenau camps. According to Bayer, the film "asks questions about how a place such as Auschwitz can retain its significance and yet be reintegrated into the normal life of the people after it has become a symbol for the Nazi Holocaust" (2010, 125). This becomes pertinent in Polish interpreter Ania's view of Auschwitz as her home town ("it's a normal town"), whereas Sven eventually understands that his national past has an impact on his personal, rather apolitical present. As is typical of European cinema, the film presents the audience with an open ending: will Sven remain in Auschwitz to complete his service; will Mr Krzemiński still be allowed to prevent the suitcases (symbolic for a first generation's memory) from disintegrating; and will Sven and Ania's relationship continue?

The film has been nominated for Best Film at the German Film Awards in 2008 and was among the pre-selected films of the German 2008 nomination for the Academy Awards ('the Oscars') in the category Best Foreign Film. Critics consider the film as a highly observational film on the subject of a potential German-Polish normality "beyond any trepidation and truism" (*Lexikon des internationalen Films* 2007). However, it is the educational potential of this film that immediately jumps out, especially for viewers with a sound awareness of contemporary Germany and the process of coming to terms with its Nazi past. The film narrative is carried by the relationships of its key personnel, each of them representing a specific position or generation which mirrors typical attitudes to be found in the German public: Sven Lehnert, the 19-years old German *Zivi* did not actively choose to spend his civilian service in Auschwitz but received the position as a result of his application to spend his service abroad. Thus, unlike a substantial number of *Zivis* during the 1980s willing 'to atone' for German guilt in sensitive locations, Sven accidently ends up in the most notorious setting of Nazi crimes; one that has become synonymous with the Holocaust. The young German is a representative of the third post-war generation and does not come across as overly political although educated in the meaning of Auschwitz for German memory. He understands the complicated relationship of Poles and Germans, certainly that of Jews and gentile Germans, as a result of WW II. Nonetheless, to him it is rather a matter of textbook-history as his life has been shaped by a borderless Europe and a reunited Germany apparently removed from its Nazi past. Sven does not share feelings of guilt, nor does he feel defensive about German history. In a sense, he acts as the film's neutral observer among the group of individuals connected with the memorial site. Other third-generation characters are Polish siblings Ania and Krzystof Lanuszewski, who are both born and bred in Oświęcim. Sven and Krzystof meet at a local rock concert and their love for music initially seems to create a bond between the two young men until Krzystof returns to his original anti-German sentiments of Germans as bossy and militaristic. Ironically, these anti-German views are essentially a mirror-image of German stereotypes about Poles: the fact that unreliable Krzystof cannot hold down his job in a local German-run chemical company perpetuates the long-established cliché of the 'lazy Pole'. Ania, on the other hand, lets herself not be ruled by outdated discernments. Unlike Krzystof, who adopts a Polish-victim role (feeling subjugated to German bosses 'again'), she is unfazed by the memory of the past regardless of her daily work at Birkenau (or because of it?) and seems in control of her future. She also represents the changes to gender roles and expectations brought about in Poland by female emancipation and altered economic conditions.

Mr Herold, Sven's boss at the International Meeting Centre, and Mrs Schneider of the German-owned chemical plant located on the Auschwitz III site (the concentration camp's former external site operated by German chemistry and pharmaceutical giant *IG Farben*) are the film's representatives of a second post-war generation who are seemingly more interested in demonstrating political correctness by acknowledging a duty to remember preferably confined to museum space, which results in empty gestures and an appetite for media coverage rather than real compassion or concern for the locality as an actual place of ethnic cleansing, the victims and survivors. This, and the company's main interest in economic gain, becomes disturbingly clear in a scene where Holocaust survivor Krzemiński gives a speech on the dedication of a new memorial site on Auschwitz III grounds: as he speaks ponderously about witnessing Nazi physicians' bored attitudes during the selection process prisoners had to undergo regarding their profitability on their arrival to Auschwitz, he gets interrupted by Mrs Schneider and the premature applause of present dignitaries. Thus, now as in the past Krzemiński is treated as a commodity by the Germans in charge, who are apparently indifferent to his eyewitness testimony and personal memories. Sven, who has grown increasingly critical of a commercial memory culture, is irritated by Mrs Schneider's excuse for her interruption: "Ich hatte das Gefühl, dass sein Vortrag an Wirkung verlor."[11] It remains unclear if Polish Krzemiński is Jewish or not as he does not identify with ethnic or religious categories beyond his nationality. Apart from the massive space of the camp sites and a village built on a former external site, the urban space of Auschwitz town, displayed only on brief occasions in the film, holds no physical references to a Jewish past or presence (e.g. no synagogue) but is marked by a skyline of churches. In that way, the film avoids presenting Jews as 'the other' yet invites criticism "for not giving Jewish suffering a more prominent position beyond the

[11] "I had the feeling his talk failed in effect."

silence of the [Jewish] names written on suitcases" (Bayer 2010, 127). As Bayer reminds us, survivor Krzemiński's main aim is to keep the past present by obsessively replacing the broken pieces of the suitcases but thereby removing original material, which brings him into conflict with the museum curators who preserve the original. On Sven's insistence that Krzemiński's personal Holocaust memories are now as important (if not more so) than ever, the old man cynically replies: "Zeigen Sie denen *Schindlers Liste*, das macht mehr Eindruck."[12] Thus, the main 'border' the film describes is a symbolic one signifying a seeming inability of later generations to 'cross' into the terrain of traumatic memories of the survivor generation and demonstrates the necessity of finding their own strategies for dealing with personal memories that have been passed down to them as cultural memory.

Actual physical borders are rarely shown and are mostly of the fences and watch towers of the concentration camp's compounds usually viewed from the 'outside' perspective of those passing by, which contrasts the freedom of current generations in a pacified Europe with the devastating experience of the former imprisoned camp inmates during WW II. Interestingly, cultural borders do not feature strongly in the narrative with the young protagonists having more in common than that which might differentiate them: Ania and Sven's ability to move freely between EU nation-states is but one example; the unifying role of music (in Polish and German) is another and evident when Sven loses himself in the rocking crowd at a concert or during his car journeys with Krzemiński for which Schubert's romantic songs provide the soundtrack. The fact that Krzemiński's sister Rosa shows no awkwardness chatting in fluent German to Sven and the frequent soundtrack of song choices from Franz Schubert's lieder cycle "Schwanengesang"[13] illustrate the close bond between German (high) culture and German historical crimes with Polish space, and Auschwitz in particular. Furthermore, Krzemiń-

[12] "Show them *Schindler's List*, that's more impressive."

[13] "Swan Song"

ski's favourite Schubert song "Abschied"[14] together with his sister's proposition to leave his camp's living quarters for the peaceful surroundings of a Polish village, points towards some sort of closure or a longing for reconciliation. The memory of the Holocaust and the victims will not be forgotten or denied by later generations (of Germans), the film suggests, as can be seen in Sven overturning his decision to leave and instead directing yet another German school class to the camp museum site in the film's final sequence. And while a teacher praises him a role model because of his service at the Auschwitz meeting centre, Sven hardly listens and gets on with 'normal' routines such as buying bus tickets (in flawless Polish) for the group. In consequence, by avoiding the spectacle of the Holocaust and opposing formulaic German *Betroffenheitskultur* ('dismay culture'), the film's main message is to demonstrate the ethical challenge in finding the right balance between "presenting traumatic memories and connecting these to the reality of later generations without turning them into nostalgic commodities" (ibid., 216).

Belfast and Troubles Fiction

Generally speaking, Troubles fiction is as old as the Troubles and can be traced back in various literary genres to the 1916 Easter Rising, which eventually led to the division of Ireland. Specifically, however, the number of literary and cinematic narratives focusing on the conflict in a realistic and postmodern representative way increased steadily since the 1970s, which mark the outbreak of the violence euphemistically called the Troubles. Realistic Troubles narratives are strongly characterized by their life-likeness in displaying the impact of the violent conflict on the population. In the tradition of 19th-century French Realism, realistic Troubles narratives aim to portray all the varieties of human experience, insisting on "accurate documentation and sociological insight, [and] sub-

[14] "Farewell"

jects were to be taken from everyday life, preferably from lower-class life" (Drabble, Stringer & Hahn 2003, 532). This thematic focus on the conditions of the 'lower' or working class is rooted in the fact that most of the violence took place in working class areas, whereas the middle and 'upper' class areas were less segregated and also less prone to violent behaviour due to residents' higher levels of education and a common interest in protecting a more privileged economic status quo. Thus, in Belfast spatial borders are enforced by social class boundaries which 'double-segregate' the city's population. Postmodern Troubles narratives, on the other hand, are characterized by their hybridity (the use of various literary styles and genres within one text), carnivalization (the use of parody, satire and irony) and polysemy (the use of ambiguity and multiperspectives) (cf. Schwerter 2007, 15f.). This often leads to a discontinuous style of narration. By employing the stylistic means of parody, satire and irony, an unbearable and intolerable existing state of affairs becomes portrayed as absurd and ridiculous. However, it is not the victims of the Troubles or the conflict as such which are ridiculed but rather the perpetuation of stereotypes and tribal myths that fuel the conflict, and alternatives are sought or presented often by way of intertextual references to other narratives.

The city of Belfast has long been neglected as a topos in Irish or British cultural contexts unlike the portrayal of cities such as London, Dublin, or Paris. In Irish narrative contexts, this was mainly due to the prominent position of Dublin in the works of James Joyce which dominated the academic discourse. In addition, the Irish Republic's economic boom of the 1990s and early 2000s intensified literary interest in a modern Dublin. It is not surprising then that Belfast, first and foremost, became a topic of cultural interest with the onset of the Troubles which led to an exploration of the impact of political conflict on local people's lives. Especially during the 1980s and 1990s, attention to Belfast as the epicentre of Northern Irish violence increased: the city became firmly anchored within Troubles fiction as a lawless space, a nightmarish necropolis, and a locus of the 'Northern revival' in Irish literature (cf. Schwerter 2007, 2).

Similar developments can be stated for the cinematic representation of Belfast although cinema was slower than television drama to respond to the growing turmoil. By now, feature films set during the Troubles have become a sort of sub-genre in their own right and whereas for most of these films the Troubles merely serve as a backdrop to generic, often exploitative and simplistic gangster and love-story plots, some of the more distinguished films helped to bring events in the conflicted region into far sharper focus for home and international audiences alike, bearing testimony to the suffering of the people in Northern Ireland. What most of these conflict-films have in common is their apparent lack of a shared narrative: nobody agrees about anything, least of all history. In a way, this makes Troubles films universally appealing, as director Paul Greengrass states with reference to his 2002 *Bloody Sunday* film's international resonance:

> Although it was about a small city in a conflict, an event that took place many years ago, if you watched in France or Germany or Italy or America, it spoke to the September-11 world. It was about what can go wrong when you're faced with these conflicts and how easy it is to overreact. (quoted in Macnab 2009)

'71

This debut film by French-born British director Yann Demange is a historical narrative set in Northern Ireland at the start of the Troubles in 1971, the year lending the film its title. Typical for the genre of the so-called 'Troubles films', its theme is inseparably linked to British and Irish history and the fictional film plot could have been based on true events. It predominantly deals with the conflict and the collusion between elements of the British Army and Loyalist paramilitary gangs, is partly filmed in a documentary-like and linear style (e.g. 'hand-held camera' perspectives in certain sequences) and can be considered as representative of the realist category of Troubles fiction. Its action-movie plot makes the film attractive viewing for a general audience. However, it takes some background familiarity of the conflict to understand the dealings of the many paramilitary groups and British undercover agencies involved in the film plot:

Next to a regular unit of the British Army providing support for the local Belfast police (the then Royal Ulster Constabulary, RUC), there are members of the Military Reaction Force (MRF), i.e. the covert counter-insurgency unit of the British Army, as well as representatives of the rivalling Irish nationalist Republican paramilitary groups OIRA (Official Irish Republican Army) and PIRA (Provisional IRA or 'Provos'), and Loyalist (pro-Union) paramilitary gangs. For the non-initiated viewer, the number of different players and the politics they represent is somewhat confusing and the film offers little explanation about the ideological differences of the two Nationalist/Republican groups, who both stand for a united Ireland free from British control.[15] Thus, the viewer is left to his/her own devices to figure out the 'who is who' and 'what's this all about' to exactly the same extent as young Gary Hook (Jack O'Connell) is, the new English recruit to the British Army who becomes separated from his platoon during a riot sparked by brutal house searches within a Catholic neighbourhood in a Loyalist/Nationalist interface area in West Belfast. In an attempt to save his life behind 'enemy' lines, not knowing the local geography of Belfast's back alleys or the ideological stance of the people he meets, Gary navigates through a fractured, sinister city and becomes a witness to the collusion between MRF and Loyalists, to power struggles between OIRA and PIRA, and meets ordinary people trapped like him in the midst of horrendous violence. The film ends with casualties on all sides and a commanding British Army officer who dismisses what happened as a confused situation that merits no further official inquiry.

[15] However, OIRA adopts a Marxist view aiming not only at removing Northern Ireland from the United Kingdom (as promoted by PIRA also) but to create a Workers' Republic encompassing all of Ireland.

Border, boundaries and other types of limitations are at the core of this film. The very opening scenes display the physical limits young male recruits have to face and overcome in their basic training as soldiers: they manage by focusing on team work rather than relying on individual strength and ability. This 'army spirit' is reinforced by the drill instructor's shouted commands, "team work" and "help each other", throughout the sequence. For new recruit Gary, it seems the army is a means to develop a sense of tribe, a sense of home, as there is no reference to a family unit which supports him other than a much younger brother in a children's home for whom Gary is responsible. Belfast is referred to early in the film during the introductory sequence when the recruits are being told of their first ever deployment to Northern Ireland. It visibly causes fear on their faces and Gary's confused question "not Germany?" is met with the firm response "Belfast, Northern Ireland, you're not leaving the country". This not only sets the scene in a geographical sense but is also somewhat ironic as it becomes obvious that Germany, the UK's former worst enemy in WW II and responsible for some of the cruellest inhuman atrocities in history, is considered less threatening than Belfast which, in turn, is clearly marked by the officer's reply as British territory.

By crossing the natural border of the Irish Sea, followed by an aerial view of Belfast's cityscape, Gary and his regiment enter the confined environment of their army barracks in Belfast – a 'bordered' space that separates British soldiers from the city's indigenous population. The barracks are dimly lit and provisional in structure, which reinforces feelings of unsettledness and impermanence. The native population is frequently referred to as "Paddies"[16], demonstrating that even the pro-British Unionists/Loyalist in Northern Ireland are considered as Irish, and thus as non-British, by the mainly English soldiers. In a crash-course lecture observed by unintroduced MRF undercover agents, the new recruits become familiarised with the sectarian divide that segregates Belfast. To-

[16] This derogative nickname developed from the name Patrick, a traditional and common first name for Irish males irrespective of their religious denomination.

gether with Gary, the audience gets a brief glimpse of a map of the city showing coloured areas: orange marks the space of Loyalist communities and green that of Nationalist communities, with interface zones such as the Divis flats close to the Republican Falls Road and the Loyalist Shankill Road in West Belfast denoted as "the frontline".[17] Belfast is mapped as a war zone, a maze of murky neighbouring enemy areas with a population ("Paddies") not to be trusted. However, a lack of trust also seems to be circumstantial within the British army as MRF agents keep themselves apart from regular soldiers and are seen as having "nothing to do with us" as one soldier explains to Gary on his arrival. At the same time, the commanding but inexperienced Second Lieutenant Armitage shows a more idealised understanding of the army's assignment to Northern Ireland and respect for the local people – a naïve notion, which is met with sarcastic bemusement by some of the longer-serving soldiers.

When Gary's platoon is deployed to a volatile area where Catholic Nationalists and Protestant Loyalists live side by side, the troop drives through burning streets with missing street signs, removed to complicate outsiders' orientation in the vicinity. The barriers shown in this sequence are plenty: high fences, stone walls, burning cars and burned-out buses amongst which children are playing until they are called-in by anxious mothers on the soldiers' arrival. The unit provides support for the Royal Ulster Constabulary as the policemen inspect Catholic homes for firearms, shocking Gary with their brutal treatment of women and children. The soldiers themselves are shown as a human barrier standing armed in a straight line between the RUC policemen and an agitated crowd, trying to dissolve the aggressive confrontation with Catholic civil-

[17] The colour orange refers to the Orange Order, a Protestant loyalist society founded in defence of Protestant rule in Ireland since the Battle of the Boyne in 1690, where Protestant King William of Orange defeated deposed Catholic King James II. The colour green has been associated with Ireland since at least the 1640s, when the green harp flag was used by the Irish Catholic Confederation.

ians of all ages and gender. In this scene, it is clearly the RUC who starts the violence and Gary watches in disbelief how the situation gets out of control to the point that the unit aborts its operation during which a rifle gets stolen and a singled-out soldier is killed. The film sequences of a Catholic neighbourhood off the Falls Road are presented from a nationalist political perspective, i.e. nationalist collective memory is evoked by recalling the rough and discriminatory treatment of Catholics by the largely Protestant police force and by showing the women's habit of banging dustbin lids on the ground to alert their community to the arrival of the RUC and soldiers.

Subsequently, Gary becomes detached from his unit and escapes the riot by jumping walls (a direct reference to the introductory training scene) and passing through tunnels that connect the small working class houses of the nationalist neighbourhood, created as an escape route from police searches and army patrols. A sense of chaos is furthered by the hand-held camera style of filming, shot from the fugitive's perspective. The audience gets clues of orientation via the use of signs and symbols marking the displayed environment as either Catholic/Nationalist or Protestant/Loyalist: a Union Jack flag in a bar, a framed picture of Queen Elizabeth II in a backroom, a Madonna sculpture at a street corner, etc. Images like these establish the perception of Belfast as a highly bordered space and demonstrate the close link between the actual physical cartography of Belfast and secret blueprints based on collective memory in (local) people's heads.

It is a young boy of similar age as Gary's brother who comes to Gary's rescue by acting as a native scout in a territory unknown to the English soldier. The initiated viewer quickly realises the boy is from the Loyalist camp, using typical sectarian language such as "Fenian bastards"[18] when referring to Catholics and "they're on our side" when meeting men out-

[18] The term 'Fenian' originally refers to a member of the Irish Republican Brotherhood, a 19th-century revolutionary nationalist organization. They later were gradually eclipsed by the IRA.

side of a Protestant bar. It is in this bar that Gary witnesses the collusion of MRF agents with Loyalists and where the audience first becomes aware of the betrayal of one English member of the British forces, MRF agent Browning who speaks with a strong northern English accent, to another English member, Private Gary Hook from Derbyshire. By becoming a witness to the bigotry of the British actors in this conflict, Gary begins to distance himself mentally from the army's official 'protective' role which is also visually emphasised by his wearing of civilian clothes stolen during his escape.

Another powerful scene underlines the fact that Gary cannot rely on 'his own' to look for protection: wounded and collapsed, he receives medical attention from Eamon and Brigid McCaffrey, a Catholic father and his daughter who live in the Divis flats on the interface zone. Next to Lieutenant Armitage and two sensible civilian women on either side of the ethnic divide, the McCaffreys are the only empathic characters in an otherwise dehumanized society. Eamon, a former army medic himself, explains to Gary how the army exploits soldiers as "some piece of meat" and Brigid tells him about her cousins in Nottingham, Derbyshire. Thus, the very people Gary was trained to mistrust become the ones who literally care for him and with whom he possibly has much in common, whereas his army unit finds itself in a position of 'inbetweenness' by powerlessly observing the unfolding events, being dominated and made impotent by their counter-insurgency section. Even the nationalist paramilitaries, although a severe threat to the McCaffreys and Gary alike, spare Gary when a young 'Provo' gunman cannot bring himself to shoot the defenceless soldier. This part of the film plot is, of course, very unrealistic and romantic (i.e. in line with popular myths of the IRA as rebels and freedom fighters) as, time and again, the paramilitaries of both sides as well as the British forces have demonstrated a lack of mercy towards those they declared their enemy.

Belfast, as represented in the film, does not allow for a shared space or identity of the people who live there as even the most domestic spaces are violated by viciousness. Even in the aerial view of the city, space is divided into areas which remind us of any other 'normal' cityscape and disturbed areas that are burning, the fires clearly locatable in the West of the city with the spires of St Peter's Cathedral looming nearby. It seems, the only reference to something of a 'shared identity' is in the McCaffrey's flat, where human decency for a short moment wins the upper hand. The army is not so much a force for good as Lieutenant Armitage likes to see it, or bad as they are seen by most of the Belfast natives, but becomes a rather passive bystander with little comprehension of the local situation. The army is further limited in providing protection to the natives[19] by its hierarchical system with military ranks forming another sort of border or barrier, which becomes obvious in the privileged position of the MRF agents and the army's highest ranking officer's assessment of the events: "We look after our own in the army, Hook. Dismissed." Gary, whilst actively involved and personally threatened by the events, acts predominantly as an impartial observer of the tribal warfare in Belfast. One film scene supporting this view is where he escapes into Protestant territory and replies with "I don't know" to his young scout's question "are ye a Protestant?" With this response, he transcends the ethno-religious boundaries that govern Belfast but it also leaves him an alien without a tribe, without a sense of belonging. While crossing a last visible border, the Irish Sea on his return home, he liberates himself from the restrictions of military hierarchy and its false promise of belonging by throwing his identification tag over board. The film closes with a long landscape shot of the pastoral mid-England countryside uninterrupted by any visual borders, and with the reunited brothers travelling by coach under a dusky sky: here, quite literary, only the sky is the limit.

[19] Initially, the protection of the local population from sectarian attacks was a key reason for the employment of the British security forces to the conflicted region from 1968-1998. During this period the security forces were central to the conflict, with agencies from the British Army and the Royal Ulster Constabulary to MI5 and the SAS engaged in a 'dirty war' with paramilitaries.

Interestingly, the Belfast scenes of *'71* were all filmed in Blackburn or Sheffield, England, as many of the historical Belfast locations (e.g. the Divis flats) no longer exist. In an interview attached to the released DVD's extra features, director Damange states that his mission was not to preach politics but to deliver a universal, tense adventure story about "young boys in conflict". Yet, this Troubles film succeeds in touching on the politics behind the conflict by conjuring collective memory and, at times, surpasses its action-movie setting by addressing the real collusion of the army with local 'hard men' on both sides of the sectarian divide, and by questioning the role of the military in a conflict that requires political solutions.

Mickybo and Me

Director Terry Loane, a Belfast native, adapted the 1998 play *Mojo Mickybo* by Owen McCafferty for his 2004 film. The film is set in Belfast during the summer of 1970 at the start of the Troubles and the plot centres on the friendship of two young boys across the ethnic and social divide: eight-year old Catholic working class boy Mickybo (John Joe McNeill) and nine-year old Protestant middle class boy Jonjo (Niall Wright). While focusing on the children's perspective, it is in particular Mickybo's parents (Julie Walters and Adrian Dunbar) who add an adult perspective to the narrative. The Troubles are initially not the predominant experience the boys are engrossed in but rather their childhood obsession with the classic Western film *Butch Cassidy and the Sundance Kid* (Hill 1969). The film narrative offers many intertextual references to this Western which is loosely based on the glorified adventures of American Wild West outlaws Robert Leroy Parker, known as Butch Cassidy (Paul Newman), and his partner-in-crime Harry Longabaugh, the Sundance Kid (Robert Redford), on the run to Bolivia after a string of train robberies. Inspired by frequent viewings of *Butch Cassidy and the Sundance Kid*, the boys adopt the personas of the two anti-heroes and imagine Belfast as their own Dodge City they need to escape from.

Mickybo and Me is a representative of the postmodern category of Troubles fiction as it stylistically employs irony, features of magic realism, and intertextual references throughout. The atrocities of the Troubles are clearly represented and continually act as an impending threat to the boys' games but, until the end of the film, do not distract from their friendship. Instead, they provide them with an even greater opportunity to re-enact scenes from their favourite film, which allows for scenes of comic relief. In the Western's final sequences, the likeable gangsters find themselves in an inescapable death trap yet Butch suggests Australia as their final destination on their flight from law enforcement, culminating in a freeze-frame shot of the pair shooting their way out of their hideaway. Consequently, 'Australia' not only serves as the 'last frontier' but as a symbol for a highly-idealized and romanticized place, like Eden where everlasting peace and a happy ending will await. It is this place name, Australia, and the frontier myth connected to it that becomes a metaphor for a future beyond sectarianism and social class divisions the boys experience on a daily basis, with their native Belfast displayed as a claustrophobic place mapped by visual and non-visual boundaries treacherous to navigate.

The film displays a range of visible and invisible borders, boundaries and obstacles the boys have to overcome in order to form a friendship. Although at the end of the narrative we realise that it is not so much physical borders but rather 'mental' borders and barriers which lead to their failing friendship. The film opens with the soundtrack of the famous Irish children song "Belle of Belfast City" (also known as "I'll tell me Ma") with its origins in 19th-century folk music, which sets the scene in a geographical sense. The first sequence is filmed in monochrome, showing a street view, while Jonjo's little boy's voice provides an off-screen commentary. His voice-over commentary is a regular feature of the film and underlines the child's perspective of the plot. Jonjo describes his world of "four walls and few quiet streets" while the film shows him having a meal with his parents in their bourgeois dining room. The tranquil environment is painted in muted colours "until I met

Mickybo", the voice-over explains, which introduces bright colours and plenty of action to the following scenes. Unlike well-behaved Jonjo who is often framed in a grown-up and confined environment (e.g. the dining room, his parents' bedroom, on outings with his parents to an ice-cream parlour), Mickybo is the stereotypical foul-mouthed yet lovable 'rogue' boy-character often found in Irish-themed films (e.g. Neil Jordan's 1997 film *The Butcher Boy*, Mike Newell's 1992 film *Into the West*, or indeed the Loyalist kid in *'71*). He appears to be a free spirit, a romantic rebel who fearlessly does as he pleases, playing ball and riding his bike on the somewhat impoverished streets of a working class neighbourhood in an apparently nationalist area as the sequence's soundtrack "Hush, little Baby", a traditional lullaby adopted by the US civil rights movement, conveys to the audience. When Mickybo's playmates stop at a bridge that divides Catholic from Protestant areas, he runs right across it to steal apples from a garden, running into Jonjo. This leads to the protagonists' first ever escape together from the owner of the apple trees.

Tate's Avenue Bridge is the real Belfast bridge the two boys now cross on a regular basis and which serves as a 'natural' border between the two main communities: it is situated between the nationalist Falls area, the loyalist stronghold of 'the Village' (as it is colloquially known to natives) and Lisburn Road. For (international) audiences not recognizing the subtext of this location, Jonjo's voice-over helps to fully grasp its meaning: "The Bridge was the dividing line between us and them, Protestants and Catholics. I've been told a million times not to cross it. The other side was like the other side of the world." The reference to the 'other side of the world' not only brings to light the binary concept of otherness at the root of Northern Ireland's sectarian segregation but also serves as an early reference to Australia, the magical sanctum in Mickybo and Jonjo's (as well as their Western heroes') imagination. On Jonjo's first visit to 'the other side' of the bridge, both he and the audience see a very different environment to the 'few quiet streets' of Jonjo's middle class neighbourhood: a classic working class street view with a prominently positioned burned-out bus is the establishing shot of

Mickybo's home. The interior and atmosphere in Mickybo's house could also not be further from Jonjo's own experience, a modest 'two-up, two-down' house crowded with a large and noisy family. Mickybo's mother's relaxed greeting of Jonjo, "does your mother allow you down here?" reflects her immediate understanding of circumstances the boys are blissfully unaware of. On their first visit to the cinema, Jonjo is shocked to see employees having sexual intercourse, of which a streetwise Mickybo nonchalantly remarks: "Have you not seen someone shag before?" Coming from a young child, this not only refers to his 'salt-of-the-earth' social class background but, possibly, also to the crowded living conditions in Catholic neighbourhoods where large families shared few bedrooms with little privacy. Moreover, it may refer to traditional Protestant (in particular Presbyterian) prudism. Other cultural differences between the boys' families are shown in their fathers' past times: Jonjo's dad goes out dancing and chasing women whereas Mickybo's dad spends his time in the pub drinking and betting on race horses. Both mothers are devoted to their children, however, Jonjo's overly careful mother seems dependent on her son as she is on the verge of separating from her adulterous husband (with divorce an option for Protestants), whereas Mickybo's level-headed mother is expecting her six children to look out for each other which allows her youngest boy some level of autonomy.

The Troubles serve more as a framework to the narrative than as a cause for the boys' behaviour up until the end. In addition to fleeting visual references to the conflict, such as burned-out buses or Catholic men lined up against a house wall being searched by heavily-armed British soldiers, it is small scenes that remind the audience of the political circumstances the boys are oblivious to. For instance, when Mickybo and Jonjo storm into the pub to ask Mickybo's dad for money, the men at the bar freeze for an instant in fear of a sectarian attack and then diffuse the situation with typical Belfast wit: "My God, they're recruiting toddlers next!" The boys' acceptance and re-enactment of violence is not inevitably provoked by the conflict but rather by the glorification of violence in their favourite movie, which suggests the synthesis of familiar displays of (American) masculinity in the Western genre with male-dominated violence as central to the Northern Ireland conflict. For Mickybo and Jonjo, the movie serves as their 'shared space' and they adapt the violent story-plot to their own violent surroundings. This is also evident in the linguistic code the two are sharing, a mixture of Hollywood cowboy slang and Belfast vernacular. However, it is a personal matter (Jonjo catching his unfaithful father and his mistress) rather than the conflict which drives the two friends to escape to a better place – over the border to 'Australia'.

Wide open landscape shots of an unspoiled and unbordered countryside are frequently used in the illustration of this escape, the soundtrack lyric "Raindrops keep fallin' on my head [...] because I am free nothing is worrying me" underlines the sense of unlimited freedom. It is worth noticing that the exhibited landscape is not the typically lush, green Irish countryside but rolling hills of a sandy colour reminiscent of iconic Wild West landscapes. This impression of a Western-like setting is enforced through the use of the popular song "Raindrops keep fallin' on my Head", itself written and composed (by Bacharach and Stanek) for the movie *Butch Cassidy and the Sundance Kid*. Thus, the Western-type landscape signifies as a literally 'troubles-free' zone and privileged 'third' space to which the boys retreat, and its pastoral wilderness stands in opposition to the restrictive, disputed and bordered public space of Belfast. Moreover, the idyllic scenery may also be read as a testament to the children's purity and defiance of (anti-) social norms that will eventually damage their childhood. A series of unsubtle images are further employed to support the Western theme: for instance, a 'Wanted' poster with mug shots of the missing boys, their night camp on hay bales in a barn, Mickybo caught behind prison bars after his comic attempt to rob a small-town bank with a toy gun, the boys riding on horse-back on the town fair's merry-go-round are repeatedly montaged against footage from *Butch Cassidy and the Sundance Kid* that match Mickybo and Jonjo's endeavours. Their journey ends in a freeze-frame shot of them jumping into the sea in a desperate attempt to reach a boat to 'Australia', which corresponds to the Western's final still picture. The very choice of the Western genre for the film's sub-story is also important, similar to its use in Newell's *Into the West*, as a reference to the topographical West of Ireland as the least anglicized area in the island's colonial history and its relevance for the construction of a romantic 'Irish-Ireland' ideology within Irish nationalist cultural imagination.

In the boys' imagination and reality, 'crossing the border' has an insignificant spatial dimension but great metaphorical meaning, namely transcending territorializing notions of borders as well as religious, class, political and generational boundaries by replacing accepted ideas of community-belonging with that of the liberalized identity of the Western genre's 'outlaw'. This is irrespective of the fact that their adventures actually take Mickybo and Jonjo over the invisible green border from north to south, where they are eventually captured by Gardaí policemen in the Republic of Ireland. Only on their return to the North do we see a border post between northern and southern Ireland, referred to as "Checkpoint Charlie" by the Irish Garda who hands the boys over to his northern counterparts – very much like the exchange of captured spies on Berlin's Glienicke Bridge in yet another (formerly) divided country. Back in Belfast, the reality of the Troubles catch up with the boys in a heart-wrenching scene of magic realism: transcending the border between life and death, Mickybo has a dream-like conversation with his father in the local pub and only on Mickybo's retreat does the audience grasp the tragic reality of his father having been killed in a sectarian shooting of the bar. This scene marks the turning point in the boys' relationship: Jonjo is sent home by Mickybo's disillusioned mother, "go back to your own." When they accidently meet at 'their' cinema, Mickybo no longer protects Jonjo from their common enemies, a group of older Catholic youths, but joins in with their beating of Protestant Jonjo. The 'third space' of a metaphorical Australia and, even more so, the obliviousness to territorial borders and ethno-cultural boundaries that marked their childhood friendship and created a shared identity as 'blood brothers' has become destroyed by the effects of 'real' violence in a 'real' conflict and, through this, by the strengthening of 'borders' akin to the prejudiced assessments of their respective community. In a visual manner, the change is accentuated by the closed gates of peace lines that were open when the boys were still friends. Childhood is the main signifier of a 'third space' in this film, which becomes dissolved in the off-voice commentary too as the little boy's voice morphs into that of a grown Jonjo stating: "Back in the 1970s the whole world knew that Belfast was a divided city."

In its final sequence, the film shows an adult Mickybo reading a letter and looking at a photo sent from Australia by his estranged friend Jonjo which, it could be argued, reduces their once close friendship and shared experience of growing up in a tribal warfare zone to a sentimental childhood affair. In doing so, the film conforms to clichés of childhood innocence as a typical component in the representation of children within the Troubles genre. However, paradoxically, it is the men's shared memories of their childhood friendship that may advocate an alternative 'third space': a post-Agreement Belfast with a majority population eager to move beyond the atrocities and limitations of the Troubles.

Conclusion and the use of Film in Education

In order to strengthen democracy, education systems need to take into account the diverse character of society and aim to contribute actively to peaceful coexistence and positive interaction between different cultural groups. To attempt this, there have traditionally been two main approaches: multicultural education and intercultural education. Multicultural education uses learning about other cultures in order to produce acceptance, or at least tolerance, of these cultures. Intercultural education aims to go beyond passive coexistence to achieve a developing and sustainable way of living together in diverse societies through the creation of understanding, or respect, and dialogue between different cultural groups. As films are, by and large, authentic cultural products and tend to be culture-bound, they can be used in educational contexts to promote mutual understanding between disparate cultures. Thus, films are a great medium to employ in order to facilitate multicultural, intercultural and/or transcultural[20] learning.

Fictional films in particular have to be contextualized and placed in their historical, social and cultural dimensions. In so doing, film analysis can become a tool in aiding students in their reflection upon the intercultural encounters as displayed in films: transcultural contact through films may enable students to understand other peoples' behaviour and to develop empathy towards those who differ from us. Films also represent cultural misunderstandings or display roots of xenophobia and racism. Moreover, a visual (and aural) narrative approach through the use of feature films, particularly when opportunities for first-hand experience are limited, may be essential to develop effective transcultural sensitivity. While feature films also have distinct disadvantages for their use in educational settings, notably time constraints, there are a number of significant advantages: film-based study projects "allow the integration of academic concepts, promote a visualization of theory, provide a specific cultural focus missing from the more traditional techniques" (Tidwell 2001, 7). The concept of 'connected learning' (Bluestone 2000) has become a key objective of many educational curricula and films linked conceptually to curriculum contents will increase students' involvement by reinforcing perceptual, conceptual, and executive skills. In addition, most students of today's digitalized generation have substantial practice in understanding and analysing film. Because film is such an integral part of their experience, educators rarely have to spend much time explaining how to 'read' a film. However, film analysis may also

[20] Latest research has established the term 'transcultural' rather than inter- or cross-cultural learning; the latter, as Gesche and Makeham note, tend to assume that one's own cultural orientations remain unchanged. 'Transcultural', on the other hand, is characterized by constant renewal and adaptability to change (see Gesche & Makeham in Hellstén & Reid 2008, 243).

encourage students to think about their own intercultural and *critical* media literacy. The application of a philosophy involving transnational film theory combined with an emphasis on social justice issues, to stimulate transcultural debate and help bring about transformative changes in attitudes and values, strengthens the position of film in education programmes and internationalized curricula with the key outcome of being 'internationalized', which is a core intercultural competence.

Film narratives dealing with transcultural encounters are often set in urban spaces or in other types of public spaces such as leisure facilities, parks or roads (e.g. especially evident in the Road Movie genre), schools or holiday destinations, sight-seeing and memorial sites, etc. This is no different for the examined films: Auschwitz and Belfast serve as the real or imagined spaces featuring in *Am Ende kommen Touristen*, *Mickybo and Me* and *'71*, whereas it is the holiday destination of Lake Balaton that stitches together personal with national memories in *Westwind*. Whilst the locations, terrains and memories conveyed in these films are clearly linked to specific regions and to historical traumatic events effecting the communities concerned, it can be argued that these films also contribute to the body of a transnational cinema which directs the focus away

> from clearly delineated national cinemas toward a more expansive system of cinema, in which locally specific stories can cross national borders, and distinct national cinemas become increasingly hard to grasp and define (Yeates *et al.* 2011, 76-77).

A transnational cinema's key argument is the necessity for a redefinition, or even rejection, of the concept of a national cinema by claiming that notions of national identity have been postulated as an 'imagined community' (Anderson 1983) which in reality is formed of many separate and fragmented communities defined more by social class, sexuality, gender, generation, religion, ethnicity, political belief and trends than nationality. Thus, the limiting nature of national cinema is reworked to accommodate a more fluid definition of 'the national' by specifically examining the relationship between the local and the global: in the German film examples, this becomes manifest in the fact that both historical events (the Holocaust and the *Wende*) and related 'collective' memories are linked to more than one nation involved, and in both cases Germany is not even the films' location. The Irish film examples exhibit the rather universal experience of violent conflict and its disastrous effects on the opposing communities, especially children.

Also, *Mickybo and Me* adopts a spatial frontier discourse regarding the conquest and settlement of the Wild West and global places further afield (here Australia) linked to immigration to New World destinations. This is echoed in *'71* where an outsider's survival depends on native 'scouts', thus employing a similar frontier context with strong references to the recruitment of native Americans by colonists in the 17th-century and US military forces during the 19th and early 20th-centuries in America. The crossing of borders prior to German unification in *Westwind* corresponds with the root cause of the conflict in Northern Ireland, i.e. Ireland's division into two jurisdictions. The Troubles as a central element in the narratives of both Irish films, in turn, reflects the process of coming to terms with a very recent traumatic past similar to the complex route to Holocaust remembrance in a unified Germany's public discourse since the early 1990s, which is the subject matter in *Am Ende kommen Touristen*. The film landscapes serve as *aide memoirs*, recalling the sights, sounds and smells of past times and events that hold a special place in audiences' recollections, reminding us that borders, borderlands or transitional zones are spaces where identities harden as well as change, and the extent to which memory and stories help people to mark and root themselves within a 'personalised' landscape. 'Third spaces' appear when binary thought-structures are broken down and interactions between different cultures occur, or as Bhabha (1994) defines it: a place where identities can become renegotiated. In the four discussed films, it is those places where the protagonists escape the dilemmas of dichotomies and hierarchies, e.g. the neighbourhood cinema and scenes of childhood idyll in *Mickybo and Me*, the holiday destination and young love in *Westwind*, the site of post-war commemoration and newly established Polish-German relationships in *Am Ende kommen Touristen* as well as the more metaphorical 'space' of human integrity experienced in the shelter of a small flat amid a violent milieu in *'71*. What is more, it is the common characteristics and similarities of the protagonists that accompany the creation of third spaces, such as an international youth culture, a shared childhood, life-changing incidents or mutual affection, which confirms the significance of a preceding will to cross boundaries in the first place. In the cinematic processing of specific life-experiences (e.g. childhood and survival during the Troubles, love across the divide, post-war relationships), the concept of 'third space' is utilized as a guide for a global re-mapping of the narratives, leaving behind the binary division of West versus East, Catholic versus Protestant or oppressor versus oppressed, and it becomes a space for mediation.

Film can offer a space for criticism and ethical reflection, and allows questions about the function of cinema as a cultural institution within a memory-obsessed culture at a time when reliance on post-memory and mediated image is becoming increasingly prevalent. As Fuchs *et al.* remind us,

> Germany has now entered a new phase of historical consciousness. This does not mean that memory of the Third Reich can be abandoned but that other topics are beginning to reclaim their space in the public discourse. (Fuchs et al. 2016, 17)

Irish national cinema's attempts to explore the political realities of Northern Ireland (e.g. Alan Clarke's 1989 art film *Elephant*; see McLoone 2009, 1) are still likely to become the subject of controversy, while those narratives that explore the human cost of the political instability, whatever their artistic merit, are more likely to receive a favourable critical response. Consequently, cinema serves as a framing devise of society's status quo and is a privileged geopolitical medium which is at once topographical and geographical, and that responds to border issues as a local and global reality by not only illustrating various borders, boundaries and frontiers but by actively constructing and deconstructing them. This includes selective representations of 'collective' memory. Paradoxically, borders that divide also unite and produce cultural exchange, which may in turn lead to transcultural in-between or third spaces that enable new positions to emerge. The study of contextual films aids this process of renegotiation.

References

Adelson, L. (2002). Against between: a manifesto. In Salah M. Hassan & Iftikah Dadi (eds.). *Unpacking Europe*. Rotterdam, 244-255.

Anderson, B. ([3]2006). *Imagined Communities. Reflections on the Origin and Spread of Nationalism*. London & New York.

Bayer, G. (2010). After postmemory: Holocaust cinema and the third generation. *Shofar: An Interdisciplinary Journal of Jewish Studies 28 (4),* 116-132.

Berghahn, D. (2006). Post-1990 screen memories: How East and West German cinema remembers the Third Reich and the Holocaust. *German Life and Letters 59 (2),* 294-308.

Berghan, D. & Sternberg, C. (eds.; 2010) *European Cinema in Motion: Migrant and Diasporic Film in Contemporary Europe*. Basingstoke.

Bhabha, H. K. ([2]2004). *The Location of Culture*. London.

Bluestone, Ch. (2000). Feature films as a teaching tool. *College Teaching 48 (4),* 141-146.

Demange, Y. (2014).*'71*. DVD: Studiocanal, 2015.

Drabble, M.; Stringer, J. & Hahn, D. (eds.; 2003). *The Concise Oxford Companion to English Literature*. Oxford.

Fuchs, A. & Cosgrove, M. (2006). Introduction: Germany's memory contests and the management of the past. In A. Fuchs, M. Cosgrove & G. Grote (eds.). *German Memory Contests. The Quest for Identity in Literature, Film, and Discourse since 1990*. Rochester, 1-25.

Gansera, R. (2011). *Republikflucht im Käfer.* Online: http://www.sueddeutsche.de/kultur/im-kino-westwind-republikflucht-im-kaefer-1.1135017 [last accessed 09 June 2016].

Gesche, A. & Makeham, P. (2008). Creating conditions for intercultural and international learning and teaching. In M. Hellstén & A. Reid (eds.). *Researching International Pedagogies*. Dordrecht, 241-259.

Halle, R. (2014). *The Europeanization of Cinema. Interzones and Imaginative Communities*. Illinois.

Hirsch, M. (2012). *The Generation of Postmemory: Writing and Visual Culture after the Holocaust*. Columbia.

Loane, T. (2004). *Mickybo and Me*. DVD: Universal Pictures, 2005.

Macnab, G. (2009). *Classic films with the Troubles in mind.* Online: http://www.independent.co.uk/arts-entertainment/films/features/classic-films-with-the-troubles-in-mind-795354.html [last accessed 20 February 2017].

Mavroudi, E. (2013). Creating geographies of hope through film: performing spaces in Palestine-Israel. *Transactions of the Institute of British Geographers 38 (4),* 560-571.

McLoone, M. (2009). *Film, Television and the Troubles. A Troubles Archive Essay*. From the collection of the Arts Council of Northern Ireland. Belfast.

Schwerter, S. (2007). *Literarisierung einer gespaltenen Stadt: Belfast in der nordirischen Troubles Fiction vom Realismus zur Karnevalisierung*. Trier.

Thalheim, R. (2011). *Westwind*. DVD: Credofilm, Laokoon Filmgroup and ZDF, 2012.

Thalheim, R. (2007). *Am Ende kommen Touristen*. DVD: Warner Home Video, 2008.

Thrift, N. (2004). Intensities of feelings: towards a spatial politics of affect. *Geografiska Annaler. Series B. Human Geography 86 (1),* 57–78.

Tidwell, Ch. H. (2001). *"Fools Rush In": Developing cross-cultural sensitivity using film-based group projects.* Online: https://www.researchgate.net/publication/234557620_Fools_Rush_In_Developing_Cross-Cultural_Sensitivity_Using_Film-Based_Group_Projects [last accessed 22 February 2017].

Turan, K. (2015). *'71 delivers 100% tension amid 'the Troubles' in Ireland.* Online: http://www.latimes.com/entertainment/movies/la-et-mn-71-review-20150227-column.html [last accessed 14 June 2016].

Yeates, H.; McVeigh, M. & Van Hemert, T. (2011). From ethnocentrism to transculturalism: a film studies pedagogical journey. *Cultural Studies Review 17 (2),* 71–99.

Zeitschrift Filmdienst und Katholische Filmkommission für Deutschland (ed.; 2007). *Lexikon des internationalen Films: Das komplette Angebot im Kino, Fernsehen und auf DVD.* Marburg.

Chloé Faucompré

Cross-border cooperation between a researcher and teachers to optimise the teaching of the neighbour's language

Introduction

If you come from an inland area of France, there is a ready tendency to associate the border regions with bilingualism, mainly due to France's proximity with other countries. In the Upper Rhine cross-border region that is the subject of this study, joint bilingual courses are in place on both sides of the French-German border with the neighbour's language being systematically taught as the first foreign language (cf. Geiger-Jaillet 2013). However, there has been a mutual decline in interest in learning the neighbour's language in recent years (cf. Huck, Bothorel-Witz & Geiger-Jaillet 2007). This was the inspiration behind the present study, which undertook to reassess the educational practices in the region in order to try to remedy this alarming situation. The study took place in the two cities of Strasbourg (Alsace) and Freiburg (Bade-Wurtemberg). As such, I, as the researcher, was immersed in a resolutely French-German approach. A European border region like the Upper Rhine is primarily characterised by the daily cross-border flow of its inhabitants, which influence the representations on both sides in terms of the neighbour's language and culture (cf. Putsche 2016, 48). These representations, which are not always positive owing to a continuous cohabitation with the Other, should thus be taken into account in the teaching and learning of German and French in this context (cf. Putsche 2011; Raasch 2002; Faucompré & Putsche 2015). The starting point for my reflections was therefore a theoretical model that incorporates this element and promotes what is intended to be a cross-border educational approach (cf. Raasch 2005 & 2008). My reflections focused on how to concretise such a theory in order that the teachers on the ground might directly implement it. It seemed to me that such a research problem could not be tested without the cooperation of those who were teaching the neighbour's language on both sides of the border. Indeed, it is not possible to be part of a process of change without setting up cross-border cooperation between a researcher (me, in this case) and the teachers who are directly concerned.

The aim of this article is therefore, on the one hand, to highlight the research methodology selected for this study, which allowed me to achieve my principal objective of proposing a concretisation of Raasch's model, and, on the other, to draw attention to a tool that was vital in terms of achieving my second objective, which was to set up a cooperative partnership between the researcher and the teachers.

In the first section, I describe the study context. I then attempt to define the particular characteristics of both cross-border cooperation in the Upper Rhine and cooperation as a tool for collecting and producing scientific data in the second section, closing with the details of my research methodology. Finally, I move onto the empirical section, where I present concrete examples from my study to illustrate the comments I have made.

The Upper Rhine and the teaching of the neighbour's language: state of the art

The Upper Rhine region represents a particularly interesting research context for the domain of language didactics. The proximity that is maintained with one or several other languages and cultures makes this region a real research laboratory for the teaching and learning of the neighbour's language and culture. A number of different studies have succeeded in pointing out why border regions – or more precisely the French-German border context – represent a unique environment in terms of language teaching and learning. The most salient among them have been carried out by Raasch, including most notably the study he carried out for the Council of Europe (cf. Raasch 2002) on the subject of promoting multilingualism. He explains in this study why it is necessary to use the potential of border regions in language teaching and learning and stresses the need for a specific didactics for language teaching that is suited to the geographic situation of European border regions (cf. ibid, 17). This involves a real political awareness on the part of both the teachers (awareness of the issues that this represents in the construction of a multilingual Europe) and the students. Raasch's other publications (2005 and 2008) on the same issue have proposed new theoretical directions, such as the model of five competencies[1] that have to be achieved in order to acquire cross-border competence[2]. There is this myth that the border is an obstacle, but Raasch is pointing out the absurdity of this myth with this theoretical model and allowing us to take a fresh look at the competences schoolchildren in border regions need to acquire. However, we are still currently at the theory stage because no link has yet been established between this theory and the resulting practice. Hence the present research project.

This idea of acquiring border competence can also be found in the work of Bufe (2001) and Kliewer (2005). Both these authors based their educational propositions on the development of teaching and learning objectives common to the two countries in question, such as through a pedagogy of encounter or project-based learning conducted in a space common to the border region between the two countries. Kliewer stressed the sense of regional identity that could be developed in the schoolchildren by working with the neighbouring country and ultimately living in a shared cross-border region. She thus put forward the hypothesis that by exclusively using regional teaching aids in the various different academic disciplines, the schoolchildren would be able to understand and tolerate the multiple identities present in society. This would

[1] Civilisational competence (*landeskundliche Kompetenz*), contrastive civilisational competence (*konstrativ-landeskundliche Kompetenz*), empathic competence (*Empathiekompetenz*), intercultural competence (*interkulturelle Kompetenz*), intracultural competence (*intrakulturelle Kompetenz*).

[2] According to Raasch, this means the ability to act and interact with your neighbour in a shared geographic space while being able to recognise that you share certain cultural codes.

allow the development of not only a regional but also a European competence that is turned outwards towards the Other. However, the problem lies in deciding which approach to adopt. The concept has so far neither been exported nor concretised because it is often only envisaged from one side of the border and because it has never been the product of a joint scientific debate involving both sides of the border. It therefore seems that while there has been a desire to bring about unification focused on a shared objective, no one has stopped to think that the approach might need to be differentiated as part of a real simultaneous co-construction of knowledge and know-how with the French and German teachers. In terms of this binational perspective, mention should also be made here of the French-German research project I am conducting in parallel with this study, which aligns itself fully with this idea of cross-border cooperation and aims to propose a teaching module that will raise awareness among future teachers in the Upper Rhine of an educational approach that takes into account the geographic space in which they will be teaching their neighbour's language (cf. Faucompré & Putsche 2017). As such, this is a project that tackles the root of the problem, namely the initial training of language teachers. The study being presented here, however, aims more at the continuing professional development of teachers who are already in a post in order that they become aware and active in seeking out educational solutions, which may then lead to the expansion of the approach throughout the Upper Rhine.

Cooperation: political and scientific tool

In this second section, it seems essential to review what we understand by "cooperation". I would like to organise my thinking on this subject around two points. The first consists in establishing a picture of the cross-border cooperation currently in place in the Upper Rhine by focusing on what is decided at the level of teaching and learning the neighbour's language. The second point will be presented from a more methodological perspective because I will reflect on cooperation as a qualitative tool for use in research on language didactics. In other words, I will focus on how it is structured, its characteristics and its limitations.

Cross-border cooperation and language teaching

While cooperation within the Upper Rhine has existed since the 1960s, it only became concrete with the creation of the Franco-German-Swiss Conference of the Upper Rhine on 21 November 1991 (cf. Wassenberg 2010, 95). This organisation has allowed the development of projects and activities within this region with the aim of fostering the intervention of different actors at different levels of cooperation. It should be noted that the initial objectives of cross-border cooperation are primarily economic, that is, they are aimed at establishing markets without borders. However, there is also a "pansement"[3] element to cooperation because another of its objectives is "guérir les cicatrices de l'histoire"[4] (Mozer 1973 cited in Wassenberg 2010, 96). The history of cross-border cooperation in the space we are focusing on is thus laden with meaning, and it plays a significant role in political initiatives aimed at encouraging bilingualism for lasting peace between the two countries.

The institutionalisation of cross-border cooperation has involved, most notably, the creation of eurodistricts[5]. A eurodistrict is characterised by the fact that it allows local European cross-border cooperation in sectors such as education, transport and the environment. Although the Upper Rhine comprises in total four eurodistricts[6], this study took place in two distinct eurodistricts, the Strasbourg-Ortenau Eurodistrict and the Freiburg-Central and Southern Alsace Eurodistrict. Since their creation in 2005 and 2006 respectively, these two eurodistricts have launched a

---

[3] "sticking plaster"

[4] "to heal the scars of history"

[5] A eurodistrict refers to a cross-border geographic zone that contains communes situated on both sides of the border.

[6] Regio-Pamina; Strasbourg-Ortenau; Basel Trinational; Freiburg-Central and Southern Alsace.

number of cross-border events to strengthen social cohesion with the aim of developing a regional identity between the two countries. Furthermore, working groups have been created within the Conference of the Upper Rhine, such as the *Education and Training* group, which is responsible for the promotion of bi- and multilingualism. One concrete example of the events it has established is the *Journée Trinationale des acteurs de l'éducation et de la formation/Trinationale Fachtagung im Rahmen des oberrheinischen Lehrertages*[7]. This event brings together educational specialists and other stakeholders in education from the three countries concerned to address this theme in the form of academic presentations and workshops with the aim of raising awareness of the various projects that have been set up following the Conference of the Upper Rhine's Charter to promote multilingualism (cf. Franco-German-Swiss Conference of the Upper Rhine 2013). Mention should also be made of the INTERREG cross-border programmes. These have been made possible through support from the European Regional Development Fund. INTERREG projects cover a number of areas, including the teaching and learning of the neighbour's language:

> [...] utiliser le grand potential de la région en matière de bilinguisme, tant au niveau de l'éducation scolaire et professionnelle qu'universitaire, semble revêtir une importance paticulièrement stratégique pour l'esapce du Rhin supérieur (INTERREG Rhin Supérieur 2007, 25).[8]

The following statement describes therefore what I understand by institutionalised cross-border cooperation: Funds are made available for the promotion of bilingualism and therefore the teaching of the neighbour's language within this space. However, I would like to highlight two

---

[7] Trinational day for stakeholders in education and training; http://www.conference-rhin-sup.org/fr/education-et-formation/apercu/actualite/items/journee-trinationale-des-acteurs-de-leducation-et-de-la-formation.html.

[8] "Using the region's great potential in terms of bilingualism, whether at school, university or vocational education level, seems to take on a particularly strategic importance for the Upper Rhine space."

points here. The first concerns the visibility of these projects and the cross-border agreements that are currently in place. The second relates to the gap that exists between political decision-making and the situation on the ground. Regarding visibility, I would like to talk about my own personal experience within the context of my research project. I am personally aware of these institutions and projects because I am conducting a scientific study on the subject, but the actors on the ground that I have been cooperating with had no knowledge of these projects nor even that they belonged to a eurodistrict. We therefore find ourselves in a complex situation. It is as if the situation on the ground and the scientific and political worlds are two parallel universes that only occasionally come into contact with one another. In my opinion, there is still not enough communication between the teaching world and the scientific and political institutions. If we want to extend bi- and multilingualism of this region, then we must begin by offering continuing professional development that is accessible and visible to the teachers concerned in order to make them aware of such cross-border matters at both the theoretical and the practical levels. The majority of projects that have been set up through these institutions are part of a logic of school exchanges and contact between teachers aimed at fostering supposedly cross-border language teaching. However, while they certainly represent a start, they do not go far enough because these exchanges and this contact only happen occasionally and there is no precise aim in terms of setting out the competences that the pupils and teachers concerned need to acquire. What is needed is a systematic programme of meetings and a substantial debate on the educational concretisation of a cross-border educational approach. In my opinion, this can only be done with the help of researchers in the domain, who would play the role of mediators between the two countries, establishing a link not only between theory and the practice on the ground (the search for solutions) but also between concrete political decision-making and a joint effort by researchers and teachers on the ground. Moreover, the projects undertaken within the context of this institutionalised cooperation are isolated and do not extend to all establishments. Hence, I believe it is up to institutions such as the Conference of the Upper Rhine to be more active in calling on researchers for their help and to supplement their top-down mode of operating with a bottom-up approach that comes directly from the situation on the ground.

Cooperation between the researcher and the teachers

In order to illustrate what I have set out above, the next section discusses cross-border teachers-researcher cooperation within the context of my research project.

Methodological approach

The principal objective of this study was, as previously mentioned, the concretisation of Raasch's theoretical model (2005 and 2008), which is aimed at achieving cross-border competence in the teaching of the neighbour's language. In other words, I wanted to develop teaching aids in the form of teaching units to be used in the French and German lessons delivered in the Upper Rhine in cooperation with the teachers currently in post. In order to achieve this, I conducted my research in four classes that provided lessons on the neighbour's language. These classes were selected from two secondary schools[9], one on each side of the border, in the cities of Strasbourg and Freiburg. After defining the research problem and the desired profile of the establishments, I went in search of teachers who were willing to cooperate. This was therefore a research-intervention type of approach (henceforth RI). RI is the research method of choice in the domain of management, but it also lends itself well to research in Humanities, Arts, and Social Sciences. It can be defined as follows:

[9] There will be no discussion here of why I chose secondary rather than primary schools because it is not relevant to this reflection.

> Il s'agit en somme d'une methode de recherche menée par un acteur-chercheur don't les roles d'intervenant et d'agent de changement s'harmonisent aux besoins des acteurs-participants tout comme aux caractéristiques du terrain d'étude. (Duchesne & Leurebourg 2012, 6)[10]

In other words, I am clearly distinguishing from the outset the methodological approach adopted here from an action research approach (henceforth AR). There are two reasons for this. The first is that in RI, the position of the researcher is determining because they are the only ones controlling the intervention whereas in AR, "la position du chercheur demeure extérieure à l'objet de recherche" (ibid., 5)[11]. In the present case, the supervision of the test phases was in effect entrusted to the teachers. The second reason is that, while both approaches promote action and are oriented towards change, RI focuses more on the process that is underway while AR is more interested in the results of the change initiated (cf. ibid., 8). While a certain amount of importance was attached from the outset to the results of the anticipated change at the level of the teaching practices in question, the intention was to focus primarily on my cooperation with the teachers. That is, it seemed more pertinent to analyse the actual process of co-constructing the units while taking into account the day-to-day experiences and constraints faced by those involved.

I should point out that this co-construction of teaching aids represented the third stage of my study, following on from the two data-collection stages, which were as follows:

- participant observation in the four classes;
- semi-open questionnaires to determine the representations of the learners of the neighbour's language with regard to the neighbour's language and culture and the geographic space in which they lived

[10] "It is, in short, a research method applied by an actor-researcher whose roles as participant and agent of change match the needs of both the actor-participants and the characteristics of the study context."

[11] "the position of the researcher is external to the research object"

plus semi-structured interviews to gather information on the (German and French) teachers' representations.

This research was therefore entirely qualitative in nature because it aimed to understand the actors involved and the situation on the ground within the context of a change objective.

Researcher's position and ethics in practice

The actors-researcher relationship was at the heart of this study because without the teachers' cooperation, the project could not have succeeded. Hence, it was essential to thematise everything concerning this relationship. Moreover, since the collaboration was so close and the results were entirely dependent on it, it is also essential here to provide a reflection on what Guillemin and Gillam (2004) called "ethics in practice", as distinct from "procedural ethics". Martineau drew on the publication to propose the following definition:

> [...] la recherche est traversée par deux types d'éthique: les éthiques des procédures (procedural ethics) et les éthiques de la pratique (ethics in practice). Les premières concernent les mesures misent en place pour respecter les droits des sujets, leur éviter des désagréments, gérer les événements souhaités. Les seconds concernent les dilemmes éthiques qui peuvent survenir au jour le jour dans la recherche qualitative (ethically important moments). (Martineau 2007, 75)[12]

According to Narcy-Combes, in the collaborative type of work called for in AR and indeed in RI in this case, "La complémentarité devrait être horizontale, chacun a son expertise, chacun joue son role, mais per-

[12] "There are two types of ethics running through research: procedural ethics and ethics in practice. Procedural ethics concern the measures put in place to respect the rights of the subjects, to avoid any disagreements that might arise with them and to manage unintended events. The second concern the ethical dilemmas that can arise on a day-to-day basis in qualitative research (ethically important moments)."

sonne ne peut fonctionner sans les autres." (Narcy-Combes 1998, 6)[13] However, this much-vaunted horizontal complementarity is not necessarily obvious. The researcher's substantial involvement with the actors on the ground does not come without a few tensions, which can lead to the appearance of certain dilemmas in day-to-day life. These can influence not only the production and collection of data but also its analysis and interpretation. This is what Martineau called the "relation intersubjective de proximité" (2007, 75)[14], and it raises ethical issues that go beyond those concerning the procedure itself. When we work with human subjects, it is important to take this dimension into account and to thematise it in order to offer a different perspective on our results, which have inevitably been influenced by it.

Results of the cooperation

Having situated this subject theoretically and methodologically, I will now illustrate the comments made above by drawing on the results of my cooperation with the teachers.

At the start of the project: varying attitudes

Presented below are translated extracts from the first series of semi-structured interviews conducted with the French and German teachers just before construction of the teaching units began. In these extracts, the teachers were asked if there was anything they wished to add in relation to this research project and to the production of teaching aids that might fit in with a cross-border languages didactics.

---

[13] "Complementarity should be horizontal, where each person has their own expertise and plays their own role but no one person can function without the others."

[14] "intersubjective relationship of proximity"

Extract 1a (Strasbourg)[15]

393 SEBa	there's also not really much time for cooperation I find
394 C	yes oh well=
395 SEBa	=mhm
396 C	and do you want to add anything in relation to the project or the interview?
397 SEBa	well I'm interested in:: maybe after talking it over again, having er maybe getting together with other colleagues, just to exchange the things that have worked well, to see where that could lead in concrete terms, maybe to have some directions er ideas:, some suggestions for the course, so there you go, I'm interested in the outcome of the project as well ((laughs))

Extract 1b (Freiburg)

313 FRL1	er (2.0) on the whole I find it incredibly good that we're starting with the general (.) and moving towards the specific er I'm very happy with this research in this area, so, because I think that what we've been doing up to now is not enough anymore and I'm maybe more aware of it now, er how rewarding that can be for the pupils

Extract 1c (Strasbourg)

461 SEBi	because you know, you've made me open up er, you know? and so I know, I know it's not finished, it's the common theme[16] and I'm waiting for the rest
462 C	well, yes we'll see each other again
463 SEBi	and I will of course be at your disposal and:
464 C	thank you
465 SEBi	I'm really waiting er, you know for a project er, cooperation[17]

[15] The abstracts were translated into English for an easier lecture.

[16] The French speaker used the German term *roter Faden* for *common theme*.

[17] The French speaker used the German term *Zusammenarbeit* for *cooperation*.

Two things stand out in these three extracts. The first is the teachers' realisation of the pertinence and need for the project, and the second is the need that they express for cooperation, particularly in the case of the Strasbourg teachers (extracts 1a and 1c). The first phenomenon can be explained by a conscientisation, which would have been triggered by the teachers' participation in the research project, in relation to the research subject, namely the thematization of the border space in the (neighbour's) language course. The teachers felt they were on hold but also already engaged in the project because in the first extract above, one of them even alludes to a point in time "after" the project. The process of cooperation is therefore gradually set in motion as the actors (in this case the German and French teachers) begin to feel that the project concerns them. They are no longer passive (just letting the researchers into their classrooms) but realise that they too can make a contribution and that the experiment cannot be brought to fruition without cooperation.

The second element that is pertinent to our discussion and which explicitly comes through in these extracts is the definite expression of a need for cooperation on the part of the teachers. They communicate, on the one hand, a real need to get out of the educational and pedagogical routine and, on the other, a realisation in respect of the geographic context, with all the issues that involves. The teacher from Freiburg recognises that their current practices are not enough and that putting in place a cross-border educational approach can only be a positive move as far as the pupils are concerned. This shows that she had already given some thought to this issue but that participation in the project had opened the door to change. Hence, such thoughts are made concrete.

As far as the teachers from Strasbourg were concerned, a certain reserve can be noted in terms of their involvement in the project. They seem to be waiting to see what it can deliver in concrete terms, but they do not mention their own practical involvement. Moreover, they do not mention the word "research" either. I think this is very representative of teachers' attitudes towards research. The actor-researcher relationship becomes complex from the very moment a cooperative partnership is set up because there are tacit representations regarding the functions of each party (cf. Charlier & Daele 2002). As far as the teachers are concerned, I am the researcher who has come into their world because I need data, but nothing is required of them. The comments from the teacher SEBi (extract 1c), for example, "I'm waiting for the rest", "I'm waiting to see" and "I'm waiting for a real collaboration", are a good representation of the simplistic attitude of a teacher who is waiting to see the outcome of the researcher's work. Such a teacher is most often mistrusting and does not feel they are on equal terms with the researcher but rather that they are in a different position altogether. There is the theoretical world, on the one hand, and the world of practice, on the other.

Co-construction of teaching units

A rarely horizontal actors-researcher relationship

During the development of the teaching units, minutes were taken of all the meetings that took place with the teachers involved in the project so that there would be a written record of all the exchanges and, more particularly, of all the well-defined stages of this meticulous co-construction. These minutes were supplemented with a log of the process, which allowed me to gain more perspective on the data and therefore more reflexivity, because as Baribeau rightly says, a log

> [...] assure la validité interne du processus de recherche. Il en assure aussi la validité externe puisqu'on y retrouve les traces de la subjectivité du chercheur, de ses préférences, de ses valeurs, de ses choix et de ses interpretations. (Baribeau 2005, 111)[18]

[18] "ensures the internal validity of the research process. It also ensures the external validity of the process because it contains traces of the researcher's subjectivity, preferences, values, choices and interpretations."

Hence, during the analysis of these accounts of the working meetings, three significant points emerged from the development of this teachers-researcher cooperation:

- gap between theory and practice;
- fear of innovation and pressure of the programme;
- delimitation and adjustment of roles.

The first can be explained by the meeting of two worlds that only rarely come into contact with one another. This played a significant role in the relations between the teachers and the researcher. As part of the project, for example, I had to present the theoretical model to the teachers, which I wanted to concretise to be sure that the teachers had the same information as me. The presentation of the theoretical model was perceived by all the teachers as being too theoretical and as something they did not need to take into account. They stressed their need for something concrete because they did not know how to respond to such a model. This confrontation with theory was difficult because it clearly revealed the preconceptions the teachers had of the researcher and those the researcher had of the teachers. Both parties therefore had to win the other over before we could speak the same language and continue with the cooperative work.

The second point that emerged was the teachers' anxiety and mistrust regarding what they did not know. For some, the concretisation of this model presented a challenge to their usual practices in the classroom insofar as they were confronted with a different way of doing things. It is, of course, completely understandable that it is not necessarily easy for someone to take a different perspective on what they have been doing for a number of years. Once again, the problem of hierarchy between the teacher and the researcher resurfaced. The teachers felt caught between two authority figures, that of the researcher, on the one hand, who was organising what they were to do, and the pressure of the programme, on the other. In the working meetings, this anxiety about not finishing the programme on time and their concern that the contents we were going to create together should be faithful to what was prescribed by the ministerial guidelines were their main preoccupations. Furthermore, with regard to the French school, it is important to point out that this pressure of the programme also illustrated the teachers' fear of inspections. Their decision-making during this project was influenced by their fear that their competences would be judged as soon as they departed from the prescribed framework. The teachers' discourse in relation to inspections is represented well in the following citation from Mosconi and Heideger, who wrote that inspections are generally "représenté comme un jugement quasi divin, séparant les bons des mauvais" (Mosconi & Heideger 2003, 45)[19].

The third and final point to emerge, namely the delimitation of everyone's roles during the division of labour, marked the true beginning of my cooperation with the teachers. As we proceeded to construct the teaching units, we automatically slotted into our individual places within the cooperative partnership through our attempt to arrive at this much-vaunted horizontal relationship. In other words, we left behind a certain disequilibrium between my interests and those of the teachers as well as between our respective roles to come together in our shared construction of the teaching units. Moreover, the teachers agreed during these working meetings to be responsible for testing the teaching units. It had not been very clear up to this point whether it would be I or the teachers who would conduct the test, but it had been hoped it would be the teachers so that, on the one hand, they could step into the researcher's shoes by testing the products we were going to develop and, on the other, they would have a raised awareness of their role as teachers of the neighbour's language in that particular geographic space. The teachers had been reluctant at the start of the project because this study just represented an anomaly in their daily lives. They were not as committed as I was because the primary research problem had been formulated without their involvement. The working meetings therefore represented

[19] "represented as an almost divine judgement, separating the good from the bad"

the shared formulation of our problem within an ethical framework negotiated by all involved. It was then quite natural that the teachers were proposed as the testers of the teaching unit activities. They were asked to provide feedback on the test itself as well as to give reflexive feedback on their positioning as actors and researchers who had taken on this dual role with the aim of obtaining an open-ended outcome oriented towards change (cf. Macaire 2007). The focus was no longer on the process therefore so much as on the change brought about as a result of the outcome, namely the concrete teaching units.

This episode thus represents the key moment when my RI transformed into real AR because, drawing on some of the intervention characteristics in AR put forward by Macaire (cf. 2008, 74), this is what we get for this study:

- Actors (practitioners and researchers) able to solve a situational problem through collective action that is both negotiated and flexible, similar to creation with a rationality of engagement
  ➔ *Teachers take on the role of researcher and become actors in the search for solutions*
- Regular reflexive practices to measure, in particular, the effects of the action
  ➔ *Log-keeping by the actors-researchers*
- Reinvestment of the change, in the form of either replication in other situations or new creations
  ➔ *After the project, the teachers created other teaching units within the cross-border logic of Raasch's model*
- Clarification of roles in terms of the researcher's positioning, making explicit their intentions, ambitions and modalities of action in relation to those expected by the practitioners
  ➔ *Negotiation and delimitation of roles during the co-construction of the teaching units.*

My original project therefore also became the teachers' project because the testing of the teaching activities allowed a transformation in the actors' role in the project.

By way of conclusion

I have attempted in this scientific contribution to highlight the main points as well as the limitations of a teachers-researcher cooperative partnership set up to optimise the teaching of the neighbour's language. I began by explaining why action was urgently needed in the teaching/ learning of the neighbour's language in the Upper Rhine and then highlighted the fact that institutionalised cross-border cooperation, although vital, was unfortunately not enough to remedy the situation.

In relation to the research approach implemented in this study, which aimed to improve practices in the teaching of the neighbour's language, we can see that the cooperation between the scientific world and the actors on the ground led to the "painless" development of a concrete awareness among the teachers. Moreover, this awareness was lasting because it liberated the actors (cf. Coenen 2001, 20) and allowed real professional development through the implementation of real AR (cf. Guillemette & Savoie-Zajc 2012, 17).

I also shed light on the fact that many elements have to be taken into account and re-evaluated throughout the duration of a project involving this type of cooperation between human subjects, as productive as it may be, in order to sustain a stable level of cooperation to ensure the project's success. Finally, I highlighted the fact that prompting reflexive moments, particularly through a log, allows the researcher to extract knowledge concerning the research approach and its direct implications for the production and interpretation of field data.

References

Baribeau, C. (2005). Le journal de bord de chercheur. *Recherches qualitatives hors-série 2-2005,* 98-114.

Bufe, W. (2001). Didactique des langues en région frontalière, frontière de la didactique? *Etudes de linguistique appliquée 123-124, 305-312.*

Charlier, B. & Daele, A. (2002). *La relation enseignant-chercheur en question: un cadre de réflexion, une histoire, un cas. Actes de la 2ème Biennale des Chercheurs en Education.* Louvain-la-Neuve.

Coenen, H. (2001). Recherche-action: rapports entre chercheurs et acteurs. *Revue internationale de psychosociologie 16*, 19-32.

Duchesne, C. & Leurebourg, R. (2012). La recherche-intervention en formation des adultes: une démarche favorisant l'apprentissage transformateur. *Recherches Qualitatives 31*, 3-24. Online: http://www.recherche-qualitative.qc.ca/documents/files/revue/edition_reguliere/numero31(2)/duchesne-et-leurebourg.pdf [last accessed 22 June 2017].

Faucompré, Ch. & Putsche, J. (2015). Les activités pédagogiques dans le cadre d'une didactique des langues en région frontalière: le cas d'un cours de français en 5. Klasse à Kehl, Bade-Wurtemberg. *Les nouveaux cahiers d'allemand 33-2*, 161-176.

Faucompré, Ch. & Putsche, J. (2017). Déconstruire les représentations des futurs enseignants de langues face à l'enseignement en région frontalière. In D. Elmiger, I. Racine & F. Zay (eds). *Processus de différenciation: des pratiques langagières à leur interprétation sociale.* Neuchâtel: Centre de linguistique appliquée, 227-238. Online: http://doc.rero.ch/record/11876/files/bulletin_vals_asla_2017_special_2.pdf [last accessed 22 June 2017].

Franco-German-Swiss Conference of the Upper Rhine (2013). *Charte pour la promotion du plurilinguisme.* Online: http://www.conference-rhin-sup.org/fr/education-et-formation/apercu/actualite/items/charte-pour-la-promotion-du-plurilinguisme.html?file=files/assets/Erziehung-und-Bildung/docs_fr/FR_Charte_plurilinguisme_Rhinsup_2013.pdf [last accessed 22 June 2017].

Geiger-Jaillet, A. (2013). Deutsch und Französisch in der Grenzregion am Oberrhein. *Europäische Erziehung 43*, 17-20.

Guillemette, S. & Savoie-Zajc, L. (2012). La recherche-action et ses rapports de coconstruction de savoirs et de formation dans une perspective de professionnalisation entre acteurs praticiens et chercheurs. *Formation et profession 20-3*, 41-52. Online: http://formation-profession.org/pages/article/20/3/7 [last accessed 22 June 2017].

Guillemin, M. & Gillam , L. (2004). Ethics, reflexivity and «ethically important moments». *Research. Qualitative Inquiry 10(2),* 261-280.

Huck, D.; Bothorel-Witz, A. & Geiger-Jaillet, A. (2007). L'Alsace et ses langues. Éléments de description d'une situation sociolinguistique en zone frontalière. In A. Abel, M. Stuflesser & L. Voltmer (dir.). *Aspects of Multilingualism in Euro-*

pean Border Regions: Insights and Views of Alsace, Eastern Macedonia and Thrace, the Lublin Voivodeship and South Tyrol. Europäische Akademie Bozen, 13-100.

INTERREG Rhin supérieur (2007). *Programme opérationnel INTERREG IV A Rhin supérieur. Programme communautaire de soutien à la coopération transfrontalière dans l'espace du Rhin supérieur.* Online: http://www.espaces-transfrontaliers.org/fileadmin/user_upload/documents/Programmes_europeens/PO_IVA_RSpdf [last accessed 19 July 2017].

Kliewer, A. (2005). *Unterricht entgrenzen – Interregionale Ansätze in Pfalz und Elsass.* Landau.

Macaire, D. (2007). Recherche-action et didactique des langues. *Les Cahiers de l'Acedle 4*, 93-120.

Macaire, D. (2008). De la didactique de l'allemand à une didactique du plurilinguisme: la recherche-action comme aide au changement. Online: https://halshs.archives-ouvertes.fr/tel-00554808/document [last accessed 22 June 2017].

Martineau, S. (2007). L'éthique en recherche qualitative: quelques pistes de réflexion. *Recherches qualitatives hors-série 5*, 70-81.

Mosconi, N. & Heideger, N. (2003). Des enseignantes face à des inspecteurs: une approche mendélienne du rapport d'autorité. *Revue française de pédagogie 42*, 45-54.

Narcy-Combes, J.-P. (1998). La problématique action research/recherche-action et le travail coopératif. *ASP 19-22*, 229-238.

Putsche, J. (2011). *Spracheinstellungen von Grundschülerinnen und Grundschülern in einer Grenzregion. Qualitative Untersuchung in zwei paritätisch unterrichteten ersten Klassen mit Zielsprache Französisch.* Bern.

Putsche, J. (2016). Qu'est-ce-qu'une didactique transfronalière et comment conscientiser les enseignants de langue pour celle-ci? *Synergies Pays Germanophones 9*, 47-61.

Raasch, A. (2002). *L'Europe, les frontières et les langues. Guide pour l'élaboration des politiques linguistiques éducatives en Europe – De la diversité linguistique à l'éducation plurilingue.* Strasbourg.

Raasch, A. (2005). Grenzkompetenz – Ein Weg nach Europa. Wissenschaften von der Sprache und Kontextwissenschaften im Gespräch. In R. Denk (ed.). *In Europa unterwegs. Grenzüberschreitende Modelle der Lehrerbildung im Zeichen von europäischen Identität, Kultur, und Mehrsprachigkeit.* Herbolzheim, 119-129.

Raasch, A. (2008). Von Baden-Württemberg nach Europa und zurück. Sprachenlernen und Sprachenlehren als sprachenpolitisches Handeln. In F. Windmüller (coord.). *Synergies Pays germanophones 1, L'enseignement bi-plurilingue: Educations, compétences, stratégies d'apprentissage.* Berlin, 21-40.

Wassenberg, B. (2010). Qu'est-ce-qui motive la coopération transfrontalière dans l'espace franco-germano-suisse? Approche historique. In B. Wassenberg (ed.). *Vivre et penser la coopération transfrontalière: les régions frontalières françaises*. Stuttgart, 95-113.

Mojca Ilc Klun

Thinking, teaching and learning about migration processes – The case of Slovenia

Introduction

Slovenia, much like every country, has been involved with migration processes, whether directly or indirectly. Even though Slovenia is a young and small country of only 2 million people, the area of present day Slovenia has always been involved into different migration processes. On one hand we could categorize Slovenia as an emigration country. From the middle of the 19th Century until the middle of the 20th Century the area of present day Slovenia was the place of emigration. Due to statistical data, today around 500,000 people of Slovenian descents live outside Slovenia (cf. Zupančič 1998). Secondly we could categorize Slovenia as an immigration country. At the end of the 20th Century, Slovenia was a destination country for around 70,000 people, who emigrated from different ex-Yugoslavian countries. In addition Slovenia can also be categorized as a transit country. During 2015 and 2016 Slovenia was the place of so-called Western Balkan migration route, where more than 460,000 migrants crossed the territory of Slovenia, in order to reach their destination country in either Western or Northern Europe. Since Slovenia has always been involved with different migration processes and because migrations are becoming a global phenomenon it is crucial that the Slovenian educational system implement migration processes within their curriculum.

Methodological approaches

The paper presents some of the findings of three studies, which were conducted between the years 2014 and 2016.

The first study focuses on a survey among 1,103 Slovenian students from eleven Slovenian primary and secondary schools. The survey was conducted between May 2014 and May 2015 as a written questionnaire, divided into three parts: Part A focuses on demographical issues of participants, Part B focuses on knowledge about migration processes, and Part C focuses on perceptions and personal opinions about migration processes. For the present paper we focused only on the results of one question (V4 – Have you ever thought about emigrating from Slovenia), which was included into part C of the questionnaire. In the study we were interested in perceptions and opinions of young people (primary and secondary school students) about emigration from Slovenia.

The second study focuses on 75 written unstructured essays[1], which were conducted among Geography students from Slovenia, University of Ljubljana, Faculty of Arts, Department of Geography. In that study we focused on the perception of young people about migration processes during the period 2015/2016. We investigated the positive or negative opinion of young people about recent migration processes and how they built their own opinion. While the question from the first study was direct, the second study provided students an opportunity to express their feelings and thoughts. They had no other limitations other than just to be focused on the title.

The last study was conducted among 56 people of Slovenian descent, who live in the USA, Canada, Australia and New Zealand. According to adopted biographic narrative interpretive method we wrote 56 life stories of people of Slovenian descent, through which students can learn about migration processes.

Within those three studies we combined topics about Slovenian diaspora, emigration processes of Slovenians, and migratory flows. The results of the studies can be used when educators teach about migration processes in primary and secondary schools. Especially written life sto-

[1] Unstructured essay is in-depth essay, more flexible and open, where usually just the title is defined. A person can express in this essay his/her own thoughts and feelings.

ries can be utilized and implemented within a course as additional teaching tool regarding migration, emigration, and/or immigration processes.

Slovenia has always been involved into different migration processes

Throughout its history, present day Slovenia has always been involved with different migration processes. Each are described as follows:

Slovenia as an emigration country

In the introduction we already stated that on the one hand we could categorize Slovenia as an emigration country. From the middle of the 19th Century until the beginning of the 20th Century around 300,000 people emigrated from Slovenia, mainly because of economical reasons (cf. Drnovšek 2001). At that time the major immigration destinations for Slovenians were USA, Canada, and Argentina. Nevertheless some Slovenians also emigrated to different European countries, but those were mainly short-term stops. Slovenians remained in those countries long enough to earn enough funds in order to afford a ticket across the Atlantic (cf. ibid.). At the beginning of the 20th Century Slovenian emigrants formed so-called Slovenian ethnic settlements outside Slovenia. One of the biggest and well known at that time was formed in Cleveland, Ohio, USA, where in 1910 14,332 Slovenians lived. With this statistic, in 1910 Cleveland became the third largest "Slovenian city" in the terms of the number of Slovenians – after Ljubljana, which is the capital, and Trieste, Italy. However in 1921 USA introduced a quota system, limiting the immigration of certain ethnic groups of immigrants (mainly those, coming from Eastern and Southern Europe), the number of Slovenian immigrants has dropped significantly. In 1921 only 6,426 people from Yugoslavia[2] were allowed to immigrate to the USA and in 1924, when the USA

[2] In the statistic there was no division between different etnhnic groups of people from Yugoslavia. All of them were categorized as Yugoslavians, therefore we

introduced another even more stringent quota system, only 671 people from Yugoslavia were allowed to immigrate and settled in the USA (cf. Genorio 1979). For that reason Slovenian emigration flows were redirected to other destination countries – Canada, Argentina and Brazil (between WW I and WW II 4,359 Slovenians emigrated to Canada, 3,024 to Argentina and 525 to Brazil) (cf. Valenčič 1990), and also to other European countries, especially to Germany and France. WW II almost stopped emigration of Slovenians, while after WW II Slovenia faced so-called political emigration, where Slovenians, who did not agree with the political situation, emigrated mainly to Argentina, Australia and Canada. Due to statistical data at that time, around 18,000 Slovenians emigrated from Slovenia. After that political emigration flow another so-called chain emigration flow followed, when an additional 11,000 people (relatives and family members of political emigrants) emigrated from Slovenia (cf. Zupančič 1998). At the end of the 1950s Slovenians started to emigrate to Germany, France, Sweden, Belgium, Netherlands and Luxemburg as physical workers. At first some of them worked in those countries as seasonal workers, but later many of them moved and settled in those countries permanently. Even today, Slovenia faces a small, but important emigration flow of well-educated Slovenians to Australia and New Zealand. Due to statistical data around 30,000 people of Slovenian descent live in Australia (majority of them in Melbourne, Sydney, Brisbane, Perth, Canberra and Adelaide) (cf. Čebulj Sajko 2000), and around 170 people of Slovenian descent in New Zealand (mainly in regions Auckland, Wellington and Canterbury) (cf. Abazović 2010).

Slovenian women workers in Alexandria, Egypt
At the end of the 19th Century and at the beginning of the 20th Century Slovenians from Western part of Slovenia (Goriška region) faced with one special emigration flow. Because of economical reasons in 1870

---

cannot know the excact number of Slovenians who actually immigrated to the USA in the 1920s.

Slovenian women started to emigrate from Goriška region to Alexandria, Egypt, where they worked as housekeepers, maidens, cooks, babysitters, and dressmakers. Some of them emigrated because of opportunities to earn some money, some of them because of youthful desire, some of them because after WW I they became young widows; some of them emigrated alone, others accompanied by a husband, some with a child, etc (cf. Koprivec 2013). By the end of the 19th Century Slovenian women from Goriška region established in Alexandria an important form of networking, through which new Slovenian emigrants from Goriška region moved to Alexandria on the basis of the acquaintances and recommendations of those Slovenian women who already worked in Egypt. This type of networking is nowadays strongly present, especially in the category of woman migration. As an example we could mention the Philippine who emigrate practically to all countries as housekeepers, maidens, cooks, babysitters and are, as were a Century ago, Aleksandrinke (Slovenian women migrants in Alexandria, Egypt), influenced by stigmatization and stereotyping.

In 1902 around 5,000 female Slovenian emigrants from Goriška region lived in Alexandria, Egypt. Emigration of Slovenian women from Goriška region to Alexandria reached its peak between the period 1918 and 1926. At the beginning of WW II around 7,000 Slovenian female emigrants lived in Alexandria. Majority of them emigrated back to Slovenia between 1950s and 1970s, but some of them emigrated also to other parts of the world (cf. ibid.).

According to statistics today around 500,000 people of Slovenian descent live outside Slovenia (cf. Zupančič 1998), which for a small country of only 2 million people, is a huge number. We can conclude, that during the centuries Slovenians were emigrating from Slovenia mainly due to economical and political reasons, but nevertheless some of them emigrated also because of personal, family and other reasons.

Figure 1: The number of nowadays Slovenian diaspora

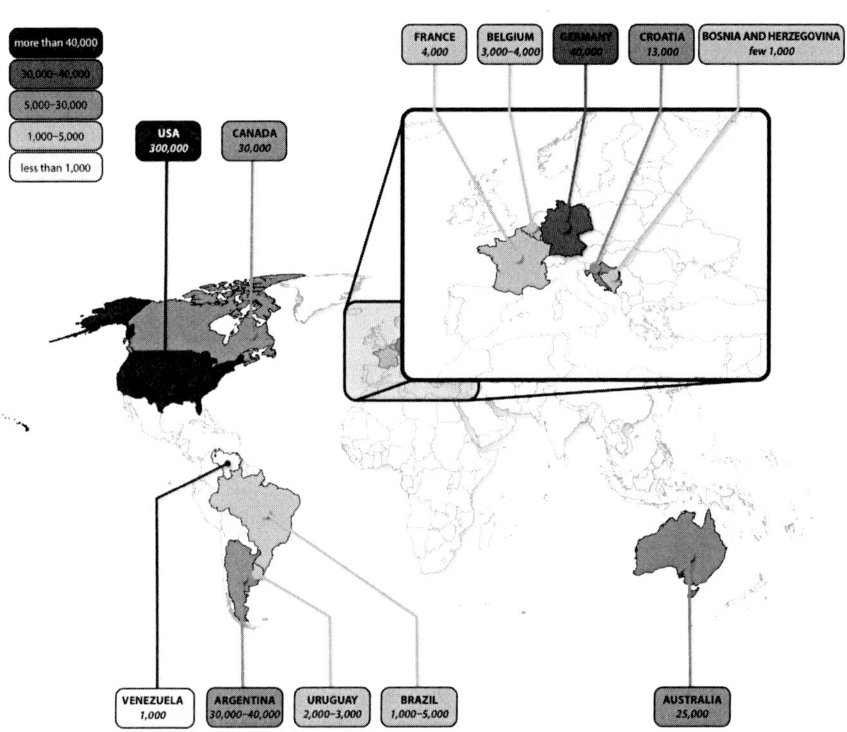

Slovenia as an immigration country

In the middle of the 20th Century Slovenia was a country of destination for some Yugoslavian migrants. Between 1961 and 1971 around 83,000 people from other Yugoslavian republics moved to Slovenia, mostly because of economical reasons. In the middle of the 1970s immigration flow from other Yugoslav republics had increased due to: a) economical improvements in Slovenia, and b) the change of immigration politics of some Western European countries. In the last decade before the split of

Yugoslavia the immigration flows to Slovenia had slowed down, mainly because of political reasons.

Table 1: Annual number of immigrants in Slovenia between 1961-1990

Year	1961	1965	1967	1970	1975	1978	1980	1985	1990
Number	6,537	10,513	9,272	7,168	11,325	12,770	11,983	8,912	7,075

After 1991, when Yugoslavia split into five countries[3], Slovenia became a destination country for around 70,000 people, who emigrated from different ex-Yugoslavian countries because of political reasons. The majority of them were emigrants from Bosnia and Herzegovina (cf. Komac 2007). In the following years emigrants from ex-Yugoslavian republics moved to Slovenia mostly because of economical and political reasons. Many of those immigrants worked as physical workers or cleaners, but on the other hand some of them found their employment also in tertiary sector. Nevertheless the image of immigrant who moved to Slovenia from one of the ex-Yugoslavian countries and found his/her employment in lower paid jobs and have a lower social status prevail among Slovenians. Today, according to some statistics, around 263,000 people from ex-Yugoslavian countries live in Slovenia, which represents around 13.4% of all people who live in Slovenia (cf. Medvešek 2007).

Slovenia as a transit country

During 2015 and 2016, Slovenia experienced a massive wave of migratory flow in what is known as the Western Balkan migration route. More than 460,000 people crossed Slovenia's borders during a span of just five months (October 2015-March 2016). This massive influx began October

---

[3] In 1991 and 1992 Yugoslavia divided into five countries: Republic of Slovenia, Republic of Croatia, Bosnia and Herzegovina, FYROM and Federal Republic of Yugoslavia. In 2003 Federal Republic of Yugoslavia was renamed into Republic of Serbia and Montenegro, in 2006 this republic was divided into two countries – Serbia and Montenegro.

16th to 17th, 2015, when Hungary decided to close its borders. As a result, migrants redirected their path across Croatia, to Slovenia, and eventually towards Austria and Germany. The largest inflow into Slovenia centered around Brežice county, where between 8,000 to 10,000 migrants arrived daily. Slovenia reacted quickly, and established migrant centers across the border (see fig. 2). It is interesting to note that while majority of Slovenian media were neutral on the topic, social media ran rampant with negativity, and that perception among young people prevailed.

Figure 2: Map of Slovenia with entry and exit points and the centers for migrants

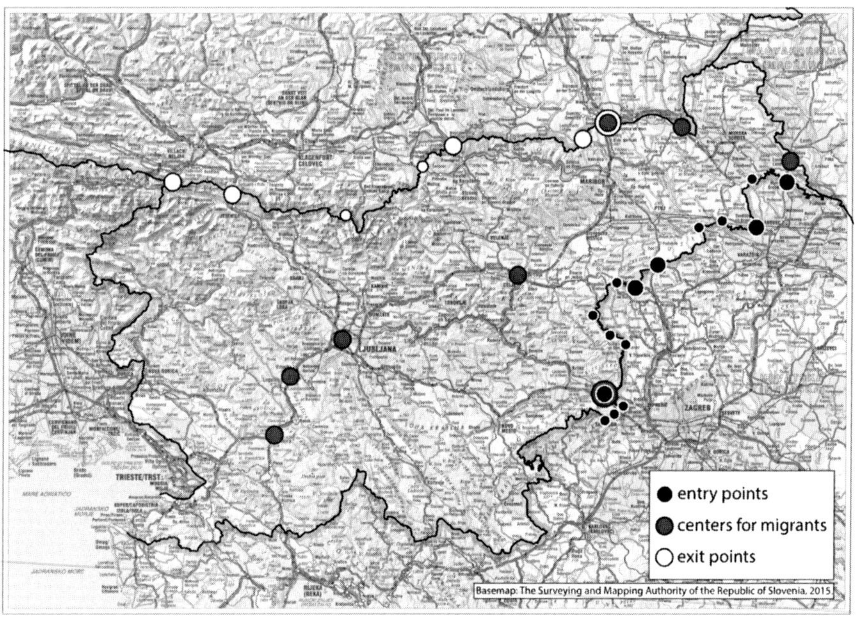

Results of the studies

Results from Study 1 – "I wish to emigrate from Slovenia!"

The first study, which was conducted as a written questionnaire among 1,103 students of primary and secondary schools in Slovenia, showed that 63.5% of students would like to emigrate from Slovenia. The study concluded that the older the students are, the more likely they are to think about emigrating from Slovenia. In the grade 6, where students are 10-11 years old, 31.5% of them would like to emigrate from Slovenia; that number jumps to 72.5% when evaluating responses from those in their 4th year of high school.

Table 2: The percentage of primary and secondary school students who would like to emigrate from Slovenia

Type of school	Grades/Years	YES, I would like to emigrate from Slovenia (%)	NO, I would not like to emigrate from Slovenia (%)
Primary school	Grade 6	31.5	68.5
	Grade 7	53.8	46.2
	Grade 8	63.6	36.4
	Grade 9	67.5	32.5
Secondary school	Year 1	69.7	30.3
	Year 2	71.9	28.9
	Year 3	69.1	30.9
	Year 4	72.5	27.5

The results of these studies showed that 54.3% of all primary school students and 70.3% of secondary school students would like to emigrate from Slovenia. It also exposed gender differences. More than 70% of all primary and secondary school female students indicated that they would like to emigrate from Slovenia, while "only" 55.4% of their male counterparts responded the same way. And what are the reasons for such a high number of students who would like to emigrate from Slovenia? What is, according to their opinions, so bad or not so good in Slovenia that would cause them to emigrate from Slovenia and live elsewhere? The majority of questioned students revealed that they would like to emigrate for economic reasons, primarily for job opportunities. Respondents believe that they can earn better wages elsewhere for the same type of work performed in Slovenia. Other responses could not be categorized as shown below; they varied from educational opportunities to learning other languages, while others simply did not specify their answers and wrote "I would just like to emigrate for no reason".

Table 3: The reasons primary and secondary school students would like to emigrate from Slovenia

Reasons	Percentage of students (%)
Economical reasons	46.9
Other reasons	42.2
Socio-cultural reasons	4.5
Spatial-locational reasons	3.2
Political reasons	3.0
Historical reasons	0.2

The study showed that a majority of questioned primary and secondary school students would like to emigrate from Slovenia (63.5%). The data provided shows a direct correlation between the age of the students and their desire to emigrate from Slovenia. In Grade 6 "only" one third of all students think about emigrating, while by Year 1 of high school that percentage already reaches more than two thirds of all students.

Results from Study 2 – "Social networks have a significant impact on opinions"

The second study was conducted among 75 geography students from University of Ljubljana, Faculty of Arts, Department of Geography. In this study we were interested in the student's thoughts, feelings, and opinions about migration flow that Slovenia experienced during 2015/2016. The study showed that social networks (especially Facebook) had a significant impact on the opinions of young people. Despite the fact that Slovenian media (TV, radio and newspapers) objectively reported on the so-called migration crisis, social networks had a significant impact on student's opinion, where a very negative perspective prevailed. 41% of surveyed students stated in their unstructured essays, that migrations would have a very negative impact on Slovenia. They revealed that people in Slovenia were afraid of migrants, associating them with the possibility of terrorist attacks. In addition, students shared opinions and concerns regarding the potential burden that Slovenia would experience if too much money would be allocated to migrants. This, among other debates surrounding the migration crisis, has caused disunity between Slovenians. 28% of all students stated in their unstructured essays that the so-called migration crisis would have very negative impacts on the European Union as a whole. The prevailing opinion was that migrants would cause economic problems as well as various other conflicts (social, linguistic, religious, cultural, political).

When both studies are analyzed, we find that young people in Slovenia are faced with two conflicting positions. On one hand they would like to emigrate from Slovenia, mainly for economic reasons. Thereby becoming migrants themselves; on the other hand, when there is a question of accepting immigrants in Slovenia, they do not want to accept them, because in their opinion, migrants would only cause problems in Slovenia. Studies such as these show us that there is a need to bring topics about migration processes into the Slovenian educational system. We should educate young people in Slovenia about migration processes, its causes and effects, as well as acceptance of cultural, religious, linguistic and other diversities in order to develop positive intercultural dialogue.

Results from Study 3 – Developing life stories as a teaching tool

In the final phase of our research we decided that there is a need to develop a teaching tool through which an educator can teach about migration processes. Since our studies revealed that young people would like to become migrants, but would not like to accept immigrants, we decided to develop a teaching tool, through which students could learn about emigration and immigration processes through the eyes of other Slovenians who themselves emigrated from Slovenia. We developed a teaching tool where we gathered 56 real life stories of people of Slovenian descent who live in USA, Canada, Australia and New Zealand. Through those real life stories students can learn about migration processes, as well as find similarities between past and present migration flows in different parts of the world. Through real life stories they could easily understand the phases each migrant has to experience from the country of emigration to the country of final destination. They would learn about migration processes, emigration, immigration, integration into new social and cultural environment via different memories of migrants or their descendants etc.

I wanted to visit homeland regularly, therefore I searched for the job in aviation (Frank)

"After the graduation from high school in 1965 I was 19 years old and I decided to visit Australia, because my aunt had already lived there. In Australia I saw beautiful girls, nice weather, tasted good wine ... so I decided to stay. I said to myself that I did not come so far just to have fun – I wanted to earn some money, a good pension and then move back to my homeland, Slovenia.

In Australia I started to work for the insurance company and I settled in a house on the beach. Afterwards I worked as a mountain rescuer. When I got the permanent residential visa, I got the same possibilities and responsibilities as other citizens – so I got a call from the army. I went to Vietnam, where I worked as an economist in air unit. I stayed there for three months. During this period I got a lot of friends, one of them is also today's governor of Australia. When I came back from Vietnam, I began to search for a permanent job. I wanted to find a job, which would allow me the regular access to Europe, therefore I thought that the best choice was a job in aviation. I applied for that job once, twice, five times, but I did not get any response from employer. Then I had enough. I wrote the letter, where I express my feelings: "If I was good enough to wear Australian uniform in Vietnam, then I should be good enough to get at least a job interview." The very next day I got a call and that is how my business career started. For two years I went to aviation academy in Melbourne and then I joined Australian airline company Qantas, where I firstly worked as a fleet controller. Then I completed additional trainings and I became a pilot. I had that job for 32 years. That job allowed me regular visits to my homeland, Slovenia. Every week I flew to Europe, especially to Paris, Rome, Frankfurt and London. From there, when I had at least one afternoon of free time, I went to Ljubljana, Slovenia.

When you move to another country, you have to integrate as soon as possible. In the case with Slovenians I realized that the biggest problem is that Slovenians do not want to socialize. I was pretty much active in Slovenian community – for many years I was a member of the board of Slovenian society in Sydney, and for several years I was also a president for that society. I wanted to integrate into Australian community as soon as possible, but on the other hand, I also wanted to stay connected to Slovenian society, culture and habits.

Slovenian poet Oton Zupančič once said: "There is only one homeland." You can create new home anywhere in the world, but you will always have just one homeland, which is deeply enrooted into your heart and memory. I always had the desire that one day I will return to my homeland, to Slovenia. In 2003 my wife and me decided to move back to Slovenia. When I came to Slovenia I went to the Institute for the Employment, where I searched for the job. But they told me, that they do not have any job for an old pilot and that Slovenia does not have any Boeing 747, which I could pilot. Instead of working as a pilot I started to run my own business. I opened a firm, where I was an interpreter and help those Slovenians, who wanted to move to Australia. But soon I had enough of that job. Now I am retired and every two weeks I get a good pension from Australian government.

> Every year I travel to Australia for a month or two. There I still have some good friends, and also my daughter lives in Australia. She is an Australian, she was born in Australia, she is married to Australian man, has Anglo-Saxon last name and she has never been thinking about moving to Slovenia."

Real life stories (e.g. Frank's story) are good examples through which we can teach young people about migration processes. Since they are short, written in simple and understandable language, and include first person emotions and experiences, students can learn about migration processes in a more "pleasant way" that is meaningful and tangible.

Conclusion

Since migration and its effects play a significant role in our daily lives, there is an important need that we introduce such topics to the school curricula. Nowadays social networks have a huge impact on opinion of young people, also when there is a question about migrations. In order to prevent that young people would built their own opinion mainly through social networks, there is a need that teachers discuss about migration processes during the lessons. One of the way through which educators can teach about migration processes are also real life stories. Our research showed that real life stories, told through the eyes of migrants, or their descendants, could foster a more positive perception, and can ultimately facilitate or even change the initial attitudes formed through social media alone.

References

Abazović, A. (2010). *Slovensko izseljenstvo na Novi Zelandiji.* University of Ljubljana, Thesis.

Čebulj Sajko, B. (2000). *Razpotja izseljencev. Razdvojena identiteta avtsralskih Slovencev.* Ljubljana.

Drnovšek, M. (2001). *Izseljevanje Slovencev v Severno Ameriko. Slovensko izseljenstvo. Zbornik ob 50. Letnici Slovenske izseljenske matice.* Ljubljana, 173-186.

Genorio R. (1979). *Problemi slovenskih izseljencev v Kanadi. 1. faza.* Ljubljana.

Komac, M. (ed.; 2007). *Priseljenci: Študije o priseljevanju in vključevanju v slovensko družbo.* Ljubljana.

Koprivec, D. (2013). *Dediščina Aleksandrink in spomini njihovih potomcev.* Ljubljana.

Medvešek, M. (2007). Kdo so potomci priseljencev z območja nekdanje Jugoslavije? *Razprave in gradivo: revija za narodnostna vprašanja 2007 53/54,* 30-34.

Valenčič, V. (1990). Izseljevanje Slovencev v tujino do druge svetovne vojne. *Dve domovini 1990 (1),* 43-82.

Zupančič, J. (1998). Identiteta je merljiva. Prispevek k metodologiji proučevanja etnične identitete. *Razprave in gradivo 33,* 253-268.

Boštjan Rogelj, Katja Vintar Mally & Tatjana Resnik Planinc

"Yugonostalgia" among young Slovenes

Introduction

The Socialist Federal Republic of Yugoslavia (SFRY) was born in the maelstrom of war at the end of 1943. It officially disintegrated in January of 1992, when members of the EU at the urging of Germany recognized the independence of Slovenia and Croatia (cf. Pirjevec 2003, 2011). Its existence and development was closely tied to the Yugoslav Communist Party, led for many years by Josip Broz Tito. Under his leadership a one-party political system and socialist socio-economic order was introduced. This new system changed Yugoslavia in the postwar period from an agrarian to an industrialized country whose citizens enjoyed a relatively high standard of social rights (cf. Velikonja 2008a). However, the communist party did not succeed in responding adequately to new economic challenges and so Yugoslavia in the last decade of its existence was confronted with increasingly intractable economic and social problems.

In the social field the communist party led a policy of brotherhood and unity through which it hoped to unite different nations into a multinational state and create a common, supranational Yugoslav identity (cf. Hodson, Massey & Sekulic 1994). Any form of public expression of national sentiment was therefore severely sanctioned. Another important pillar of social policy was formed by the policy of equality, solidarity, and decentralization, upon which the system of self-management was based. This system supported the equal rights of all citizens in making decisions. Through the creation of various administrative organs, in which the majority was composed of ordinary citizens, an impression was created of a high degree of democracy and the role of the individual in society was enhanced. The politics of solidarity ensured the provision of numerous benefits to citizens in the social field (especially worth noting are free health care and education and socially-oriented housing policy). At the same time the self-management system shaped an environment that destimulated entrepreneurship, as a result of which the entire economy began to decline and lose contact with more developed countries (cf. Woodward 1995).

Zero tolerance of political opposition was characteristic of the communist-led one-party system. Repressive agencies led by intelligence services often suppressed various political opponents using force. State terror was especially strong immediately after the end of the WW II and during the time of the dispute with the Soviet Union. Later on, and especially after Tito's death, the control of the communist party began to weaken, which ultimately led to democratization and the collapse of the state.

Yugoslavia enjoyed a great reputation in the international arena. Through a relatively independent foreign policy it succeeded in acquiring the position of an intermediate link between the two blocs. It was also one of the founders of the Non-Aligned Movement.

Over the fifty-year history of the country there were periods of rise and fall, successes and failures, lighter and darker moments. It is thus not surprising that many often diametrically opposed memories of life in Yugoslavia have been preserved. While some remember it as a country whose inhabitants lived a good life free of care, others remember hardship and the repression of political and economic freedom of individuals and nations.

Varying memories of Yugoslavia are the central subject of our research. We have focused on young people. We were interested in the kinds of memories held by a generation that grew up after the collapse of the shared state and that never had any direct contact with it. Of foremost interest was the question of whether any memory of Yugoslavia is even still present among the young. How frequently do memories of Yugoslavia come up in their everyday life? Which memories are most often preserved? How and by whom are these memories transferred to younger generations? Who are the agents of memories of Yugoslavia?

This article is divided into three parts. The introductory part is followed by a presentation of the theoretical and methodological framework for the research. In it the concept of nostalgia is presented and critically evaluated. In the second part the results of surveys and interviews performed among young people in Slovenia are presented. Based on these results we were able to provide answers to the four research questions outlined above. In the last part some key findings and concluding thoughts are presented.

Theoretical-methodological framework for the research

The research is centered on memories and their mediation from older to younger generations. We start from the findings of recent studies that warn of the inconsistency of memories and highlight the significance of the wider context in which the process of remembering occurs.

There is a general belief that assumes that memories are permanent, unchanging, and accurate, a sort of video recording from the past that is stored in our brains and can be accessed at any time. Critical approaches to the study of memories contradict this belief. In the view of Lowenthal: "Memory does not passively record the past but actively – and errantly – reconstructs it." (2015, 305) As a result, memories are frequently inaccurate or even invented. Although the reshaping of the past is inherent to the process of remembering, we tend not to question memories, since the status of eyewitness gives them the required legitimacy.

In memories, the present and the past are inseparably interconnected. Memories are strongly dependent on the wider context in which they are awakened. What and how we remember something is strongly dependent on when, where, and why certain memories are evoked. An individual's memory of a certain event can change depending on the broader circumstances in which it was evoked. At the same time, memories and the past have a great influence on our perception of the present. Everything we experience today is placed in the frame of our memories. Each individual forms their present-day expectations, aspirations, and goals with the help of the past.

> More than recapturing the past, recollection helps digest and comprehend it. Memories are selective reconstructions, remade by subsequent actions

> and perceptions, freshly envisioned by changing codes of knowledge. Memory does not preserve but adapts the past, to manage and enrich the present and anticipate the future; indeed, memory is as much the kernel of the future as the trace of the past. (ibid., 332)

In the literature for research on memories we can often see a division into individual and collective memories (cf. Fentress & Wickham 1992; Lowenthal 2015; Olick & Robbins 1998), in which more recent studies highlight that the border between collective and individual memories is unclear and frequently blurred. Memories are inherently individual/personal. Nevertheless, it happens that certain memories that we believe have been evoked from our personal experience are in fact acquired from others (cf. Halbwachs 2001, 25; Lowenthal 2015, 310). The reason for this can be found in the fact that individual memories are much harder to preserve and awaken than collective ones (cf. Halbwachs 2001, 23). People thus often collectivize individual memories and adapt them to the wider collective memory.

In interpreting the results of the research performed it should be taken into account that memories do not represent an objective recording of events from the past but that they are constantly changing, selective reconstructions of the past that are adapted to the broader collective memory. Due to the close connection of the present and the past in the process of remembering it is essential to consider also the wider context in which the research was performed. Negative economic, social and political consequences in Slovenia brought by the most recent economic crisis have had an important role in the formation and transfer of memories of Yugoslavia to the generation that was included in the study.

Besides a critical approach to the study of memories it also made sense to include the concept of nostalgia and Yugonostalgia in the research on memories, in which nostalgia should not be regarded as something negative[1] but rather as a cultural practice through which critiques of the present are developed (cf. Todorova & Gille 2010, 5). In the past decade we have witnessed a visible evocation of collective and individual memories of the socialist period in most formerly communist countries. According to Velikonja (2004, 37) nostalgia has been expressed from Szczecin on the Baltic to Trieste on the Adriatic. Post-socialist nostalgia has been given much attention by researchers (cf. Luthar & Pušnik 2010; Petrović 2013; Todorova, Dimou & Troebst 2014; Todorova & Gille 2010; Velikonja 2004, 2008b). Western observers have often viewed it with disdain, regarding it as a negative, reactionary phenomenon, but in so doing they neglect the context in which it has emerged. Its appearance is no accident, since it is closely connected with the post-transition context. It coincided with the inclusion of eight formerly socialist countries in the EU.

Inclusion in the EU represented a symbolic end to the political and economic transition of Central and Eastern Europe. With it former communist countries once again became part of the "European family" (Rogelj 2006). New conditions enabled a different view of the past. Whereas in the 1990s any sort of evocation of memories about socialist times was met with many criticisms and treated as a non-European act, after 2004 it become somewhat more acceptable. Something similar also happened in Slovenia. The political atmosphere during the initial period after independence was exceptionally unfavorable towards anything Yugoslav. Conditions began to change after 2000, when there was a normalization of relations among the former republics and when it became clear that Slovenia would be included in the first expansion of the EU into Central Europe.

[1] Nostalgia in the past was treated as a conceptual opposition to progress, as something reactionary, sentimental, and melancholic, a discouraged retreat from the present or rather a loss of faith in the future (cf. Pickering & Keightley 2006).

The rise of post-socialist nostalgia was influenced even more by the process of economic transition. This left many citizens with a feeling of loss. "Nostalgia usually appears when the present condition is experienced as worse than the previous one." (Velikonja 2008a, 172) Besides feeling a loss of security, stability, and prosperity, people were also affected by the loss of solidarity and certain forms of social life, and the vulgarity of cultural life (cf. Todorova & Gille 2010, 7). In this regard, it is interesting that the feelings mentioned were present not only among older generations and people whose economic position was significantly worsened as a result of the economic transition. Classes of people who had gained the most economically from the transition were also frequently disappointed (cf. Wieliczko & Zuk 2003). The emergence of post-socialist nostalgia coincided with a more critical attitude towards the transition process. The economic crisis that had affected Europe in the past decade further increased the feeling of uncertainty and additionally undermined faith in a better tomorrow, thereby reinforcing post-socialist nostalgia.

In the Slovenian context post-socialist nostalgia is usually labeled with the term Yugonostalgia or "red" nostalgia[2] (cf. Velikonja 2008a). The first instances of the manifestation of Yugonostalgia appeared soon after Slovenian independence, when so-called Balkan parties were very fashionable. The organization of parties at which exclusively music from the former common state was played could be interpreted as the resistance of young people to the strongly anti-Yugoslav discourse that prevailed in Slovenian society during that period. In the more recent period it can be linked to people's growing dissatisfaction with the situation in the country.

Methodologically the research is based on the results of a survey that was carried out among young people in the Republic of Slovenia in the spring of 2016. 116 respondents aged 15-30 years old participated in the

[2] Within it nostalgia for the former president of the country Josip Broz Tito holds a special place. Velikonja (2008b) calls this Titostalgia.

survey. The great majority (80%) were younger than 25, meaning that they were born after the declaration of Slovenian independence. People of both sexes were represented equally: there were 58 men and 58 women. Whereas more than a third (34.5%) had relatives in countries of the former Yugoslavia, the share of those whose parents were not born in Slovenia was very low (only 7.0%).

The survey was composed of four sets of questions. In the first set we were interested in associations with the word Yugoslavia. In the second set we were interested in whom young people get the most information about Yugoslavia from and how often the former state is talked about at home. In the third set we asked which topics were most often brought up when families talked about Yugoslavia, and how these topics were treated (positively or negatively). Finally, we wanted to know how older generations assessed life in Yugoslavia. The last part of the survey included standard demographic questions.

Results and discussion

Through the survey we hoped to gain an insight into the existing state among young people with regard to the following four research questions:

1. Is the memory of Yugoslavia still present among young Slovenes?
2. What sort of memories prevail?
3. How often do they emerge in everyday life?
4. Who passes them on to younger generations?

The survey of the younger generation of Slovenes, aged 15 to 30 years, showed that memory of the former federal state is still preserved from generation to generation, even though the majority of those surveyed due to their youth never had actual experience of life in Yugoslavia: 82% of survey participants were younger than 25 years. Among their first associations with the word Yugoslavia (see fig. 1, p. 141) were most frequently the name of the former president Tito (mentioned by 73% of respondents), a description of the political system, Yugoslav national symbols and holidays, and also socio-economic conditions and everyday life (from sport to music and food).

Figure 1: Associations with the word Yugoslavia

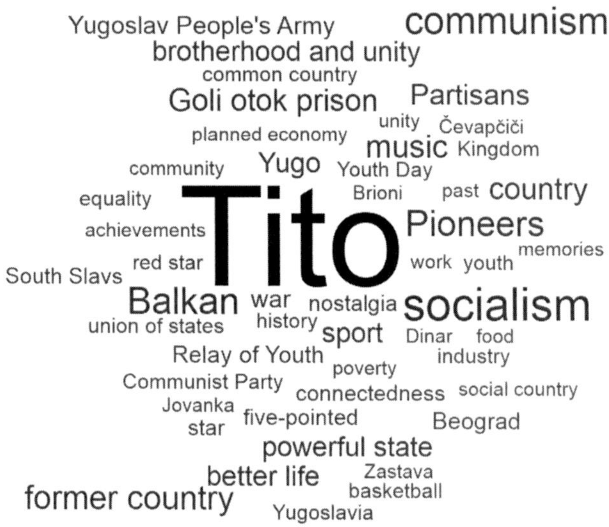

In the continuation respondents were asked to list any aspects of the existence of Yugoslavia that they remembered, and then for each one to categorize it as positive of negative. An interesting finding was that on average more positive aspects were remembered (3.3 per respondent) than negative (2.6 per respondent) regarding life in Yugoslavia. After combining responses in similar groups (coding of responses) it turned out that the majority of the positive aspects cites (see fig. 2, p. 142) related to socio-economic conditions in Yugoslavia. Most frequent were responses that noted the good economic position (nearly a third of all respondents mentioned in particular the advantages of economic stability, a high level of employment, a large common market, purchasing power, favorable terms for credit, etc.) as well as better relations in society and greater social security and equality. Many also highlighted the good international reputation of the former country, including its political power and sporting achievements. Due to the citing of various aspects of the political order and President Tito in the category of positive features of Yugoslavia, this could also be partially interpreted as nostalgia for the former political and economic system.

Figure 2: Respondents' views of positive aspects of the existence of Yugoslavia

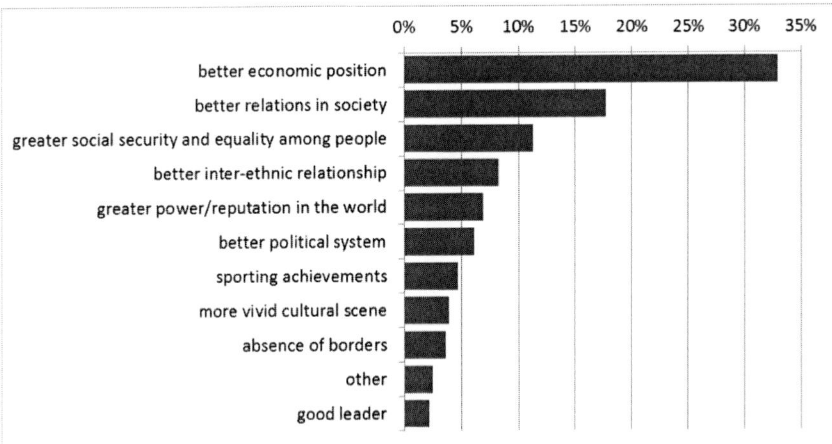

At the same time, political conditions were also evaluated negatively by the greatest share of respondents (see fig. 3, p. 143), since they cited cases of repression of political rights/freedom and civil liberties (30% of respondents) and the shortcomings of the political system (16%). Socialism, communism, a one-party system, the closed nature of the state, censorship, restrictions on freedom of speech, repression and similar were also frequently evaluated as negative. About 30% of respondents had an unfavorable view of the economic system in the former Yugoslavia, in particular due to the shortage of consumer goods and restrictions on imports. Further, the problems of centralism (with domination by Belgrade and Serbia, and anti-Slovene policies), dissension among nations, wars after the collapse of Yugoslavia, etc. were often highlighted. Through a comparison of the frequency of negative or positive evaluation we find that Yugoslav economic conditions were more often evaluated as positive, while in perceptions of political conditions negative assessments predominate.

Figure 3: Respondents' views of the negative aspects of the existence of Yugoslavia

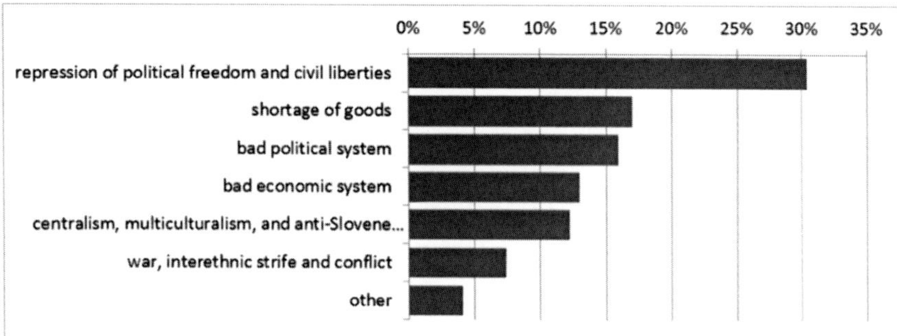

In everyday life young people in Slovenia often come across the traces of the Yugoslav past. According to the responses 30% of participants in the survey come across monuments and symbols of the former state, 24% observe cultural events of this kind, 15% of respondents see the heritage of Yugoslavia in the multi-ethnicity of Slovenia, and 15% see it in the political division. Yugoslavia and the Yugoslav past continue to be a subject of debates and discussions in daily politics, society and of course within the family even more than a quarter century after the country's collapse. According to the results of our study, conversations about Yugoslavia are occasional (33%) or frequent (12%) in 45% of families, while in only 14% of the families of respondents these topics are never discussed. As expected these types of conversations are usually begun by parents (40.7%) or grandparents (40.7%) of respondents, while only rarely (9.3%) do respondents or other younger members in the family bring them up (1.9%). It is interesting that conversations about Yugoslavia are often initiated by male family members, especially fathers and grandfathers. Topics relating to life in Yugoslavia were cited as being the most frequent subject (42%), followed by politics and the political situation at the time (18%), personal experiences of family members (13%), wars and conflicts (7%) and sport (4%).

In one of the closed questions we asked respondents to assess how often certain topics were discussed in the family (see fig. 4) and to what extent positive or negative memories were associated with them (see fig. 5, p. 145). Among the topics offered, respondents most often assessed those relating to social and economic conditions in Yugoslavia as a very frequent or frequent subject of family discussions (41% of families talk about the subject frequently or very frequently), followed by memories of the experiences of family members from Yugoslav times (40% of families bring them up frequently or very frequently), such as memories of military service, holidays, trips and similar. On the other hand, about 42% of respondents' families never or rarely talked about Yugoslav politics or political conditions or the sporting achievements of Yugoslav athletes. Mentioning initial associations also showed that sporting achievements were among the smaller elements of Yugonostalgia. Nevertheless, memories of them were distinctly positive – 71% of respondents characterized them as positive or very positive, which was the highest share of any of the topics.

Figure 4: Assessment of the frequency of conversations about selected topics

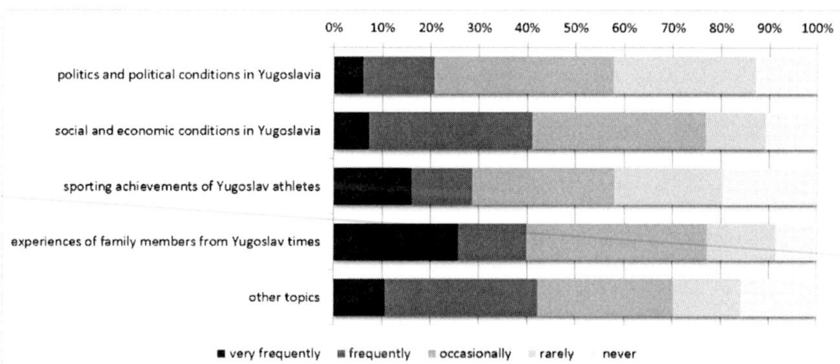

Figure 5: Assessment of memories of selected topics

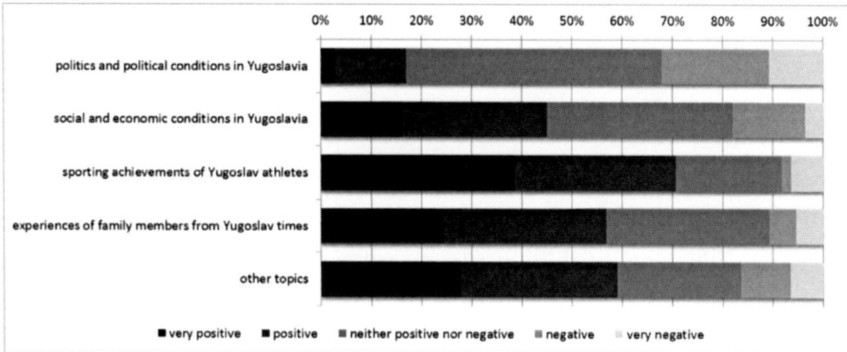

In contrast, political conditions were one of the main associations and also criticism of the former state. Although clearly the topic is less frequently talked about personally, it has a remarkably high proportion of negative and very negative memories (32%) and the lowest proportion of positive and very positive memories (17%). Thus in view of the results of our study, nostalgia for the former state only rarely includes a longing for the former political order and system, while the socio-economic advantages of the "good old days" and shared successes (as for example the successes of Yugoslav athletes, both individuals and strong teams in team sports). Predominantly positive are also memories of personal experiences of family members (a total of 71% positive or very positive memories). All this also fits in with responses to the question as to whether people lived better in Yugoslavia than today in the belief of older generations. 75% of respondents answered in the affirmative and only 11% in the negative, while the rest had trouble providing an unambiguous answer, since in their view it depended on the personal experiences of the person being talked to or the areas of life being evaluated.

Considering all the opinions gathered from young respondents, a key question is who their main source of information about Yugoslavia is. Despite a number of possible responses offered, altogether more than

70% of participants selected either parents or grandparents (see fig. 6), while clearly school and other sources (media, friends, other relatives) were of only secondary importance. Consequently, we estimate that through questions about family memories of Yugoslavia we have investigated one of the key factors in forming the perceptions of young people and the transfer of Yugonostalgia from older to younger generations. Here it is important to stress that while 35% of respondents reported having relatives living in the area of the former Yugoslavia, only in the case of 7% of respondents had their parents in fact moved to Slovenia from the area of the former Yugoslavia. We can thus conclude that for a large number of respondents, these family ties with regions of other republics of the former state did not have any influence on their memories and the evaluations and perceptions expressed.

Figure 6: Main source of information about Yugoslavia

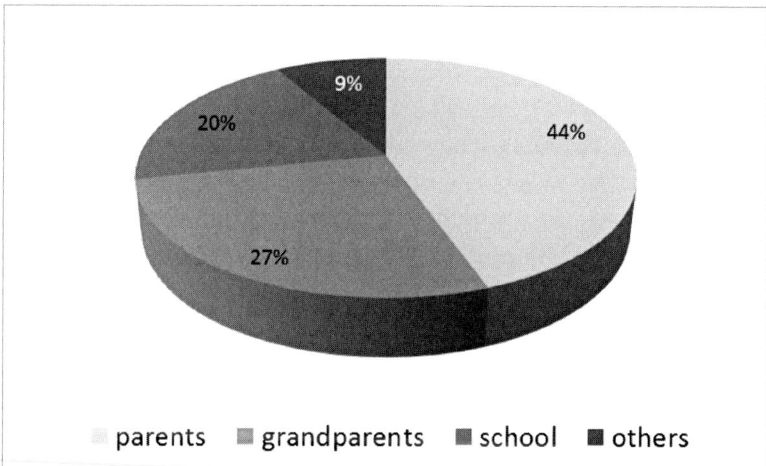

In response to the questions set out in the introduction we can conclude that the study has shown clearly that memories of Yugoslavia are still very much alive among the younger generation and these memories are to a great extent more positive than negative. A large part of Yugonostalgia can be explained by missing some socio-economic advantages and achievements of the former shared state, and certainly also by older generations' memories of their youth. Parents and grandparents through occasional family conversations still preserve and pass on these memories and in this way keep alive Yugonostalgia over the decades.

Concluding thoughts

"The masses prefer to turn to those seductive sirens whose songs / singing are easiest to understand. Those are the sirens of inherited mythological archetypes, the sirens of tribal traditions", writes Debeljak in his essay "Twilight of the Idols". This essay is a sort of lament for the destroyed Yugoslavia and for the cultural mosaic that it offered notwithstanding political ideology. In it Debeljak even back in 1993 predicted that after the wars it would again be necessary to establish contact regardless of whether the international community would force us into it. However, as he emphasizes, this of course does not mean that we must cooperate with everyone as though nothing had happened, since this sort of amnesia would be equally dangerous (cf. Milek 2003).

Yugonostalgia today as well remains an extremely complex and diverse concept which in general can be defined as a longing for the period of socialist Yugoslavia, irreversibly "lost" in a time when it represented to many Slovenes as well as other inhabitants from the area of the "former common state" a synonym for youth, frequently cleansed of many unpleasant and bitter memories. Thus Vidmar and Jež already a few months after the departure of the Yugoslav army from Slovenia stated: "Yugoslavia as a political space is dead, but not as a multicultural one," (Vidmar & Jež 2001) As early as a few months after the last ferry left with the forces of the Yugoslav People's Army (YPA) from Koper the first so-called Balkan parties surfaced, a sort of subpolitical and subcultural gathering/partying against the nationalist orthodoxy of the Slovenian establishment at that time. And they are still going on. In 2001 the youth who attended the Balkan parties in the view of Tomc no longer had any sort of relationship with the former Yugoslavia and accepted things without prejudices (cf. Jež 2001). In this case we could refer to Yugonostalgia on a non-threatening, romantic level of the former common cultural space that was definitely more authentic than the politically declared brotherhood and unity (cf. ibid.).

Perhaps it is true, as Miheljak says, that Yugoslavia in the consciousness of Slovenes is placed in timeless stories of the previous period that we try to repress, to escape, but which continue to surprise us and emerge/surface when we least expect it. Even 13 years ago he believed that interest in Yugoslavia would be preserved and perhaps even strengthened, primarily through music, film and perhaps translated literature as well (cf. Milek 2003). Of course in this regard we do not want to pass on obsolete and ineffective thinking patterns to the young, who were born in a different political and economic system in a new state.

Results of the study among young people that took place in 2016 show that Yugonostalgia is on the one hand a nostalgia for something from the past but it is not a desire for this to be revived in the present. As Pečjak found back in 2005, its charm lies precisely in the fact that it no longer exists, that it has remained in a past that can never return and is lost forever; something that is safely preserved and rediscovered in the present as needed; that exists as an example of model that we can resort to when we want to evaluate the present; since it is cleansed of bad, it remains as an ideal, model, and legitimate measure of human behavior and activity in the present (cf. Pečjak 2005).

Memories of Yugoslavia are still present even today among young Slovenes. Positive memories, which fairly frequently come up in their everyday life, predominate. The main source of information about the former Yugoslavia continue to be parents and grandparents. Thus, more than ten years later the reflection of Pečjak has been confirmed. She wrote:

> Although memory is in a constant state of change and being (re)formed, through new information, through forgetting, through being supplemented with the memories of others, etc., it appears that the (nostalgic) image of Yugoslavia remains the same – "frozen" in time and unchanging. (Pečjak 2005, 64)

References

Fentress, J. & Wickham, C. (1992). *Social Memory.* Oxford.

Halbwachs, M. (2001). *Kolektivni spomin*. Ljubljana.

Hodson, R.; Massey, G. & Sekulic, D. (1994). Who Were the Yugoslavs? Failed Sources of a Common Identity in the Former Yugoslavia. *American Sociological Review 59*(1), 83-97.

Jež, B. (2001). Samo rock'n'roll? *Delo*, 27.10.2001.

Lowenthal, D. ([2]2015). *The Past is a Foreign Country – Revisited*. Cambridge.

Luthar, B. & Pušnik, M. (2010). *Remembering Utopia: The Culture of Everyday Life in Socialist Yugoslavia*. Washington DC.

Milek, V. (2003). Leto 1991 pač ni leto nič. *Delo, Sobotna priloga*, 28.6.2003.

Olick, J. K. & Robbins, J. (1998). Social Memory Studies: From "Collective Memory" to the Historical Sociology of Mnemonic Practices. *Annual Review of Sociology 24*(1), 105-140.

Pečjak, L. (2005). *Spomini na Jugoslavijo in jugonostalgija med mladimi.* Diplomsko delo. Fakulteta za družbene vede, Univerza v Ljubljani, 69. str. Online: http://dk.fdv.uni-lj.si/dela/Pecjak-Lara.PDF [last accessed 25 June 2017].

Petrović, T. (2013). The past that binds us: Yugonostalgia as the politics of future. In S. Pavlović & M. Živković (eds.). *Transcending fratricide: political mythologies, reconciliations, and the uncertain future in the former Yugoslavia.* Baden-Baden, 129-147.

Pickering, M. & Keightley, E. (2006). The Modalities of Nostalgia. *Current Sociology 54*(6), 919–941.

Pirjevec, J. (2003). *Jugoslovanske vojne, 1991-2001*. Ljubljana.

Pirjevec, J. (2011). *Tito in tovariši*. Ljubljana.

Rogelj, B. (2006). Nazaj k Evropi – geopolitični diskurzi o Srednji in Vzhodni Evropi v institucijah Evropske unije. *Dela, 26*, 181-202.

Todorova, M.; Dimou, A. & Troebst, S. (eds.; 2014). *Remembering communism – Private and Public Recollections of Lived Experience in Southeastern Europe*. Budapest, New York.

Todorova, M. & Gille, Z. (eds.; 2010). *Post-Communist nostalgia*. New York, Oxford.

Velikonja, M. (2004). Tistega lepega dne: Značilnosti sodobnega nostalgičnega diskurza. *Bal Canis 5*(12/16), 37-40.

Velikonja, M. (2008a). "Red shades": Nostalgia for socialism as an element of cultural pluralism in the Slovenian transition. *Slovene Studies 30.2,* 171-184.

Velikonja, M. (2008b). *Titostalgija – Študija nostalgije po Josipu Brozu*. Ljubljana.

Wieliczko, B. & Zuk, M. (2003). *Post-Communist Nostalgia Among the Middle-Aged Middle-Class Poles.* Online: http://www.allacademic.com/meta/p106706_index.htm [last accessed 22 June 2017].

Woodward, S. L. (1995). *Socialist unemployment: the political economy of Yugoslavia, 1945-1990*. New Jersey.

Laila Niklasson

Social memories and identities. How staff in museum and Initial Teacher Education can create critical learning experience[1]

Introduction

As a migrant society, Sweden experience both internal migration and migration to and from the country. Thereby members of the society have generated memories from different geographical and social settings. These memories are evoked as individual memories or social or group memories. The definition of social memory used is based on Maurice Halbwachs´ (1992) definition of collective memory. In his work he suggests that a collective memory is what individuals remember, tell others and enact, in activities or in artefacts (rituals, statues). Texts and persons can uphold the memory in a variety of ways between activities where the collective memory is enacted in bigger manifestations, such as a national celebration day. Thereby there is no in-between time without content. In the in-between time there is social interaction creating the memory, as such, the collective memory is a social memory.

The focus in this article will be on how a social memory is created to uphold an identity by second and third generation immigrants. The social memory is then used for a discussion of how museums and Initial Teacher Education can cooperate and create critical learning experiences. As a starting point an investigation of the exhibition 'The Legacy' (Arvet) was be carried out. The exhibition was displayed at a regional museum, Västmanland´s County Museum in Sweden. The exhibition represents how second or third generation immigrants from Finland perceive their Finnish legacy and how they uphold it in Sweden. The exhibi-

[1] Acknowledgement: Thanks to Eva Insulander, Stockholm University, for comments on a first draft of the text.

tion is a mobile exhibition and parts of it are continually re-created with data from different local contexts in Sweden.

The text will continue with a short description of how a border was created between Sweden and Finland followed by the present situation with migration from Finland to Sweden. The change of borders in 19th century and its combination with nationalism, including collecting artefacts for museums is presented and ends with the present shift in the role of the museums. The previous studies end with a reflection of a common assignment for museums and Initial Teacher Education; that is, creating critical learning experiences.

A border between Sweden and Finland

When the second and third generations of Sweden Finns are presenting their legacy the exhibition is also, in some way, presenting a relation between Sweden and Finland and the change of border between the countries.

The change of border between Sweden and Finland is part of a context which includes relations and alliances during war in Northern Europe and Russia. During late 19th century the Swedish king Gustav IV Adolf refused to change his alliance with Great Britain which was directed towards France (led by Napoleon) and thereby countries allied with France, such as Russia sent troops to Finland in 1808 (then a Swedish territory) and Denmark – Norway declared war. The British army stopped troops from Denmark-Norway and France to enter Sweden from the south border and thereby Finland and the border to Russia became the conflict center. The Swedish-Finnish troops could not defend Finland and in 1809 the Russian troops landed at Åland, close to Sweden, and carried out raids in the eastern archipelago (Roslagen). In September 1809 a peace agreement was signed where Sweden had to leave Finland to Russia (cf. Häger 2000). Thereby a new political geographical border was created.

Especially during wartime it becomes clear that a political geographical border is a social construction by human beings. As both Swedish and Finnish language were spoken in different areas in ´Sweden-Finland' there were probably already a certain social border among language groups. But what became different was instead the orientation, the westward orientation in Finland towards Sweden changed to south-west to Russia (Finland became a self-governing territory) and the east-ward orientation for Sweden towards Finland changed to become westward, to Norway. According to Diener and Hagen (2012) a new border creates change in access, mobility and sense of belonging and a primary function of a geographic border is to differentiate space and place. The change of orientation and new political context in Finland in Sweden confirms the effect of changes in borders. The concept place is relevant in this study as it is not necessarily possible to measure (like space), but as Brusman (2011) argues, is experienced and lived. That is, the population could still perceive Finland and Sweden as a place, a meaningful place, or, as well, never perceived Sweden – Finland as a place.

Migration from Finland to Sweden

About two-thirds of the inter-Nordic migrants since 1954 have been Finnish emigrants to and Finnish returnees from Sweden (cf. Fischer & Straubhaar 1996; Statistics Finland in Korkiasaari & Söderling 2003). After WW II there was a general rapid industrialization and urbanization in Scandinavia and especially during 1960-70 the emigration from Finland to Sweden increased. Between 1860 and 1944, 45,000 persons emigrated from Finland to Sweden compared with 535,000 persons between 1945 and 1999. One important prerequisite is that there has been agreement of free mobility between Nordic countries since decades. An earlier labor migration during the 1960s changed during 1980-1990s to emigration due to personal motives as the differences in living standard in Finland and Sweden has decreased (cf. ibid.). An additional factor for emigration could be that Finland is bilingual, both Swedish and Finnish are languages spoken in Finland (cf. Språklag 6.6.2003.423).

In 2011 the most common origin country of immigrants in Sweden was Finland. Of 1,427,296 born in another country 166,723 of them were born in Finland (cf. Statistiska centralbyrån). Some of them are born in western regions in Finland where Swedish is spoken, others speak Finnish. The consequence is that there are persons born in Finland who has Swedish as mother tongue and persons born in Finland who has Finnish as mother tongue. In this case study the focus is on persons born in Finland with Finnish as mother tongue who has either immigrated to Sweden or persons with one or two parents who have immigrated to Sweden.

Since 2000 Finnish has status as official minority language in Sweden (cf. SFS 2009:724). In addition there are a so-called Finnish administrative districts in Sweden. Municipalities with a large group speaking Finnish can send a letter of interest concerning creating a Finnish administrative district within the municipality to the Government, Department of Culture. The Government has to handle the letter of interest, and thereby decide about some extra money, within a year (cf. Adell Hellström). If the application is accepted Sweden Finns can demand public administrative service and legal service in Finnish. They can also, to a certain extent, demand preschool activities and elderly care in Finnish; there are also private schools in Sweden where Finnish is spoken (cf. Regeringen 2009). Since the extensive immigration during the 1960s groups of Finnish speaking have established associations (cf. Sverigefinska Riksförbundet 2017), there are Finnish congregations within the Swedish church (cf. Svenska kyrkan 2017) and a Finnish institute in Stockholm (cf. Finska institutet). In 1977 the Sweden Finn archive (Sverigefinländarnas arkiv) was established in Eskilstuna, a choice of municipality partly due to the big Sweden Finn group in the area (cf. Sverigefinländarnas arkiv 2017).

From nationalism to multicultural perspective – museums

When the exhibition ′The Legacy′ is displaced in Västmanland′s County museum it is an example of how the role of the museum has changed from a national approach and mainly having exhibitions of collections, to an approach where exhibitions are mobile between museums and the content to a higher degree present perspectives in society from different socio-economic and ethnic groups.

In late 19th century and early 20th century Sweden as well as other countries saw a wave of nationalism. Artefacts were collected and presented within a national framework, such as the outdoor museum Skansen in Stockholm showing different regional houses and crafts (cf. Arcadius 1997). This occurred in many countries, all in the support of constructing a national community (cf. Andersen 1983/2016; Hein 1998 and 1999). At the same time there was an interest to both support local museums and create an effective organization concerning collections. Here the counties became a possibility for organizing county museums and the local museums were supposed to associate. During 1930s the first county museums were established in Sweden. The county museums were often already existing museums which were chosen to become central museums. In 1861 an association for ancient artefacts was established in Västmanland and 1889 the collections were located to Västerås Castle. Successively the museum became a county museum, Västmanlands Museum (2017). Most of the museums in Sweden are actually regional, local museums (cf. Sveriges muséer).

During decades of democratization during 20th century new groups have got power and demand that their history and cultural identity should be respected and displayed. This has increased interest in social history and is also affecting how exhibitions are created (cf. Lundberg & Ågren 1999). There are still showcases with artefacts but in addition more and more exhibitions show individual and family life, but with less written text, instead there are scenes, videos and workshops. According to Rosander (1996) the role of the museums in society has been a constant debate and reason for enquiries. During late 19th century the discussions were focusing on relations between national museums and local museums, during 20th century the discussion seems to be more oriented towards how a multicultural society could and should be displayed.

Even though suggestions mainly are directed towards museums financed by the state, directives will influence other museums. The Swedish National Heritage Board serves since 17th century as a central administrative agency in the area of cultural heritage, cultural or historic environment (cf. Riksantikvarieämbetet). Museums are directed by assignments followed by finance – there is no 'museum act', but concerning the assignment, museums in Sweden adhere to the definition of museum from International Council of museums:

> A museum is a non-profit, permanent institution in the service of society and its development, open to the public, which acquires, conserves, researches, communicates and exhibits the tangible and intangible heritage of humanity and its environment for the purposes of education, study and enjoyment.

The mission of Västmanland´s County Museum is stated as:

> The purpose of the museum is to extend our understanding of the rich diversity of Västmanland's cultural heritage, to communicate with people and to stimulate public opinion, increase people's insights into our history and to enrich our perspective on life today and in the future. We work in a variety of areas: cultural heritage, archives & libraries, collections of objects, art, events, education and exhibitions, as well as communication and visitor service. (Västmanlands museum 2017)

Learning environments – museums and Initial Teacher Education

If the relation to an audience in 19th century was to 'show', successively the relation to audience has change from *an* audience to *the* audience. There is a change from transmission of information to creation of learning situation which are meaningful for the audience (cf. Hooper-Greenhill, 1999a). This does not mean that an educational role for the museum was not in focus earlier, already from the start in middle of the 19th century museums were among the institutions that was supposed to provide “education for the masses” (Hein 1998, 4).

There is also a demand for relating to democratic values (cf. Hooper-Greenhill 1999b). A museum can contribute to democracy by being accessible for the audience but further discussions are needed in what way, or if, museums also should create a ‘democratic audience’ (cf. Niklasson 2001). There has to be a reason to visit a museum, as Hooper-Greenhill (1999b) notice, of all social institutions, museums are easy to avoid.

However, the audience has become more and more important and this includes education. Hooper-Greenhill (ibid.) argues that the educational role of a museum includes education, interpretation and communication. There is an educational potential in museum if there is a holistic view, not perceiving education only as lessons for pupils from schools in a lecture room. In addition the educational potential is supported by using a constructivist approach to learning. This approach is used by museum educators when asking questions, offering alternative points of view, personalizing objects and references and using complementary images and sounds (Hooper-Greenhill 1999a, xi).

As Hooper-Greenhill (1999b) argues, an idea of a metanarrative with an underlying consensus has changed to an idea of fragmentation and diverse approaches. In this fragmentation the displays have to be perceived as meaningful to an audience. What constitutes meaning is both individual but also social as individuals are affected by communities to which the individual belong. In addition the personal and social meaning making is affected by the socio-economic circumstances and values, that is, a display in a museum is also embedded in politics of culture. Education is about ‘facts’ but also about emotions and creating an identity.

More and more the concept of education is changed to the concept of learning; that is also the case for museums as well as for Higher Education. Opening up for a learning approach can also include a critical pedagogy perspective, mentioned above, and a constructivist learning approach. Hein (1998 and 1999) argue that there is a need to combine theory of knowledge (epistemology) and theory of learning (pedagogy / didactics). If the constructivist learning approach is used there is an understanding that knowledge as constructed by the learner in interaction with the social environment and a learning situation is organized as experience to be sorted out and organized by the learning. This is in alignment with the trend that the focus should be on the audience and its experience, not on the content of the museum (cf. Hooper-Greenhill 1999c; Hein 1998 and 1999).

If a museum should use a constructivist approach then the display will

- have many entry points
- provide a range of active learning models
- present a range of point of views
- enable visitors to connect with objects (and ideas) through a range of activities and experiences that utilize their life experiences
- provide experience and material that allow students in school programs to experiment, conjecture, and draw conclusions (cf. Hein 1998, 35)

As a constructivist approach is concerned with experiences and ideas learners´ already have, they will try to design an environment with which the learner can make connections. As Hein describes it: family reference, object, idea, or activity that will allow the learner to engage with the issue (cf. ibid., 38)

With this presentation of one of the roles of museum a suggest is made that there is a common assignment for museums and Initial Teacher Education, which is, creating critical learning experiences. All Initial Teacher Education in Sweden is designed based on national learning goals presented in a Higher Education Ordinance (1993). The learning goals are both general for academic exam and designed for work in different school forms. Apart from knowing their own learning goals on a national level, and local goals for Initial Teacher Program and courses, the Student teachers have to know the learning goals for their school form and the common value ground for all school forms. In the curricula for school forms, such as preschool and compulsory school, upper secondary (cf. SKOLFS 1998:16; SKOLFS 2010:37; SKOLFS 2011:144), there are different goals which are especially noteworthy concerning exhibitions like "The Legacy", such as the value base about democracy and phrasing like knowledge about history. In Initial Teacher Education there are often student teachers with emigrant background and some are themselves, second or third generation of a certain ethnicity. During practice in practice schools, the student teacher will meet new immigrants or immigrants living in Sweden for a long time, second and third generation families and not the least, newly arrived unaccompanied children.

Thereby an exhibition like "The Legacy" can be useful for critical discussion both directly in the Initial Teacher Program and for training for in-service teachers.

Data-collection

The focus, and aim of this study is on how a social memory is created to uphold an identity by second and third generation immigrants. As presented earlier the definition of social memory is what individuals remember, tell others and enact, in activities or in artefacts (rituals, statues) (cf. Halbwachs 1992). The manifestations of social memory occurs at certain times, such as when the Sweden Finns celebrate the Sweden Finn day, but in the meantime individuals and groups can create activities in their everyday life, such as creating certain workshops based on songs from Finland for younger children

The definition of social memory and the earlier presentation of context and concepts inspired the research questions:

- How is meaning of place and memory produced?
- How are individual memories changed into group memories?
- What didactical implications are there to be found for Initial Teacher Education?

To answer the question several data collections were carried out. First of all an observation of the exhibition of 'the Legacy' at Västmanland´s County Museum was carried out autumn 2015. Photos and notes were taken. Then documents from the exhibition were gathered. A brochure with interviews of second and third generation Finns (cf. Sverigefinländarnas arkiv 2015) and additional interviews (not in the brochure) were read. Some of these interviews are used in the exhibition as basis for roll-ups, but not all. Personal information in person, by telephone or mail, concerning the exhibition was given by the educator at Västmanland´s County Museum (cf. Engström Englin), the project leader for 'The Legacy' who is also manager of Sverigefinländarnas arkiv (cf. Vuonokari) and persons engaged in language course (cf. Heinonen; Puranen). Lastly additional documents about 'The Legacy' in Sweden Finn archive (Sverigefinländarnas arkiv) were read during 2017.

A mobile exhibition

'The Legacy' is an example of a temporary, mobile exhibition in the museum. It is partly in contrast to an idea of "acquire and conserve" which can be perceived as a mean to have a permanent collection "against the destructiveness of time" (Elsner & Cardinal 1994, 1). From a social constructivist perspective the very idea of designing 'The Legacy' can be perceived as both acquiring individual memories and also conserve an idea that second and third generations have a (living) Finnish heritage. The individual memories are mainly based on memories of experiences and perceptions and the presented persons are not perceived as regular 'collectors' of artefacts (cf. Blom 2003) in this study.

The exhibition is created by the Sweden Finn archive. The main theme is to show challenges and possibilities for Sweden Finns to transfer their language and culture to next generation. Another theme is to show the variety of professions among the group as the curator argue that there has been a perception of the group as blue collar workers with low status. The representatives have occupations as for example teacher, artist, musician, politician, musician, actor, manager for theater, chef de cuisine, and author.

It was first presented at Västmanland´s County Museum in 2011. During summer 2015 the exhibition returned. The exhibition is still displayed and currently, May 2017, shown in Finland at Tornedalen museum in Torneå. Torneå and the Swedish town Haparanda is very close, a small bridge is connecting the cities in northern Sweden and Finland.

In 2015, the exhibition was placed in a large area on the entrance level at Västmanland´s County Museum. The visitor could walk around freely, no special path, and look at text and pictures displayed on roll-ups, there were short films, music, a video with a language course in Finnish and other documents. That is, the content was displayed in several modes. The content on the roll-ups and the documents showed facts about migration, life stories of second and third generation Sweden Finns and pictures of them. As a special local contribution children had drawn pictures of their own memories of Finland.

How is meaning of border and memory produced?

Besides from that the exhibition in itself is contributing to a social memory, the documentation of life stories presented on the roll ups and the interviews in the brochure give information about how the persons are upholding a 'legacy'. After rereading the life stories several times some themes can be found: language, visits, older relatives, children, school, shame, proud, not only Finns-additional identities, culture (plays, music, literature, art, food) and support to Finnish legacy.

Most of the persons presented in the exhibition bring up language as an important issue. Some of them have been born in Finland and immigrated to Sweden. In some families it has been a tradition to speak Finnish at home and the language has also been used if they have participated in daycare where Finnish was spoken, a Finnish speaking preschool or class in compulsory school. Some are also active in Sweden Finn associations and attend cultural activities where Finnish is spoken. To practice the language they also visit relatives in Finland and some of the original places where they, or their parents, came from. These visits are remembered and much appreciated. They notice that there is a change since 1960s when it was more common to adapt and speak Swedish. Some recall an earlier feeling of shame of speaking Finnish. Today several of them are proud of speaking Finnish and they work actively so their children could practice the language, even if only one parent speaks the language.

Successively during the years it has become more accepted to have Finnish speaking education for children and younger ages and in some job opportunities speaking another language, such as Finnish, is regarded as a merit.

The impression from the exhibition is that it was the first generation who had to make a hard choice, whether to speak Finnish or not. An example is a parent who had come to Sweden as a child during WW II (Swedish families received smaller children to care for – some successfully, some with negative consequences), then returned to Finland without knowing the language any longer, and then returned to Sweden again and married and got children. Finnish was not spoken in the family, but some of the children got mother tongue lessons at compulsory school (in Sweden). Memories from Finland during WW II are issues which are brought up and mentioned as hard to handle for older generations.

The exhibition leaves an impression of a second and third generation who present themselves as both Swedish and Finnish, but some "feel" more Finnish. The identity issue is not only a question between a choice of identity of being or feeling Swedish or Finnish; other cultural origin is also in play. An example is the Romani group where families or individuals have emigrated from Finland to Sweden. They can have three different languages: Finnish, Romani and Swedish. The Romani group is represented in both countries (Finland and Sweden) and has so been for a long time. In addition there are marriages where one parent is from Finland or have Finnish heritage but the other is from for example Iran. For all, those who are bi-lingual or tri-lingual, all languages are important, especially from a cultural aspect and several of the participants in the exhibition work in the cultural sector. Some of them work with Finnish speaking events, but some of them are choosing to create events which are performed in both Swedish and Finnish. In addition some are influenced by their third language.

How are individual memories changed into group memories?

The exhibition is displaying individual memories but all together, in display, the memories show a social memory from a group. When the exhibition arrives for display, the introduction of the exhibition is made by a representative for example from municipality and is noticed by local mass media, such as in Degerfors municipality in 2016 (cf. Karlskoga tidning). This way of underlining a social memory for a group is also shown in activities parallel to the exhibition. The exhibition can be shown in addition with other events, such as when it was presented on the Day for the Sweden Finns in Oxelösund municipality in 2016 (cf. Oxelösunds tidning) or when a partly autonomous district in a municipality with many Finnish speaking inhabitants were established in the municipality Smedjebacken in 2015 (cf. Dala Demokraten). When Finland commemorated 100 year of independence, 2017, the exhibition was showed in Motala municipality by initiative from the local Sweden Finns´ association (cf. Motala Vadstena Tidning). The exhibition is also commented on and scanned digitally in the Sweden Finn archive (Sverigefinländarnas arkiv 2017). As can be noticed, the exhibition is created to last and be renewed during several years. Museums have basic exhibitions which they rearrange continuously and this exhibition, although mobile, can be perceived as such for the Sweden Finn archive.

Time is used in various ways, showing the long relation between Sweden and Finland with migration, but also that there is a living social memory. By re-creating the exhibition during several year it could be perceived as an example that a social memory is socially constructed by using time, individual memories, social gatherings (associations for Sweden Finns), formal acknowledgement (autonomous administrative districts) and events (Sweden Finn day) to construct and supplement a social memory.

Discussion – didactical implications for Initial Teacher Education?

As was presented earlier, both museums and Initial Teacher Education aim at creating critical learning experiences. By visiting and critically discuss exhibitions in museums, there is a chance for the student teachers to both be reminded of the possibility of visiting a museum and increase their own knowledge about certain issues.

An exhibition like ´The Legacy´ creates several opportunities for critical discussion and reflection. As an entrance of a discussion, a definition of social memory can be used and presented, such as Halbwachs (1992). Then the student teacher could have discussions in groups and discuss in what way individuals remember, tell others and enact, in activities or in artefacts (rituals, statues). In this case it is also possible to discuss whether or how a memory is kept and enacted in bigger manifestations, such as a national celebration day (such as the Sweden Finn day).

It is possible that a discussion, as suggested above could create a learning situation where the student teachers have different opinions about many issues. First of all they can be critical concerning why the Sweden Finns´ are getting this attention. This can lead to a search for how other (minority) groups in Sweden are presenting themselves. The staff at the museum can be at help here and clarify the role of the museum and the student teachers can compare it with teacher´s role in a society which have several socio-economic and ethnic groups.

Secondly, the discussion can be extended to presentation of concepts like inter-cultural relations and multiculturalism and whether second generation immigrants are what Catarci calls "being poised between two cultures" (2017, 8). With help of an exhibition like 'The Legacy' it is possible to discuss the situation where not only two cultures are found in the family, but sometimes three cultures (such as Swedish, Finnish and Romani). The phenomenon of having more than one cultural identity could be perceived as considered in Catarci´s suggestion that citizenship education should be intercultural, in his suggestion 'citizens of the world'. A ´citizen of the world´ approach further on be discussed in relation to the fact that Sweden is a member of the European Union and that Swedish citizens are European Union citizens. A feeling of belonging is possible both in accordance with territorial/political borders and cultural groups.

Both possibilities presented above can create a situation where the student teachers are 'talking about' issues, but not necessarily take a standpoint and further on reflect on what their own standpoint´s are based on emotionally and cognitively. Grannäs and Ljungquist (2017) argue that student teachers in Sweden often are 'politically correct', concerning democracy issues or value issues. They know that they have to follow the value ground which is stated in the curricula for the different school forms. This approach can cause difficulties when the student teachers meet different opinions in the classroom, also controversial and not in line with the value ground. As Ljunggren (2017) suggests, if (student) teachers argue that they cannot handle a situation with students coming from different socio-economic and ethnic background, then they can be carriers of potential controversies, where individuals and groups risk to stand apart or against each other. As a class room can be perceived as a semi-public space, Ljunggren argues that it is important that participants in a dialogue (student teachers as well as students), have self-insight about own political and moral value basis for their opinions. The question of moral value basis is also brought up by O´Flaherty and Gleeson (2017) when they argue that student teachers can be less aware of that decisions made in the classroom often are based on ethical and moral reasons. To increase the level of awareness moral dilemmas can be used in Initial Teacher Education and discussions on ethical and moral values can be carried out. In contrast to an individual self-reflection O´Flaherty and Gleeson argue that self-reflection could go beyond individual level and that the student teachers could be discussing what is ´good´ from a societal level. This is also in line with Ljunggren´s (2017) approach when he is highlighting the concept ´public space´ and its possibility for discussing issues concerning society. A museums could be perceived as a public space, and as such the exhibition ´The Legacy´ is an act of contributing to our knowledge of varieties of sense of belonging and constructing social memories in a public space in society.

As a conclusion, by presenting the exhibition ´The Legacy´ based on Sweden Finn´s social memories it was possible to discuss possibilities for staff at museum and teacher educators to cooperate and create critical learning experiences for student teachers in Initial Teacher Education. The learning experience could be individual self-reflection, but also deeper reflection expanding to questions about public space and ´common good´ for society. The issues discussed, border and social memory, will continue to be controversial issues, which student teachers and in-service teachers, as well as staff at museums, have to be aware of and able to create discussions about.

References

Andersen, B. (1983/2016). *Imagined communities*. London.

Arcadius, K. (1997). *Museum på svenska*. Stockholm.

Blom, P. (2003). *To Have and To Hold. An Intimate History of Collectors and Collecting*. London.

Brusman, M. (2011). Plats. In J. Syssner (ed.). *Perspektiv på turism och resande*. Stockholm, 147-168.

Catarci, M. (2017). Citizenship Education from an Intercultural Perspective: Theories, approaches and practices in the Italian context. In N. Palaiogou & M. Zembylas (eds.). *Human Rights and Citizenship Education: An Intercultural and International Perspective*. Newcastle upon Tyne (forthcoming).

Dala Demokraten. *Homepage*. Online: http.//dalademokraten.se/dalarna/smedjebacken/arvet-en-granslos-utstallning [last accessed 05 June 2017].

Diener, C. A. & Hagen, J. (2012). *Borders. A Very Short Introduction*. Oxford.

Elsner, J. & Cardinal, R. (1994). Introduction. In J. Elsner & R. Cardinal (eds.). *The cultures of collecting*. London, 1-6.

Finska institutet. *Homepage*. Online: http://www.finlandsinstittutet.se/sv/ [last accessed 06 May 2017].

Grannäs, J. & Ljungquist, S. (2017). Berättelsern som forum förkontroversiella frågor. In C. Ljunggren, I. Unemar & T. Englund (eds.) *Kontroversiella frågor. Om kunskap och politik i samhällsundervisningen*. Lund, 149-168.

Häger, B-Å. (2000). Frihetstiden och den gustavianska tiden 1718-1809. In H. A. Larsson (Ed.). *Boken om Sveriges historia*. Stockholm, 181-218.

Halbwachs, M. (1992). *On collective memory*. Chicago.

Hein, E. G. (1998). *Learning in the museum.* London.

Hein, E. G. (1999). The constructivist museum. In E. Hooper-Greenhill (ed.). *The Educational Role of the Museum*. London, 73-79.

Higher Education Ordinance (1993:100). Stockholm.

Hooper-Greenhill, E. (1999a). Preface. In E. Hooper-Greenhill (ed.). *The Educational Role of the Museum*. London, x-xiii.

Hooper-Greenhill, E. (1999b). Education, communication and interpretation: towards a critical pedagogy in museums. In E. Hooper-Greenhill (ed.). *The Educational Role of the Museum*. London, 3-27.

Hooper-Greenhill, E. (1999c). Museum learners as active postmodernists. In E. Hooper-Greenhill (Ed.). *The Educational Role of the Museum*. London, 67-72.

International Council of museums. *Webpage*. Online: http://icom.museum [last accessed 16 August 2017].

Karlskoga tidning. Homepage. Online: http://nwt.se/karlskoga-degerfors/2016/03/08/arvet-har-invigts [last accessed 05 June 2017].

Korkiasaari, J. & Söderling, I. (2003). *Finnish Emigration and Immigration after World War II.* Åbo.

Ljunggren, C. (2017). Det offentliga rummet. In C. Ljunggren, I. Unemar & T. Englund (eds.) *Kontroversiella frågor. Om kunskap och politik i samhällsundervisningen*. Lund, 25-43.

Lundberg, B. & Ågren, P-U. (1999). *Historiebilder. Om intention och reception i museer*. Umeå.

Motala Vadstena Tidning. Online: http://www.mvt.se/nyheter/motala/nya-nut gravningar-infor-dubbelsparet-om4680286.aspx [last accessed 05 June 2017].

Niklasson, L. (2001). Ett demokratiskt museum eller en demokratisk besökare? *Svenska museer*, 1/01, 18-19.

O´Flaherty, J. & Gleeson, J. (2017). Irish student teachers´ levels of moral reasoning: context, comparisons, and contributing influences. *Teachers and Teaching: Theory and Practice*, 23:1, 59-77.

Oxelösunds tidning. *Homepage*. Online: http://www.sn.se/nyheter/utstallningen-arvet-invigdes-pa-sverigefinlandarnas-dag/ [last accessed 05 June 2017].

Regeringen (2009). *Lagrådsremiss*. Online: http://www.regeringen.se/49bafb/contentassets/fcc5cac1e2ba45989ff9fd852ea40bf1/fran-erkannande-till-egen makt---regeringens-strategi-for-de-nationella-minoriteterna [last accessed 05 June 2017].

Riksantikvarieämbetet. *Homepage*. Online: http://www.raa.se/in-english/ [last accessed 28 May 2017].

Rosander, G. (1996). Museerna och tidsandans förändring. *Nordisk museologi*, 1, 13-22.

SFS 2009:724. *Lag om nationella minoriteter och minoritetsspråk*. Stockholm.

SKOLFS (1998:16). *Läroplan för förskola*. Revised 2011. Stockholm.

SKOLFS (2010:37). *Läroplan för grundskola, förskoleklass och fritidsaktiviteter*. Stockholm.

SKOLFS (2011:144). *Läroplan för gymnasiet*. Stockholm.

***Språklag* (Act on language) 6.6.2003.423**. Online: http://www.finlex.fi/sv/laki/ajantasa/2003/20030423 [last accessed 01 July 2017].

Statistiska centralbyrån. *Utrikes födda*. Online: http://www.scb.se/sv_/Hitta-statistik/Artiklar/Finland-vanligaste-ursprungslandet-for-utrikes-fodda [last accessed 26 May 2017].

Svenska kyrkan. *Homepage*. Online: https://www.svenskakyrkan.se/finskaforsamlingen [last accessed 05 June 2017].

Sverigefinländarnas arkiv. *Homepage*. Online: http://www.arkisto.org/digitala-arkivet/historisk-utstallning-2 [last accessed 27 May 2017].

Sverigefinländarnas arkiv (2015). *Arvet. Utställning om en ny generation*. Eskilstuna.

Sverigefinska Riksförbundet. *Homepage*. Online: http://www.rskl.se/framsida.html [last accessed 01 July 2017].

Sveriges muséer. *Homepage*. Online: http://www.sverigemuseer.se/press meddelanden/2015/10/museiutredningens-forslag/ [last accessed 26 May 2017].

Västmanlands museum. *Homepage*. Online: http://www.vastmanslands museum.se/pages.asp?PageID=460&MenuID=417 [last accessed 26 May 2017].

Västmanlands museum. *Historia*. Online: http://www.vastmanlandslans museum.se/pages.asp?PageID=208&MenuID=197 [last accessed 28 May 2017].

Personal information (personal meeting, e-mail or by telephone):

Adell Hellström, Erik, Swedish Government, Department of Culture

Engström Englin, Lena, educator at Västmanland´s County Museum

Heinonen, Irina, contributed to language course used in 'The Legacy'

Puranen, Lina, contributed to language course used in 'The Legacy'

Vuonokari, Erkki, project leader for 'The Legacy', manager of Sverigefinländarnas arkiv

Tracey McKay

Crossing Borders in Initial Teacher Education: a case study on students' perceptions of the Orange Order and education in a conflicted society

Introduction

This BE-SMaRT case study was inspired by a paper which appeared in the UK academic journal, Progress in Human Geography, 2006, 'The lines that continue to separate us: borders in our 'borderless' world', by David Newman. In this paper Newman, pointed out how

> we live in a world of lines and compartments. We may not necessarily see the lines, but they order our daily life practices and strengthen our belonging to, and identity with places and groups, while [...] perpetuating and re-perpetuating notions of difference and 'othering'. (Newman 2006, 1)

While many people (my Geography students included) will be familiar with the concept of a 'border 'as a line on a map, whose primary function is to delineate and demarcate territory, Newman's paper called for a much broader appreciation of 'borders' as dynamic human phenomenon, socially constructed, and strongly influenced by perceptions. The north of Ireland exemplifies a range of border issues including a sovereign / territorial dispute over the contested border which separates the northern six counties (of Northern Ireland) from the 26 counties of the Republic of Ireland (cf. Nash, Reid & Graham 2013). At the same time the deeply divided nature of society in the north of Ireland means that ethnic / cultural 'borders', to one extent or another, impact on most aspects of daily life, including education. While peace lines and indeed other 'territorial' markers on the cultural landscape speak of inclusion, exclusion and belonging, they are also symbolic indicators of the 'borders' that exists in the minds of citizens separating the 'us' from the 'them', the 'insiders' from the outsiders'. In the context of Northern Ireland physical, tangible 'borders' really matter but so too do the perceptions that shape the 'borders of belonging' that exist inside people's heads.

The Orange Order is a Protestant fraternal organisation founded in Ireland in 1795 to defend Protestant interests. According to its official website, it is both a Protestant and a patriotic organisation, with members required to pledge adherence to the principles of the Reformed (Protestant) faith and loyalty to their country. While the Order claims worldwide membership, it is mostly based in Northern Ireland. The Orange Order has attracted its fair share of global publicity, much of which has been associated with tension and conflict arising from its tradition of public commemoration and parading. For those outside the organisation, most especially those from a nationalist / Catholic background, perceptions of the Orange Order tend to be unfavourable: it is perceived as a 'secret society', as an overtly anti-Catholic institution, and a sectarian organisation. Indeed part of the ritual of joining the Orange Order requires new members to read the qualifications of an Orangeman which remind him of his obligations to "strenuously oppose the fatal errors and doctrines of the Church of Rome, and scrupulously avoid countenancing (by his presence or otherwise) any act of Popish worship" (Jess 2007, 12). June 2015 saw a new chapter for the Orange Order with the official opening of the Museum of Orange Heritage, a self-driven initiative intended to bring the Order's own narrative to a wider public audience, to tell the story of the Order's foundation and development, its traditions, and its role in British, Irish and World society. The opening attracted significant local and regional media coverage, including a speech delivered by Mary McAleese (former President of Ireland, who grew up and was educated in Belfast) when she suggested that the Museum would be a place where those of a nationalist perspective could learn more about the Orange tradition, and her hope that this would lead to a better understanding of Orange culture:

> It's important to be here because this place is built with a view, first of all, to celebrating Orange culture, but also to explaining it to a wider audience [...] I think good neighbours should know about each other, should respect each

other, and part of that respect is being interested in each other. (BBC News 24th June 2015)

The Orange Order: Outreach and Education

According to the Grand Orange Lodge of Ireland the Museum initiative is simultaneously an attempt at self-representation and an opportunity for outreach and engagement with wider civic society. To that end the Museum is part of an ongoing process of engagement and outreach by the Orange Order which began in 2004 with the appointment of its first community education officer. Indeed for well over a decade the education and community outreach officer has been contributing to curriculum delivery, mostly around themes of cultural diversity, mutual understanding and citizenship education in some schools in Northern Ireland. This work has been undertaken in both the Protestant (Controlled) and the Catholic (Maintained) sectors; interestingly figures available from 2014 suggest that 58% of that work was undertaken in the Catholic / Maintained sector, 33% to schools attended mostly by Protestant students and 8% within the integrated sector (BBC News 5th November 2014). Some of this work has taken place in schools that are located in areas where community relations, particularly during the Orange 'marching season', are fractured. With regards initial teacher education, there are well established links between the Museum of Orange Heritage and Stranmillis University College, Belfast (the largely 'Protestant' teacher education college in Northern Ireland). For the first time in the century and more since the Dominican Sisters began training teachers at St Mary's College on the Falls Road in Belfast (the main training provider for the Catholic maintained sector in the north of Ireland), the Orange Order's education officer was invited in 2016 (under the auspices of this BE-SMaRT Project) to work with student teachers from the mainly Catholic tradition. This BE-SMaRT case study reports on some aspects of that experience. A more detailed publication (McKay forthcoming 2018) which takes as its core theme, 'crossing borders' and 'encountering memory' within the context of initial teacher education in a deeply divided society builds on work presented here and a visit by the student teachers to the new Museum of Orange Heritage. Here though the focus is on the perceptions of and attitudes towards the Orange Order held by albeit a small group of students from a mainly Catholic / nationalist background, currently enrolled in a four year initial teacher education programme at St Mary's University College, Belfast. This short case study seeks to contextualise the students' responses and considers the extent to which 'memory' has contributed to those perceptions, it concludes with a short reflection on the implications for initial teacher education as it strives to play its part in the realisation of the 'shared society' set out in the Good Friday Agreement.

Case Study Research Context

This case study research was conducted with a very small number of second year students enrolled in a four year initial teacher education degree programme at St Mary's University College, Belfast. 13 students in total were invited to participate. 7 of the students were enrolled in the BEd Primary pathway with a main subject specialism in Geography programme, while 6 were following the Post-primary BEd pathway, where Geography was their subsidiary subject. For those training to be primary school teachers their learning programme focused on cross-curricular links between the World Around Us (Geography strand) and Personal Development and Mutual Understanding (PDMU), while for the Post-primary students the focus was links between Environment and Society (Geography strand) and Learning for Life and Work (LLW). In the revised Northern Ireland Curriculum (2007) statutory citizenship education content is embedded within PDMU (Primary Curriculum) and LLW (Post- primary curriculum). The workshop was delivered by the Education and Outreach Officer with the Grand Orange Lodge of Ireland and was conducted in the students' familiar learning environment in St Mary's University College. It lasted approximately one hour and explored the following: the background to the Orange Order; its links with key events in European, British and Irish history; the evolution of the organisation including its global outreach; what its members believe the organisation represents; an overview of the Order's public traditions, including parading and marching and finally some reflection on key celebrations including the Twelfth of July. The presentation was followed by some informal discussion and feedback.

The workshop atmosphere was one of mutual respect and when invited to do so the students asked questions pertaining to 'softer' issues which included key historical events and geographical locations associated with the Battle of the Boyne, the context within which the Pope blessed William of Orange, as well the complex familial/political relationships of late seventeenth century Europe. There was no attempt by the students to discuss harder-edged issues like anti-Catholicism (the basis upon which the organisation was founded) or contentious parading issues linked to marching through 'nationalist/republican' areas. Nor did any of the students ask questions about: the 'closed' nature of the Institution; the fact that Catholics are excluded from membership; that there is a ban on members attending Catholic services such as weddings and funerals; its gender bias; its rituals, symbols or traditions or question pertaining to its relevance as an organisation today. Before the workshop commenced 12 students completed a short questionnaire (1 student was absent due to illness). In the sections that follow the aim is to outline and contextualise the students' responses.

Contextual Background Information on the Respondents

11 females and 1 male completed the questionnaire. At the time of completion all of the students were either 19 or 20 years old, meaning they were born into a post-ceasefire Northern Ireland and just before the signing of the Good Friday agreement, thus forming part of the so-called Good Friday Agreement generation. All of the students were born in one of the six counties that constitute Northern Ireland. All came from places

where parading by the Orange Order has been an issue and/or where Orange Order halls have attacked or burned in sectarian violence. Significantly none of the students came from areas that have experienced highly contentious parading issues such as north Belfast or Portadown. In terms of their backgrounds and identity, 11 out of the 12 students attended Catholic primary and post-primary schools. 1 student had attended an integrated primary and post-primary school. All students identified themselves as Catholic; with 10 of the 12 students stating they were actively involved in the religious life of their parish. The students were free to select the labels that best described their nationality; 8 expressed their identity exclusively as Irish, while 4 selected Northern Irish. Significantly no student saw their identity as British. The students were asked to identify if they belonged to the GAA (all-island Gaelic sporting and cultural organisation strongly associated with an Irish identity): 6 students were active members of the GAA and 6 were not. The students were asked to identify their family's socio-economic status: 7 said they came from a working class background; the remaining 5 students identified their family background as middle class.

Students' Knowledge and Perceptions of the Orange Order; its foundation, symbols and 'purpose'

As Jess suggests,

> the Orange Order is one of the most intriguing and controversial religion based organisations in Europe, if not the world. It was born out of bloodshed, has been sustained by sectarianism and remains shrouded in secrecy. (back cover to Jess 2007)

It emerged in County Armagh in the late 17th century out of a violent sectarian conflict between agrarian vigilante gangs, the ruthless Protestant Peep o'Day Boys and their equally ruthless rivals the Catholic Defenders. One local skirmish – the Battle of the Diamond – was to prove particularly significant. The Protestant victors identified their victory at the Battle of the Diamond with William of Orange's victory at the Battle of the Boyne (just over a century before) and clarified the need for a society to protect and advance the cause of Protestantism and Protestants in Ireland. So it was that on the 21st September 1795 in front of Dan Winter's cottage (which was located in the vicinity of the aforementioned Battle of the Diamond) a collection of men from Protestant denominations linked arms and agreed to form a brotherhood declaring loyalty to the crown, country and the reformed Protestant faith (cf. Jess 2007, 15). History records that some days thereafter the first formal meeting of Orangemen took place at Sloan's Inn, Loughgall, Co Armagh.

As might be expected all of the students who participated in the survey were aware that the Orange Order existed. However, when probed around a number of questions pertaining to when it was founded, where it was founded, and key historical figures and events surrounding the early history and development of the organisation what emerged most clearly was the students' lack of 'factual' knowledge/understanding. Before proceeding to review the survey findings it's imperative to bear in mind research by King who cautions that

> despite widespread agreement concerning the social, academic, and civic benefits to be gained from discussing controversial public issues within the classroom, empirical research reveals that doing so is a rare occurrence (2012, 215).

When asked to outline what they knew about when the Orange Order was founded: most said they nothing, 1 student thought (correctly) maybe after the Battle of the Boyne and another thought (incorrectly) it was "maybe sometime during or after the Troubles". When asked to outline what they knew about where it was founded: no student was able to identify the place(s) associated with its foundation: 8 said they didn't know; 1 said "Belfast but really were not sure"; while 2 others thought either Northern Ireland or England. When asked to identify the reasons **why** they thought the Orange Order had been formed in the first place: 9 said they didn't know; 1 correctly identified links to the commemoration of "King William's Victory in the Battle of the Boyne", while 2 correctly identified the protection of Protestantism and Protestants "to protect Protestants and to stick up for the rights of Protestants and Unionist people" [...] "to stand up for Protestants". The students were then asked to identify historical figures they considered were significant for the Order: 7 suggested William of Orange (or rather the vernacular, King Billy), while 1 said Ian Paisley. Ian Paisley, although an iconic figure in the pantheon of modern Ulster Protestantism, was never a member of the Orange Order. When asked to name any battles or military campaigns they considered important for the Orange Order, only 2 responses suggested "the Battle of the Boyne", 1 suggested "The Troubles, maybe?"

Anti-Catholic or pro-Protestant?

The qualifications of an Orangeman are clear and explicit: they state that "he should strenuously oppose the fatal errors and doctrines of the Church of Rome, and scrupulously avoid countenancing (by his presence or otherwise) any act or ceremony of popish worship". Orangemen are also told to refrain "from all uncharitable words, actions, or sentiments" (Jess 2007, 12) towards Roman Catholics. To that end the organisation's anti-Catholic founding principles and ideology reflects the broader religious, political and cultural issues and interests of the times. During the late eighteenth and throughout the nineteenth anti-Catholicism was a potent, virulent and multifaceted force. The rejection of Catholicism was and still is an essential feature of Protestant identity. As Mitchel notes

> Protestants have a very particular relationship to the Roman Catholic Church, one that is distinct from any other church. However much it may make some Protestants uneasy, it is 'Mother Church', and evangelical-Protestant theology and identity has been, and continues to be, intrinsically shaped by that family relationship. (2015, 170)

Thus anti-Catholicism was never just a superficial prejudice nor a coherent ideology, but rather a frame of mind – an integral part of the religious, political and social belief and experience of many Protestants, not only in Ireland but in Great Britain, Europe and around the globe (cf. Wolffe 1991). During the late 18th and throughout the 19th century anti-

Catholicism helped shaped the British psyche. From the mid 19th century onwards it took on a specifically anti-Irish dimension too – as the Irish were predominantly Catholic – and was linked with famine-induced mass migration from Ireland to Great Britain and the Empire. This contributed to traditions of intolerance not only in Great Britain and Ireland but also around the globe (cf. MacRaild & Hughes 2014). The Orange Order was part of and actively contributed to this potent mix. During the 19th and early 20th centuries the society grew rapidly – as did its Catholic rivals – but its growth was not uninterrupted. Yet for the most part the theme was one of growth and burgeoning economic, political and cultural influence for the Orange Order in Ulster.

The students in this survey were unable to demonstrate knowledge of the broader historical context out of which the Orange Order emerged or developed. Asked what they thought about the **popularity** of the Orange Order today, half of the students thought it was very popular and enjoyed widespread support, while the other half suggested it didn't command widespread support. However, none of the students were able to identify how many people actually belonged to the Order today. Membership of the Orange Order today is estimated at about just over 30,000 which is significantly down from a peak in the 1960s when it boasted more than 90,000 members (cf. Irish Times 14 July 2014). The Order is exclusively Protestant and male; it is an increasingly ageing organisation too. In recent years it has failed to attract new members, with younger men being more attracted to the loyalist flute bands rather than the Orange Order. The Orange Order in Ireland is made up of over 1,000 local lodges, which provide the localised 'power base' of the institution, through to the apex of the organisation which is the Grand Lodge of Ireland, with its headquarters in Belfast. Members join their local 'lodge', the equivalent to a branch or a club. Local lodges are run by a worshipful master and deputy master, the equivalent to a chairman and deputy chairman. Lodge meetings take place in Orange halls which are to be found dotted across the landscape in rural and urban areas. There is a strict gender boundary within the Orange Institution; women cannot join it. If they wish to join an 'Orange' fraternity, they must look to the Women's Loyal Orange Order, but it is not officially part of the Orange Order. Women are not permitted to attend lodge meetings and must be invited by their male counterparts to participate in Orange parades. Yet to most Orangemen and their families the Order represents a way of life.

> The lodge provides conviviality and companionship; its rituals have a meaning and a rhythm [...] and its halls are often the focal point for local communities and serve as a venues for a wider range of gatherings than those that are strictly Orange [...]. The lodges frequently raise money for charities and often provide welfare services for members who suffer bereavement, illness and hardship. (Haddick-Flynn 2002, 91)

Orange Rituals, Symbols and Identity

The fact that many founding members of the Orange Order were also members of another fraternal society – the Freemasons (cf. Roberts 1971) meant that this organisation provided a transferable template for the early development of the Orange Order. The organisational structure of lodges, membership and governance (the language of degrees for progression through the organisation), the development of early Orange symbols, rituals and ceremonies, as well as the architecture of Orange halls and buildings all borrowed significantly from Freemasonary. According to Haddick-Flynn "the rituals of the Orange Order are derived from Freemasonry, which has a long history in Ireland. The Grand Masonic Lodge in Dublin is the second oldest in the world" (2002, 50). That the Orange Order should have borrowed heavily from the Freemasonry probably shouldn't be that surprising; as Jess (2007, 54) points out it was a common enough practice for organisations forming at the end of the eighteenth century to look the example of others and follow their lead. While the Orange Order clearly borrowed heavily from Freemasonry, over time its structures, rituals and ceremonies evolved to reflect a more Orange way of doing things. Furthermore, the Orange Order is unequivocally Christian and forthrightly Protestant whereas Freemasonry is De-ist (cf. Haddick Flynn 2002, 50). Ritual and symbolism have a very prominent role within the Orange fraternity and folklore has played its role in perpetuating myths of Orangeism. As Jess points out "with meetings held behind closed doors, where ancient rituals are enacted, Loyal orders, like the Black and the Orange leave themselves open to allegations of dark dealings and mischievous goings on" (2007, 72). Those embryonic links with Freemasonry, initiation ceremonies, passwords, and fraternal handshakes endure in the popular consciousness of 'outsiders', especially those from a Catholic/nationalist background. Historically the Catholic Church (especially in Ireland) has been hostile to Freemasonry for amongst other things the secret-oath associated with the organisation, its deistic view of creation, its supposedly Satanic-inspired rituals as well a plot to oversee the destruction of the Holy Church of Rome. The links between these two fraternal societies has reinforced popular perceptions of the Orange Order as something sinister and deeply threatening to its non-Protestant 'other'.

This survey tried to ascertain the students' level of familiarity with the Orange Order's material presence in their locality, their awareness, knowledge and perceptions of the Order's cultural traditions, rituals and symbols. As Jess (2007, 51) captures: it for an 'outsider' looking into the Orange Order today and trying to grasp what it's all about can be a bit like peering through a dirty window on a foggy day. To those on the 'outside' looking 'in' the Order can seem highly visible as evidenced through their public parades and their meeting halls which are clearly marked and usually prominent buildings on the cultural landscape. When asked if the Orange Order had a material presence in their local community: 8 students said Yes, 3 said No. However, the students' answers were geographically and materially inaccurate because in 2 of the 3 'negative' responses, the Orange Order does in fact have a very strong presence through (lodge and orange halls), suggesting that the students are simply not aware of it in their locality. One student said they didn't know. The students were then asked to identify and describe the traditions and rituals they associated with Orange Order; they were free to write as many as they knew about. All of the students' responses related to the Order's traditions of public commemoration, marching and parading, one student highlighted the collective act of "gathering and meeting at the Orange Hall" but no reference was made to the internal workings or culture of the organisation itself. The students results are really not that surprising given that what happens behind the closed doors of Orange halls remains (centuries later) a mystery to many on the outside. There is no doubt that ritual is integral to the Order and the workings of a lodge, symbolically linking the past with the present but to those on the outside they remain either unknown or shrouded in mystery. For those who don't feel threatened by the Order its fraternal rituals and ceremonies are viewed with a mixture of amusement and bemusement, as archaic 'oddities' from a bygone age (cf. Jess 2012, 52). However, for critics and those antipathetic to Orangeism, what happens within the confines of an orange hall tends to be viewed with grave suspicion. The students surveyed here had clearly given little thought to the internal workings or culture of this organisation.

The students were asked if they could identify any symbols associated with the Orange Order. The Orange Order has 6 official symbols: the holy bible; the crown; Aaron's Rod; the Ark of the Covenant; the swords of the Lord and Gideon and King William. These symbols are usually displayed prominently on the Order's building architecture and the regalia worn by members while on public parades. The symbols of the Royal Arch Purple Order (another level of belonging that members of the Orange Order can progress towards) has a far greater range of symbols with a much closer affinity to Freemasonry. A small number of students correctly identified King William as an Orange Order symbol. The other responses focused on artefacts which they considered to be symbolically representative of the order: William of Orange's white horse; wearing a 'uniform' i.e. the Orange Order sash and orange collaret; flags and banners, including one respondent who mentioned the Orange Order flag specifically. One student identified 'Diamond Dan' a superhero mascot introduced by the Order a number of years ago to appeal to younger members. The questionnaire then turned to the annual 12th of July celebrations, students were asked if they could explain/outline why the 12th July is considered an important day for members of the Orange Order. Ten students did not know exactly why the 12th of July event was significant for Orange Order, while two said (correctly) it was important because it commemorated the Protestant victory at the Battle of the Boyne.

Parades, Marching and the Annual Twelfth of July Celebrations

The first Orange Order parades reportedly took place in Portadown, Lurgan and Warringstown on the 12th July 1796, just a few years later parades were being held in a number of other settlements including Belfast and Lisburn (cf. Jess 2007, 87). Each year on the 12th of July William's victory at Battle of the Boyne is commemorated by Orangemen as the definitive event that secured the Protestant faith (and Protestant ascendancy) in Ireland. While the public act of parading to commemorate the Williamite victory at the Battle of the Boyne actually predates the foundation of the Orange Order, public displays of Protestant religious and cultural identity were and remain critical to the organisation. The Williamite victory at the Battle of the Boyne provided the basis of a powerful and enduring myth about the supposed 'ethnic superiority' of the Protestant people (cf. Roe 2005, 62). Today the Twelfth represents the high point of the Order's public commemoration and parading, with 18 demonstrations taking place in towns and villages across Northern Ireland, the Republic of Ireland and Scotland, with longest and normally largest parade taking place in Belfast. Each year thousands of supporters line the six mile route in Belfast to watch Orange men and 60 marching bands 'remember' this victory and celebrate Protestant culture and identity. In rural towns and villages the same level of popular support can be seen lining the route of the parade (and weather dependent!) in 'the field' afterwards for the speeches. It is routinely claimed that up to half a million people participate in the annual 12th commemorations and the Orange Order points to the growing popularity of the event for international tourists (cf. Belfast Telegraph 12th July 2017). In recent years the Order has tried to promote the Twelfth as 'Orangefest', a faith-orientated festival (similar to those seen in other European countries) and its economic benefits for the cultural tourism economy of Northern Ireland. In this survey none of the students were aware of the concept of Orangefest.

As Branniff, McDowell and Byrne (2012) explain, the 'cult of memory' is at its most pronounced during the marching season. 2016 represented a highly significant commemorative year for both traditions in the north of Ireland; it was the centenary of the 1916 'nationalist' Easter Rising against British rule in Ireland and the centenary of the WW I Battle of the Somme. The 2016 Twelfth of July parade included a wreath-laying ceremony at the Cenotaph Memorial (in the grounds of the City Hall) to commemorate the Battle of the Somme and, in particular, the contribution of 36th (Ulster) Division. As the historian Eamon Phoenix (2016), writing in the Irish News, explains the Battle of the Somme is seared into Unionist and loyalist consciousness in the north of Ireland, with 36th (Ulster) Division, remembered as the 'lost generation' whose blood was shed for the Union with Great Britain (cf. Irish News 30th June 2016). There can be no doubt that Orange parades are large complex events, drawing together diverse Protestant groups with diverse political and socio-economic interests; it is also the case that these groups have significantly different relationships both with the Catholic community and with the British state (cf. Bryan 2000). In recent years the term 'respectable' Orangeism has enjoyed popular currency as a means of differentiating the religious and traditional meanings of Orangeism, including claims that the institution while pro-Protestant is non-sectarian, from those likely to engage in anti-social behaviour and disturb the status quo (cf. ibid.). As Kauffman explains "the lack of respectability of many bandsmen highlights the clash between traditional Orangeism and the new loyalist youth culture" (2007, 294), a point echoed by Dudley Edward's (2000) study of 'respectable Orangeism' in her book, The Faithful Tribe.

Perceptions of Orange Culture

When asked if they had ever attended an Orange Order outreach event, none of the students had done so. Similarly none of the students had close friends or wider family who were members of the Orange Order. Only 5 were aware of the presence of an Orange hall in their local community. When asked if they had ever visited an Orange hall, none of the students had been inside an Orange hall. The students were then asked if they had personal memories or first-hand experience of Orange Order parades. 7 said yes and 5 said no. Those students who said YES said they had witnessed bands playing and Orange Order parades in local towns as they've been going about their daily business and highlighted the inconvenience this represented when roads were closed and traffic restrictions were put in place. For those who had this first-hand experience they described the atmosphere as "standoffish", noting feelings of exclusion, detachment and perception of the 'other' projecting their superiority. The students were asked to reflect on what it is they mostly associate with Orange Order parades, including the 12th of July events. The students were free to write down as many individual things as they wanted to. Only 8 students provided details and all of the responses related to public parading and traffic disruption. A couple of the responses mentioned the 11th night tradition of lighting bonfires. These events are not organised by the Orange Order but they are widely seen as part and parcel of the Twelfth celebrations and usually includes burning effigies and symbols significant for the nationalist community. A small number of students cited anti-social behaviour (including excessive consumption of alcohol and heightened social tension), and rioting with the 'other' side as things they associated with the Twelfth. One student mentioned the political speeches in favour of political and cultural unionism that take place 'at the field' during the Twelfth demonstrations, while another documented their family's annual response to the 12th of July which was simply to "get out of Northern Ireland, to be on holiday so as to miss everything to do with the 12thJuly".

When asked if their perceptions of the Orange Order parades were mostly positive or negative: 11 students said their perceptions of Orange Order parades were mostly negative. Only one student suggested a mostly positive impression which was based on good relations in the local town where the student had grown up. This student could not recall any negative memories of the Orange Order, nor had any negative representations been passed on from their family. For those students who cited a mostly negative impression the questionnaire sought to ascertain the extent to which this has been influenced by family 'memories' and wider social contexts. The students' family portrayal of the Orange Order (as very negative) and word of mouth from people they knew informed their negative impressions. Perceptions of 'crude' behaviour which they associated with some of those who came out to support Orange Order parading events, as well as memories of tensions and disputes over Orange Order parades when they were growing up, fed into their negative perceptions; "I'm looking at these parades from the 'other' side (as an outsider, who doesn't belong); "Catholics are not allowed to become members of the Orange Order"; "it's sectarian"; "there's usually lots of violence during the 12th holidays between the two communities in my local area"; "it just seems to be regular tensions and violence" (associated with the parades, that's why my perceptions are mostly negative); "as with most marches in my area and all over NI there is always negative news/publicity and controversy in the media".

The students' responses could be said to mirror 'nationalist' perceptions of Orange Culture, particularly parading and the annual Twelfth. Even the most moderately-minded and culturally tolerant 'nationalists' find many aspects of the Twelfth spectacle deeply uncomfortable. Observing Orange Order members resplendent in sashes, collarets and bowler hats, accompanied by musical bands wearing militaristic-styled uniforms, publically processing behind banners depicting symbols and scenes affirming 'Protestant' supremacy can be deeply challenging. Indeed the very public relationship between the Order and what are popularly known as 'blood and thunder bands' and 'kick the Pope bands' (bands whose public musical repertoire includes provocative, anti-catholic/sectarian lyrics and tunes) does not help foster favourable opinions amongst nationalists (and it must also be acknowledged amongst some members of the Protestant community too), especially when links to loyalist paramilitarism are part of that public pageantry. As Neill Jarman, Institute for Conflict Research Director, explains

> the menacing nature of some of these loyalist bands, and particularly the crowds of alcohol swilling supporters who follow them, can present one of the less attractive elements of a parade. Many Protestants as well as Catholics who find themselves in close proximity to these bands on parade can feel intimidated. (quoted in Jess 2007, 85)

Thus for many people within the Catholic/nationalist/republican tradition, Orange Order parades and marching are perceived as little more than public acts of triumphalism and projected supremacy. What the Orange Order sees as a public demonstration of their Protestant faith and loyalty to the British Crown, those on the 'other' side of the cultural border perceive as 'coat trailing' i.e. displays of power and supposed supremacy intended to rub salt into historical wounds and grievances, the roots of which go back centuries to the Plantation of Ireland by the British Crown. Thousands of Orange Order marches are held each year across the north of Ireland every year, the majority of which are 'tolerated' by nationalists as inconveniences and pass off relatively peacefully or at least without serious incident. Throughout the 1990s nationalist opposition to Orange Order parades grew, especially those which passed through nationalist communities but along what the Orange Order calls its 'traditional routes'. Around the time the respondents to this survey were born, these contentious, 'flash-point' parades brought global media attention to places like Drumcree (a hamlet in Co Armagh); the Garvaghy Road (in a town called Portadown in Co Armagh), the Lower Ormeau Road (an arterial road in Belfast); Ardoyne (a neighbourhood in north Belfast). The cultural borders that divided people in the north of

Ireland for centuries laid open like putrid sores for a global audience to see.

When asked about the sources that had most influenced their (as it turned out, mostly 'negative') perceptions and understanding of the Orange Order; the media was by far the most popular response, followed by family views (4 students cited family). The students were provided with a scale and asked to rate their family's opinion on the Orange Order. 11 students responded: 7 students cited that their family view on the orange order was either wholly or mostly negative, while 4 felt that their family's position was neutral. For those coming from a largely nationalist background the Orange Order has historically been perceived as a unifying force for Protestants, most especially in relation to the exercise of political power and control. From a nationalist perspective the (geo-political) 'border' that separates the northern six counties from the Republic of Ireland which created 'Northern Ireland' simultaneously created a 'Protestant state for a Protestant people', or as Michael Farrell's 1980 book captured it in the title: 'Northern Ireland: the Orange State'. The unionist political elite including all those who held the position of Prime Minister of Northern Ireland were members of the Orange Order. A point echoed by Neil Jarman:

> I think the Order is probably the one organisation in Northern Ireland that's held the Unionist/Protestant community together to an extent. It remained open and accessible to all shades of political opinion within that community. (quoted in Jess 2007, 67)

From a nationalist perspective, the annual 12th is when that 'unified' Protestant identity goes on public display. The concept of 'respectable Orangeism' has entered the local lexicon as a means of somehow differentiating those associated with the traditional and religious 'values' of the organisation from those likely to engage in anti-social behaviour. Indeed good relationships between some Orange men and their Catholic neighbours is a reality in many places, particularly in farming communities; anecdotes abound about Catholic farmers looking after the farms of their Protestant neighbours to allow them to attend 'the Twelfth'. Thus one of the students in this survey reported a mostly positive impression of the Orange Order which was based on good relations in the largely rural area where the student had grown up. Significantly this student could not recall any negative personal memories associated with the Orange Order, nor had any negative representations been passed on from their family.

Formal Education: Teaching and Learning about the Orange Order

As discussed above the most striking thing to emerge from this very short, snapshot survey is the students' poor, almost non-existent knowledge and understanding of the history, heritage and culture of the Orange Order. This reflects the low levels of wider political and historical knowledge amongst this particular age cohort more generally. It is not something that's specific to this particular group of students, who by a variety of academic attainment indicators (including the highest A-level entry grades for admission to initial teacher education courses) are amongst the 'top-achievers' in the north of Ireland. The fact that most of the students could recall learning nothing about the Orange Order when they were at school (only one student was able to recall something having learned about the Orange Order in the context of Irish History in Year 8, Key Stage 3 but stated the recollection was vague) suggests more about the curriculum and the formal education system they have experienced than the students as individual learners *per se*. One student (who had attended an integrated post-primary school) said that they were aware that pupils in their school and their families were members of the Orange Order because the pupils talked about the Orange Order. However, the student couldn't recall specific lessons where the Orange Order was discussed as part of the curriculum. Finally, the students were asked to describe their predisposition towards the forthcoming programme (workshop and visit to the Museum of Orange Heritage) to be hosted by the Orange Order. Only one student said they were not really that interested in the visit but all of the other responses were positive suggesting the students felt: open minded about the visit to the Museum of Orange Heritage (6 responses indicated this); interested in learning more about Orange history and heritage (5 included this in their responses); they were curious to see what the Museum was like and what they would be doing there. On balance, they were eager to learn more about the Orange Order, to be open minded and curious about cultural 'otherness' and to see how this learning might enhance their knowledge and understanding of cultural diversity which they recognised as an important aspect of the Northern Ireland Curriculum.

Case Study Concluding Thoughts

Participation in the BE-SMaRT Project, with its heightened perspective on cognitive border thinking (i.e. the borders we carry in our heads that informs our thinking and behaviour), and the links with memory, provided the stimulus to embark on this case study research. The case study I suggest can be read on a number of levels. At one level it is an exemplar of action research undertaken by a teacher-researcher within initial teacher education which focused on one type of border and explored connections with personal and family memories. This work could be replicated and extended across many other 'borders' and connected to a much wider range of memory issues pertinent to student teachers in different contexts. At another level, and with regards to the results of the actual survey, a number of things emerge. The first is the students' relatively low level of historical literacy in relation to the Orange Order. While it would be easy to suggest that this limited interest in local politics might reflect an increasingly globalised, individualistic and materialistic culture that brings different priorities and identities to the fore in the lives of young citizens, the explanations are more complex. They are linked to the realities of growing up in a divided society as well as the education system in Northern Ireland. In part it could be argued that the students' 'knowledge deficit' reflects the very real challenges of meaningfully embedding education about diversity, mutual understanding and reconciliation within the context of a deeply divided society (cf.

Richardson & Gallagher 2011). Studies have shown how teachers in the north of Ireland have historically (and with good cause in light of the conflict) been reluctant to engage with divisive identity issues in the classroom. While many schools have taken risks to cross difficult and challenging borders, it remains the case that controversial, difficult or sensitive topics have been and continue to be side-stepped or avoided (cf. Loader & Hughes 2016). The explicit inclusion of Citizenship Education within the Northern Ireland Curriculum (2007) seeks to encourage active reflection on 'otherness', overcome entrenched identities and build up more positive inter-group identities. However, the findings here suggest students have not had opportunities to learn about or engage with a key institution of cultural 'otherness' i.e. the Orange Order. As a result the students have limited awareness of the roots of the grievances and conflicts which have shaped Northern Irish history, identity and culture. The research also points to the role played by the media and family-based memories in shaping perceptions. This was a very small-scale study with all its attendant limitations; a much larger sample would be necessary before more definitive conclusions could be drawn.

The Good Friday Agreement heralded a commitment to a shared and better future for all citizens; it is clear that education has an important contribution to make in building the peace and a shaping a more socially inclusive and equitable society. The Northern Ireland Curriculum (2007), with its strong commitment to citizenship education and building good relationships, provides a solid framework. However, realising the type of society envisioned by the Good Friday Agreement will require an ongoing commitment to address difficult and contentious content related to 'borders' 'memories' and identity. Indeed as recent research on 'shared education' initiatives has shown schools have to deal sensitively with "the boundaries of what the local community might find acceptable" (Hughes 2011, 842). Relationship building across borders remains a key priority for education in the north of Ireland. Optimistically the student teachers surveyed here demonstrated a readiness to think cross cultural borders, to be open-minded, eager to listen, reflect and learn. To return to the words of the former President of Ireland, Mary McAleese, at the opening of the Museum of Orange Heritage:

> The culture of the Orange is not my culture but it is the culture of my neighbours and we who are the children of the Jacobites and the Williamites we share this space, we share this island...We haven't always shared it happily with each other but we have decided that we want to share it happily for the future... "I think good neighbours should know about each other, should respect each other. Part of that respect is being interested in each other and what each other believes and where we come from and what their values are, what our values are..." (Mary McAlesse 24 June 2015 Belfast Telegraph)

Those involved in initial teacher education play an important role in helping to prepare student teachers for their role as the citizenship educators of tomorrow. One aspect of this work must be to provide opportunities for student teachers to reflect on and learn about the significance of 'borders', 'memory' and identity in their respective contexts and to facilitate their crossing of borders in pursuit of learning.

Bibliography

Branniff, M.; McDowell, S. & Byrne, J. (2012). *Violence, Space and Memory in the New Northern Ireland (3).* Online: https://www.opendemocracy.net/opensecurity/maire-braniff-sara-mcdowell-jonny-byrne/violence-space-and-memory-in-new-northern-irela [last accessed 13.07.17]

Bryan, D. (2000). *Orange Parades: the politics of ritual, tradition and control.* London.

Dudley Edwards, R. (2000). *The Faithful Tribe: An Intimate Portrait of the Loyal Institutions.* London.

Farrell, M. (1980). *Northern Ireland: the Orange State.* London.

Haddick-Flynn, K. (2002). *A Short History of Orangeism*. Mercier Press.

Hughes, J. (2011). Are separate schools divisive? A case study from Northern Ireland. *British Educational Research Journal 37 (5),* 829-850.

Jess, Mervyn (2007). *The Orange Order*. Dublin.

Kaufmann, E. P. (2007). *The Orange Order. A Contemporary Northern Ireland History.* Oxford.

King, J. T. (2012). Teaching and Learning about Controversial Issues: Lessons from Northern Ireland. *Theory and Research in Social Education 37 (2),* 215-246.

LeVon, L. (2015). Seeing/Being Orange: Perceptions and the Politics of Religion in County Armagh, Northern Ireland. *The Canadian Student Journal of Anthropology (2),* 33-44.

Loader, R. & Hughes, J. (2016). Joining Together or pushing apart? Building relationships and exploring difference through shared education in Northern Ireland. *Cambridge Journal of Education,* 1-18

MacRaild, D. & Hughes, K. (2014). Anti-Catholicism and Orangeism in nineteenth-century England and Scotland: Militant Loyalism in action. In A. Blackstock & F. O'Gorman (eds.). *Loyalism and the Formation of the British World.* Woodbridge, 61-80.

Mitchel, P. (2015). The Influence of Vatican II on the Protestant Churches in Ireland. In Coll. N. Ireland and Vatican II Essays Theological, Pastoral and Educational. Columba Press, 169-184.

Nash, C.; Reid, B. & Graham, B. (2013). *Partitioned Lives: The Irish Borderland: History, Heritage and Identity.* Farnham.

Newman, D. (2006). The lines that continue to separate us: borders in our borderless world. *Progress in Human Geography 30 (2),* 1-19.

Northern Ireland Curriculum Council for the Curriculum, Examinations & Assessment [CCEA] (2007). *The Northern Ireland Curriculum*. Belfast.

Pheonix, E. (2016). The Somme – 20,000 men walked slowly to their death on the first day. Irish News 30th June 2016. Online http://www.irishnews.com/news/2016/06/30/news/the-somme---ulster-unionism-s-blood-sacrifice-584061 [last accessed 13.07.2017].

Richardon, N. & Gallagher, T. (2011). *Education for Diversity and Mutual Understanding: the experience of Northern Ireland.* Bern et al.

Roberts, D. A. (1971). The Orange Order in Ireland: A religious institution? *The British Journal of Sociology 22 (3),* 269-282.

Roe, P. (2005). *Ethnic Violence and the societal security dilemma.* London.

Wolffe, J. (1991). *The Protestant Crusade in Britain, 1829-1860*. Oxford.

Web-references

Orange Order: *Former Irish president praises new museum.* http:///www.bbc.co.uk/news/uk-northern-ireland-33262065 24th June 2015 [last accessed 13 July 2017].

Orange Order: *Educational visits prove a hit with Catholic schools.* http://www.bbc.co.uk/news/uk-northern-ireland-29912790 5th November 2014 [last accessed 13 July 2017].

A concise History of the Orange Order. The Irish Times. http://www.irishtimes.com/news/ireland/a-concise-history-of-the-orange-order-1.1855664 5th July 2014 [last accessed 13 July 2017].

Orangemen marching to Richhill for big Twelfth parade. http://www.belfasttelegraph.co.uk/news/northern-ireland/orangemen-marching-to-richhill-for-big-twelfth-parade-35864333.html 26th June 2017 [last accessed 13 July 2017].

McAleese hails Orange Order Museum. http://www.belfasttelegraph.co.uk/news/northern-ireland/mcaleese-hails-orange-order-museum-31327159.html 24th June 2015 [last accessed 13 July 2017].

Olivier Mentz (dir.)

Memorandum of the BE-SMaRT project on Border and Memory Education in Teacher Education Curricula

BE-SMaRT
Border Education – Space, Memory and Reflection on Transculturality

"Can the European Union still be saved?"

The above quote is a newspaper headline from 2016, to name but one of many similar international headlines. This dark vision of a possibly failing EU contrasts with 60 years of progressive integration of countries into the EU while borders and barriers were opened and abolished.

It was 60 years ago when the European Community was created in Rome – which marked the beginning of the longest period of peace in European history. The Treaties of Rome, the Schengen Agreement and the Economic and Monetary Union paved the way for a common market, where people, goods, services and capital can circulate freely, and a transnational community which promised prosperity, peaceful cooperation, freedom, democracy, equality and solidarity. Thus, a wonderful and inspiring project, and the achievements of the EU are a reason to celebrate.

The opening of borders has been one of the main objectives from the beginning of the European project, with more borders falling in the context of EU enlargement. Nevertheless, evidence shows that many people continue to think in national terms due to their personal experiences, memories or socialisation. In the course of the last 15 years the stance of the European citizens turned from a 'permissive consensus' in favour of the EU to a 'constraining dissensus', which expresses an increasingly critical or even rejecting attitude towards continuous European integration. The defenders of the EU seem to be increasingly unable to overcome the barriers in people's minds, which arose due to physical distance, memories, identities, prejudices, and stereotypes.

History teaches us that in times of political crisis the 'culprits' are often very quickly identified on the other side of a 'border' – no matter if this is a national border of a country or a social boundary. For this reason, borders are often rightly associated with conflicts and hostilities. The last few years have shown that, despite historical experience, European citizens are deeply divided when it comes to abolishing and overcoming borders in Europe. This does not remain without consequences for the political sphere.

One such consequence of this deplorable situation will keep the EU busy at present and in the near future: the result of the 'Brexit' referendum in the UK. It has been largely celebrated in England, whereas Scotland and Northern Ireland have been actively looking for ways to stay in the EU. Meanwhile, the rest of Europe finds itself in a state of confusion as people question the very idea of a European union. For the first time in EU history, the question will not be which potential candidate countries want to join the European house, but how a country can leave it.

However, 'Brexit' does not mark the beginning of the crisis but positions it centre stage, similar to the failure of political elites. The people in favour of 'Brexit' share a concern with many other citizens in Europe: the EU, so their complaint, undermines nation state sovereignty, is costly and bureaucratic, threatens the welfare state and undermines democracy. It reflects the crisis of confidence in the European project and conversations return once again to national borders. Debates characterized by nationalistic visions are gaining ground in various European countries, and, stimulated by the migration issue, populist parties and movements are on the rise.

The leaders of populist parties and movements claim to know the 'true' will of the people. They win the favour of the electorate with simple answers to difficult questions. Even if these answers are restricted to an ideological minimum, there is one key point: the focus is placed on the people, who 'must' defend themselves against 'corrupt elites' (vertical dimension) and 'the others' (i.e. refugees as well as religious and ethnic minorities; horizontal dimension) who are not considered as part of 'the people' deemed to be a homogenous entity.

The current feeling of insecurity in society plays into the populists' hands. People are afraid of the consequences of globalisation, the erosion of traditional value patterns and, coupled with this, the loss of identity. At the same time, trust in politics and media disappears, in particular in institutions and elites on a European level. Many people share the feeling of being left behind. In their view, the EU presents itself as bureaucratic and non-transparent, thus lacking legitimacy. The individuals' options of exerting influence seem to become gradually reduced, and this seems to be valid for the national level too. This impression became particularly reinforced during the Euro crisis. As a solution to the crisis, processes aiming at deepening integration were quickly initiated but in an atmosphere marked by an increasingly Eurosceptic public opinion. It was, however, the refugee debate that gave a decisive stimulus to populist parties and movements. A part of the European citizens perceives the EU as a gateway for large-scale immigration and the fear of becoming overwhelmed by culturally adverse foreigners and acts of terror, motivated by Islamist fundamental ideas, is apparently immense.

The rise of especially right-wing populist parties shows that these concerns should not be underestimated and taken seriously instead. If, in the past, parties such as the *Front National* in France were classified as extreme right-wing groups, today they present themselves as 'de-demonized' and gain more and more support of voters from the midst of society. There is also an increasing number of examples of how right-wing groups try to monopolise issues such as Islam, immigration, EU criticism and cultural identity.

In Poland *Prawo i Sprawiedliwość* came to power, a party which underlines Polish sovereignty, acts in an anti-European way, reduces media freedom and the division of powers. The Hungarian Prime minister Viktor Orbán considers immigration as a security risk and takes extreme measures against this phenomenon. In Austria and the Netherlands right-wing populists, such as Norbert Hofer's *Freiheitliche Partei Öster-*

reichs (Austrian Freedom Party) and Geert Wilders's *Partij voor de Vrijheid* (Party for Freedom), narrowly missed an election victory. In France, Marine Le Pen's *Front National* managed to get to the second round of the presidential election and lost it, but presented it as a victory as she got one third of the votes. In Germany, too, the *Alternative für Deutschland* (Alternative for Germany) has succeeded in gaining much support. More countries and their right-wing parties could be added to this list. This phenomenon emerges not only on a national but also on a European level. Under the leadership of the *Front National*, right-wing populists and extremists founded a new right-wing political group "Europe of Nations and Freedoms", which obtains considerably more rights and funding than ever before in the history of the European Parliament.

When it comes to seeking answers to complex questions, many citizens of Europe do not think of the EU in the first instance but instead they think of nation states, which appear on the surface to provide easy answers through isolationism. Of course, this orientation towards the nation is neither new, nor is it likely to become less attractive in the future. Irrespective of day-to-day politics, this issue will require our full attention. Negative perceptions and stereotypes of others (i.e. 'mental borders') are omnipresent, thus the need for taking action against isolationism is pressing. What could be helpful in this situation? Today, globalisation is continuously diminishing the nation states' room for manoeuvre. It is therefore necessary to launch a pan-European debate with well-thought-out concepts how to shape European integration in the future. Above all, more focus should be placed on European citizens' participation and education. If we want to prevent populist and post-factual slogans, we must equip citizens with knowledge-based skills they need to analyse political and social developments on a rational and argumentative level. This requires critical, free-thinking and informed citizens, who are able to look beyond their own national horizon.

These reasons alone require us to address this issue immediately or we may be facing the end of the road to the European dream!

Teacher Education around Europe

However, there is one field in Europe where, contrary to political, economic and social integration, national borders always persisted: Teacher Education. All over Europe, teachers are trained in line with nationally oriented criteria. All over Europe, and despite all trends towards internationalisation, Teacher Education remains firmly located within national borders (cf. as examples Clerc 2017 for France, Lillemägi 2017 for Estonia, Niklasson 2017 for Sweden, Raith 2017 for Germany, Resnik Planinc 2017 for Slovenia, Vaupel & McKay 2017 for Northern Ireland). Even if the Bologna process aimed for more mobility in third-level academic education, and even if teacher students do go abroad for some time during their studies – no teacher education program requires a *compulsory* stay abroad as part of the study programme. Teacher education in European countries is focused on disciplinary approaches rather than on comparative issues which might lead to a better understanding of others.

Different countries might adopt different approaches to education, however, one aspect persists in European systems: school education aims to educate responsible citizens. These citizens are expected to know the values of democracy and be capable of critical reflection. Thus, these skills cannot be isolated to a national context only, they must be transnational. Therefore, Teacher Education must not be inward looking or nationally myopic but needs to be values-based, outward looking, inclusive, transnational and integrative. The timing has never been more urgent or critical to address these concerns.

As mentioned before, across the EU today there are no statutory cross-border (international) mobility requirements for student placements in Initial Teacher Education (ITE) programmes. While some internationally-minded ITE providers and enthusiastic student teachers do seek out cross-border school-based experiences through Erasmus+ and other like-minded mobility programmes, there is no general requirement for students to have cross-border experiences as part of their teacher education studies. However, as already mentioned, **we need** teachers capable of critical reflection and with in-depth knowledge of values-and-democracy education. **We need** teachers who think beyond their national horizons, examine problems from a European and global perspective, and thus actively contribute to overcoming barriers in their pupils' minds. **We need** teachers who are open to and aware of all these issues as their everyday task in their profession is to educate responsible citizens of their country, their state, and of Europe.

It is therefore imperative that we examine carefully the education we provide for tomorrow's teachers, and it is most pertinent how we address internationalization in our professional practice. In order to bring this issue closer to young people, it is in the first instance necessary to raise future teachers' awareness of this context and to provide them with a sound education on the discourse. This does not only concern teachers of politics, because they likely have already acquired proficient knowledge regarding the discourse. All teachers need opportunities to reflect on and develop competencies linked to these complex and demanding issues, which should be addressed in a cross-curricular and interdisciplinary manner.

The BE-SMaRT Project's annotated bibliography

In the context of the academic project "Border education – Space, Memory and Reflections of Transculturality" (BE-SMaRT) these very issues were tackled and the project consortium commenced work in 2014 by undertaking research for an annotated bibliography (cf. Vaupel 2017). The 'return' of borders to Europe has led scholars from many disciplines to focus their attention on the interstices of borders and national memory. Although drawing on diverse theoretical and methodological perspectives, the field of Border Research seeks answers to basic questions, such as: What exactly are borders? What do borders do? Why do borders matter? The annotated bibliography provides a guide for grappling with those issues and offers an account of the research discourse on the interdisciplinary disciplines of Border Studies, Memory Studies and (Teacher) Education: the reviews collected in this volume connect a variety of approaches such as education for diversity and inclusion; borders, memories and their representation in the media; Museum Studies and pedagogy; the history of specific 'borderlands' and the possibly changing perceptions among their populations. Thus, the bibliography intends to specifically aid educators teaching or researching these issues in their sourcing of significant academic material. The book chapters offer a wealth of information and material that refers to major socio-historical events, which shaped European regions and dominated public debate. More generally, the reviews give an impression of the rich diversity of memories, border contexts, and socio-historical cultural developments in different areas of Europe. The annotated bibliography gives an account of the research that has been done in the field of the Border Education in relation to memory and space. It is a listing of research sources and serves as an important tool within the familiarization process about (inter-)national discourses of certain fields of knowledge and, in the specific context of the BE-SMaRT project, connects innovatively three key areas: Border and Memory Studies with Education and/or Teacher Education.

As the focus of BE-SMaRT is predominantly on teacher education, i.e. targeting teacher students as Europe's professional teachers of tomorrow, the bibliography serves as a tool within the project's Teacher Education Module, for instance, as study material in the educators' lesson planning. Thus, individual literature reviews presented in the bibliography may feature as actual study material in the delivery of the module: the reviews demonstrate that borders are as much a 'real-existing' boundary as they are a complex and dynamic mental phenomenon, (re)produced through the creation of binary distinctions between the I/We and the Other(s)/Them. They exhibit in many cases how people construct (invisible) borders, influenced by diverse personal experiences or merely as a socialised concept (e.g. through media, education, local culture), and thus how people practice inclusion or exclusion. Furthermore, the reviewed literature offers examples of how borders could be studied not only from a top-down perspective but also from the bottom up, with a focus on individual border narratives and spatial experiences (e.g. memories/life-stories), reflecting the ways in which borders impact on notions of otherness and the daily life practices of people living in and around 'borderlands' and trans-boundary transition zones.

Last, but certainly not least, the publication of this bibliography is a contribution to an international discourse of border research as a fairly new academic discipline and will, therefore, have a bearing beyond the BE-SMaRT project's life span. It seeks to reach a target audience of academics and professionals working in project-relevant disciplines and contexts, i.e. staff and students in ITE programmes, Higher Education libraries and relevant (research) institutions as well as in-service teachers looking for suitable key readings. The bibliography is one of the project's responses to timely issues with the current rise in nationalism in mind. By studying and/or familiarizing themselves with the wide range of the selected literature and themes, the bibliography's target audiences will become stimulated to critically think about the role of (mental) borders in everyday life actions and practices of European citizens. Readers are given concrete examples of significant key texts for their national contexts respectively, and international contexts for possible comparison, which may challenge perceptions and taken-for-granted assumptions, seeking to make young people more reflective in their encounters with others.

The BE-SMaRT Project's survey

Parallel to the research on the annotated bibliography, the BE-SMaRT consortium focused on an online survey as another preliminary step in the project's lifetime. The survey was conducted among university students in Estonia, France, Germany, Northern Ireland, Slovenia, and Sweden. Its main aim was to identify students' perceptions and attitudes towards borders and bordering. The survey outcomes enable to answer

three key questions as relevant to the discourse outlined above: Which borders play the most important role in students' everyday life? How do students perceive these borders? Do they regard them as something positive/negative? Are there important variations in students' perceptions and attitudes towards borders and bordering between different countries?

The results of the survey revealed important differences in how distinctive borders impact the life of students in different countries. For students in Belfast ethno-religious borders have the biggest impact. For students in Freiburg language borders are the most significant and in Ljubljana as well as in Tartu national borders are identified as the most important. Social class borders are most significant for students in Västerås and Lyon. The survey also revealed important distinctions in students' perceptions regarding the role of borders in a modern world. While some believe that the existence of borders – especially national borders – is vital for the protection of their identities, others strongly disagree. While some strongly support reinforcement of border control and restrictions in immigration within the EU, others support open borders for refugees and economic migrants. However, probably the most important finding of the survey is that a vast majority of students believe that their current university study modules do not provide them with a good understanding of border issues and a good insight into the current migrant crisis in Europe. Thus, a large majority of future teachers are insufficiently aware of 'borders' or the salience of what might be usefully thought of as 'mental maps' of bordering that they carry around in their heads. The results of the survey indicate that ITE students desire and expect from their study course a provision of profound knowledge regarding border issues; knowledge, which will enable them to better understand the current processes that are taking place in Europe.

The BE-SMaRT Project's case studies as a way to increase awareness

In a next step, the BE-SMaRT consortium focused on a series of case studies strongly linked to local or regional issues of borders and memories with the aim to move the discussion (for ITE students and teachers) beyond the physical and highly visible lines of 'border' separation towards a much richer inter-disciplinary appreciation of the bottom-up 'bordering processes' affecting the lives of people on an everyday basis in different parts of Europe. The BE-SMaRT project recognises the enduring relevance and importance of geo-political/territorial borders in Europe, while at the same time it calls for the need to understand traditional border concepts (largely associated with the demarcation of tangible space) as one aspect of a more fluid, interdisciplinary and multifaceted discourse. This thinking is reflected in the range of individual case studies developed during the project; the project contributors reflect on the manner that borders create (or reflect) difference and constitute separation lines not only between states and geographical spaces but also social and cultural distinctions between the 'us and them', the 'here and there', and the 'insiders and outsiders'. We recognise the importance of border demarcation as the process through which the criteria of belonging (or not belonging) is defined; be that citizenship of a country, membership of a specific social or economic group, or religious and cultural affiliation.

The case studies examine the much broader process of 'bordering' and the ways in which different types of 'borders' are demarcated, constructed (often in peoples' minds) and managed, and the categories of difference or separation they create and maintain; in this respect the link with Memory Studies is critical. The case studies seek to provide a broad inter-disciplinary understanding of 'borders', incorporating the critical intersection with Memory Studies, in an effort to better understand how individuals and groups perceive and experience the borders and boundaries in their everyday lives. Using the diverse 'border' experiences of partner countries, the case studies seek to provide rich and accessible opportunities for ITE students to connect 'borders' and 'memories' through engaging with a wide range of 'border narratives'. The theme of 'crossing borders' (be they economic, political/territorial, social and/or cultural, linguistic, gender) has been to the fore in both academic and popular discourse; with respect to the latter much of the discussion had been couched in quite negative vocabulary, as if 'border crossing' was something to be deeply suspicious about. This has been most evident in mass media representations of recent 'border crossings' by refugees fleeing into Europe. While it is true that some 'borders' are extremely difficult to cross, a range of other 'border' types can and are regularly 'crossed'. The metaphor of 'bridges', as points of contact for border crossing, is significant and by introducing this through the BE-SMaRT case studies we aim to facilitate critical reflection on the possibilities for encountering difference across a wide range of borders. As Newman's paper suggests

> discussion concerning the nature of borders as bridges and points of interaction is of relevance in the sense that borders can become transformed into the frontiers (in the most positive sense of the term) where people or groups who have traditionally kept themselves distant from each other, make the first attempts at contact and interaction (Newman 2006, 8).

In a similar vein, and until relatively recently, the concepts of 'borderland', 'frontier' and 'transition zones' were largely restricted to discussions of real tangible spaces where lives were 'divided' or 'marked out' by territorial borders. More recently these spatially grounded concepts have been applied to a wide range of border crossings by people whose lives have hitherto been divided by 'borders' of one kind or another. None of this should be taken to mean that the act of border crossing will necessarily lead to positive and life affirming outcomes; indeed as Newman (ibid., 9) makes clear, the experience of meeting the 'other' for the first time, especially after a long period of fear, suspicion and distrust can heightened the mutual feelings of animosity. What is significant about the diverse case studies examined through the BE-SMaRT project, is that they extend the 'borderland' concept to wider critique to include consideration of border crossings by, and across, different groups (social, ethnic, religious, cultural and gender).

The BE-SMaRT case studies employ a range of methodologies intended to uncover the meaning and significance of 'borders' in a range of European contexts. They are attentive to the life-stories and experiences arising from the unique situations within the partner countries. They seek to uncover the real-life, diverse, and lived experience of different people in different parts of Europe that will have resonance for students within ITE. They incorporate a wide range of 'borders narratives' and 'border' representations in cultural media, film, museum spaces, textbooks and indeed the lecture theatre and the classroom. Significantly, these individual case studies have formed the basis of the 'dilemma' approach utilised within the BE-SMaRT Border Education module. However, it is also the case that each individual case study stands in its own right as a contribution to learning and teaching in higher education.

Traditionally borders have constituted barriers, their function being to prevent 'us' from crossing to 'there'; as such, what lies on the other side of the border remains only partially visible and mostly unknown. In this context ignorance or at best partial knowledge, often inaccurate and biased, is left unchallenged to fuel perceptions and contribute to mindsets. However, as Newman (2006) points out when borders are opened or efforts are made to cross them, the 'other' – that which hitherto had been mysterious and unknown – is encountered for the first time. The BE-SMaRT case studies believe these highly significant border 'crossing experiences' are worthy of closer scrutiny because they help to throw light on what happens when the mystique of the 'other' is brought into a more normalised reality. This is particularly important where the 'other' has been perceived in negative, threatening or indeed violent terms as exemplified in those case studies where conflict and war has been a feature of the lived experience.

Given recent media discourse one could be forgiven for thinking that the only borders that matter in Europe today are political or territorial. However, for many people in Europe the borders that are most apparent in their lives are often invisible. All borders, both tangible and intangible, start with an idea that they are needed; thus all borders are social constructs, intended to meet a perceived 'need'. For many people it is the intangible or invisible borders, deeply etched in their thinking that inform perceptions, which in turn, temper feelings and attitudes and drives behaviour. As the BE-SMaRT case studies demonstrate just because a border cannot be seen (or pointed out in tangible space) does not mean that it does not exist or have very real impacts; "if we really want to know what borders mean to people, then we need to listen to their personal and group narratives" (ibid., 12).

The rationale of the BE-SMaRT Project has been to understand Europe from the lived experiences and practices of students (future citizens of tomorrow's Europe) and their families. By adopting a bottom-up approach, with a focus on individual border narratives and experiences, reflecting the ways in which borders impact on daily life practices we endeavour to exemplify through the individual case study contributions that 'Europe' is not simply an abstract topic to be learnt about. Rather, it is a work in progress, based on past and present heritages, one where all types of borders, and the memories that inform and sustain them, really do matter. By drawing upon the students' experiences we hope to engage their curiosity, promote critical thinking and encourage them to become active citizens empowered by knowledge, enlivened by critical debate and interdisciplinary thinking. It is hoped that the inclusion of the individual case studies within the BE-SMaRT Border Education Module will lead to new approaches regarding the understanding of, and in turn, education on borders helping to challenge some of the more outdated thinking. We hope that the inclusion of these case studies from the various partner countries will stimulate student-teachers and teacher-educators within ITE to think more expansively about 'borders', to challenge static conceptions of borders only associated with fixed legalities on a territorial map and to begin to appreciate them as fluid, constantly changing entities, being (re)produced through everyday life performances/experiences and individual/collective memories meaningful for the pupils and students they will teach.

Recommendations for a future and European-oriented Initial Teacher Education in Europe

After three years of intensive work on linking Border Education and Memory Studies, the partners of the BE-SMaRT project find it necessary that ITE has to change, has to overcome the national borders that do constrain the development of future teachers which will be tasked with the education of their countries' future responsible citizens who will also have to become responsible for an on-going peaceful process of mutual understanding in Europe. We wish to contribute to the development of today's young people into tomorrow's critical and self-confident citizens. Against the backdrop of an increasingly heterogeneous society, which is subject to diverse linguistic, cultural or other influences, it is important that teacher education gives thought to the development of ways of thinking about borders and difference, and how they relate to and intersect with experiences of space, collective and personal memories. As a multinational and diverse European team with professional backgrounds in Higher Education, ITE, post-primary and vocational education, we developed study modules based on national dilemmas which will enable (future) teachers to reflect on their national 'border-related' problems, to acquire skills for addressing these and, at the same time, to think about European options for taking action.

For the political environment this should not remain at a mere theoretical level only, there has to be a political will to implement new changes to Initial and Continuing Teacher Education also. Politics and educational policies must actively support this idea and carry the demand further. We therefore call on policy and decision makers to set a framework for Teacher Education, which stipulates the following aspects:

- **A European-oriented teacher has a profound knowledge of Europe.** This means that all future teachers in EU countries should have gone through a teacher education programme in which a sort of *studium generale* includes binding elements connected to knowledge about Europe (cf. Mentz 2010):
  * The ITE student/teacher needs to possess factual knowledge about geographical aspects of Europe and to learn about them through contrastive capacity thinking.
  * The ITE student/teacher understands the role of Europe in its globalised dimension. This should include an ability to give shape to the European space and to wish to continue the construction of the European house (cf. Dahrendorf 1996, Giolitto 1993, Foucher 1993).
  * ITE students/teachers should be familiar with European history, which means that they should be able to understand European history as effecting current European developments. Future teachers need to be aware that Europe has been a basis of the world's main development, as well in the negative (e.g. colonialism or World Wars) as in the positive (e.g. 70 years of a largely peaceful continent with the EU or its influence as a global 'peace-maker') (cf. Schäfer 1993)
  They should be aware of the political impact of Europe. This signifies, for instance, to be acquainted with European institutions, to know their way of functioning, how they are structured and what options one has to take an active part in the democratic process and in the development of the EU as a global player. A mature and responsible citizen of Europe is able to conceive the role of nation states, regions and local authorities in the European subsidiarity principle. (cf. Gasser & Mentz 2004, Foucher 1998)

- **A European-oriented teacher is engaged in the multicultural nature of European society.**
  A European Teacher engages with the multicultural nature of European society. He/she has an active relationship with his/her own culture and is open towards other cultures. He/she knows how to behave in other cultures in a

> confident and non-dominant way. He/she works with heterogeneous groups, sees heterogeneity as valuable and respects any differences. He/she copes with the challenges of the multicultural aspects of the knowledge society and works to promote equal opportunities. (Schratz 2014, 19)

Based on Schratz's definition, multicultural openness and the experience of difference must become a compulsory part of ITE programmes. Lived experience can only be realised when going abroad. Thus, not only the opportunity for a stay-abroad period through Erasmus+ should be given, but ITE curricula must provide a compulsory study-stay abroad of at least one term of six months. This might enable the students to develop a European cultural 'literacy', to be able to 'read' European cultures, to note differences and similarities, and to live heterogeneity as an added value to their everyday life. (cf. Mentz 2007b and 2007c, Ferguson 2003, Sweet 2003)

- **A European-oriented teacher is able to speak more than one European language.**

  Language variety is an asset for the EU. Learning other languages is a source of personal development and a cultural skill for the young generation. Knowing different European languages is key to deeper cultural understanding. Access to cultures cannot be successful by remaining monolingual. It should be a normal procedure to leave school with the educational language of the country, English as one vehicular language and at least one additional language. Future teachers should therefore acquire skills in another language as part of their studies. As Europeans live in an environment of language-multiplicity, they should consequently educate their children (at whatever age this might be) in several languages (cf. Konrad 2003).

  Learning more than one language could lead to an increasing number of bilingual courses. This would enable teacher students as well as their future pupils to examine material of different languages and thus learn by comparatively contrasting national positions and presentations with those existing in other countries. (cf. Helbig 2000, Mentz 2005, Language Policy Division of the Council of Europe 2006)

- **A European-oriented teacher perceives of a European identity.**
  Future teachers in and for Europe see themselves as individuals within a society where everybody has roots in one particular (country's) culture but is, at the same time, belonging to a bigger entity than a country – that is, a "greater European whole" (Schratz 2014, 18). Thus, a coexistence of a national identity with, on the one hand, a regional or local one (mostly linked to the place of living or origin) and, on the other hand, with a European identity that keeps an open mind toward the world at large.
  Possessing an identity of different levels leads to transnational awareness and provides reflexive perspectives on key questions of present day societies dealing with, for instance, matters of heterogeneity, diversity, migration, equality, etc. Providing teacher-students with the skills for such reflection is a major step to live-up to the European slogan "unity in diversity".

- **A European-oriented teacher acts as a European citizen.**
  Europe has shared values such as respect for human rights, democracy and freedom. Europe puts a major focus on mutual solidarity. Through their critical teaching, future teachers in whichever European country should be prepared to foster citizens of a Europe of tomorrow who are autonomous, mature, responsible, reflective and active.

We therefore ask political and educational stakeholders to vouch for a change in ITE in Europe. We call on policy and decision makers to create frameworks for ITE that involve:

- a compulsory study stay abroad of a minimum of six months including a practice phase;
- a compulsory *studium generale* including elements of history, geography, political sciences, with a view to increase students' ability to reflect on borders and memories, and thus to appreciate the active role played by both in the construction of otherness and the perpe-

tuation of stereotypes, which must be overcome in pursuit of a socially cohesive Europe;

- a compulsory study part on Europe-oriented civic education for all teacher students, irrespective of their chosen discipline/subject;
- compulsory modules on the connection of borders and memories with the aim to overcome national-oriented reflection and to bring the students face to face with critical social issues of being and belonging, of social inclusion and exclusion in contemporary European society.

The implementation of such conditions to ITE curricula will ensure the addressing and questioning of exclusive and closed identities, and to benefit from the richness of encounters with others or otherness. By doing this, young and dynamic EU citizens (i.e. the teacher s of tomorrow) will experience meaningful dialogue about othering, will be encouraged to see mutual understanding as basis from which to shape and build a more socially just, inclusive and successfully functioning European society.

References

Clerc, P. (2017). *The French Educational System.* Online: https://sites.google.com/site/besmartproject/Project-Outputs/memorandum [last accessed 07 August 2017].

Dahrendorf , R. (1996). *Why Europe matters. A personal view.* London.

Ferguson, M.W. (2003). *Dido's Daughters: Literacy, Gender and Empire in Early Modern England and France.* Chicago.

Foucher, M. (dir., 1993). *Fragments d'Europe. Atlas de l'Europe médiane et orientale.* Paris.

Foucher, M. (1998). *La République européenne. Entre histoires et geographies.* Paris.

Gasser, A. & Mentz, U. (2004). *Gemeindefreiheit in Europa. Der steinige Weg zu mehr kommunaler Selbstverwaltung in Europa.* Baden-Baden.

Giolitto, P. (1993). *Construire l'Europe*. Paris.

Helbig, B. (2000). *Das bilingual Sachfach Geschichte, Eine empirische Stuide zur Arbeit mit französischsprachigen (Quellen-)Texten*. Tübingen.

Konrad, H. (2003). Entwurf einer "europäischen Sprachenordnung". *Zeitschrift für Interkulturellen Fremdsprachenunterricht [Online, 8 (2/3)*, 157-175. Online: http://tujournals.ulb.tu-darmstadt.de/index.php/zif/article/view/542/518 [last accessed 06 June 2017].

Language Policy Division of the Council of Europe (ed.; 2006). *Plurilingual education in Europe.* Strasburg.

Lillemägi, I. (2017). *Teacher Education in Estonia*. Online: https://sites.google.com/site/besmartproject/Project-Outputs/memorandum [last accessed 07 August 2017].

Mentz, O. (2005). Do you speak European? or: Why even Geographers should know more than English. In K. Donert & P. Charzynski (eds.). *Changing Horizons in Geography Education.* Torun, 252-257

Mentz, O. (2007a). Europalehramt – teacher training for a European future. In K. Donert, P. Charzynski & Z. Podgórski (eds.). *Teaching in and about Europe.* Torun, 20-24.

Mentz, O. (2007b). Europe Matters! 10 Reasons why school Geography should teach a European Dimension. In K. Donert, P. Charzynski & Z. Podgórski (eds.). *Teaching in and about Europe.* Torun, 25-35.

Mentz, O. (2007c). Poetic Geogaphy or Geographic Poetry? – A Way to European Cultural Literacy. In S. Catling & L. Taylor (eds.). *Changing Geographies: Innovative Curricula. The Conference Proceedings. IGU CGE / Herodot London Conference April 10th to 11th, 2007.* Oxford, 194-200.

Mentz, O. (2010). The European Challenge – How to integrate European competences in Geography in Higher Education. *European Journal of Geography 1 (2010)*, 61-69.

Newman, D. (2006). The lines that continue to separate us: borders in our "borderless" world. *Progress in Human Geography vol. 30 (2)*, 143-161.

Niklasson, L. (2017). *Teacher Education in Sweden.* Online: https://sites.google.com/site/besamrtproject/Project-Outputs/memorandum [last accessed 07 August 2017].

Raith, M. (2017). *Becoming a Teacher in Germany.* Online: https://sites.google.com/site/besamrtproject/Project-Outputs/memorandum [last accessed 07 August 2017].

Resnik Planinc, T. (2017). *Teacher Education and Education System in Slovenia.* Online: https://sites.google.com/site/besmartproject/Project-Outputs/memorandum [last accessed 07 August 2017].

Schäfer, H. (1993). Europas Einheit: Herkunft, Ziel, Form. In P. Kirchhof, H. Schäfer & H. Tietmeyer (eds.). *Europa als Idee und rechtliche Form.* Berlin, 9-34.

Schratz, M. (2014). The European Teacher: Transnational Perspectives in Teacher Education Policy and Practice. *Center for Educational Policy Studies Journal, Vol 4.*, 11-29.

Sweet, N. (2003). "Under the subtle wreath": Louise Bogan, Felicia Hemans, and Petrarchan Poetics. Online: http://www.erudit.org/revue/ron/2003/v/n29/007714ar.html#biblio. [last access: 20 August 2017].

Vaupel, A. & McKay, T. (2017). *Teacher Education in Northern Ireland.* Online: https://sites.google.com/site/besamrtproject/Project-Outputs/memorandum [last accessed 07 August 2017].

Vaupel, A. (2017). *Borders, Memory and Transculturality. An Annotated Bibliography on the European Discourse.* Münster.

The editors and the authors

The editors

Tracey McKay is a Senior Lecturer at St Mary's University College, a College of Queen's University Belfast. She teaches at both undergraduate and postgraduate level contributing to courses in geographical education and curriculum studies. Her research interests include: the history and philosophy of geographical education; teaching and learning in the world around us; the European and global dimension in education, and Catholic teacher education. She is a member of the UK Higher Education Academy.

Olivier Mentz is Dean of the Faculty of Cultural and Social Sciences of the University of Education Freiburg and a Full Professor for French Literature and ist Didactics. His research areas include French adolescent's literature, bilingual teaching and learning, and internationaisation of teacher education. He is director of a German-French binational and bilingual Teacher Education program for primary school teachers.

The authors

Hans-Peter Burth is an Associate Professor in Political Science and Civic Education and coordinator of the European Teacher Education program at the University of Education Freiburg. He holds a PhD in Political Science and a Postdoctoral Lecture Qualification in Political Science and Practical Philosophy. His current fields of research are: European Union and European Citizenship Education, European Teacher Education, Didactics and Evaluation of Democracy Learning, Didactics of Politics and Philosophy, Prevention of right-wing attitudes by Civic Education.

Alexander Drost is a Teaching/Research Assisant at the Ernst-Moritz-Arndt-University Greifswald. He is academic coordinator of the International Research Training Group "Baltic Borderlands: Shifting Boundaries of Mind and Culture in the Borderlands of the Baltic Sea Region" (2010-) and combines hereby innovative conceptual border research with his studies of early modern Southeast Asian history. His postdoc project concentrates on European bordering and differing spatial concepts in merchant communities throughout Southeast Asia in the 17th century.

Chloé Faucompré is a Teaching/Research assistant at the Institute of Romance Languages at the University of Education Freiburg. She is writing her PhD under international joint supervision at the University of Education Freiburg and at the University of Upper Alsace Mulhouse. Her research interest focusses language teaching and learning in the Upper Rhine Metropolitan region and in particular the development of teaching sequences for the acquisition of cross-border competence in the neighbour's language class.

Mojca Ilc Klun is an Assistant at the University of Ljubljana (Faculty of Arts, Department of Geography). Her teaching and research deals with the didactics of geography along with various aspects of regional and social geography, especially the topics of migration and Slovenian emigrants.

Laila Niklasson is a Senior Lecturer at Mälardalen University where her teaching is mostly in the Teacher Programme, Head Master Programme and in courses about evalution. She is interested in studying changes on an individual and organisational level, but also planning a learning environment and evaluation.

Tatjana Resnik Planinc is an Associate Professor at the University of Ljubljana (Faculty of Arts, Department of Geography). Her teaching and research work focuses on didactics of geography and regional geography of North America, Australia and Oceania.

Boštjan Rogelj is an Assistant at the University of Ljubljana (Faculty of Arts, Department of Geography). His teaching and research deals with political geography, geography of migrations along with various aspects of regional geography, especially regional geography of Southeastern Europe.

Angela Vaupel is a Senior Lecturer in International Studies at St Mary's University College, a College of Queen's University Belfast. She mainly teaches on aspects of European culture, such as the representation of (minority) identities in film and literature. Her research interests are interdisciplinary and draw mainly from Cultural Studies, Film, Exile and Identity Studies. She has frequently collaborated within international research projects regarding the promotion of transnational education.

Katja Vintar Mally is an Assistant Professor at the University of Ljubljana (Faculty of Arts, Department of Geography). Her research focus is on sustainable development and environmental protection as well as on world regional geography.